EROS AND THE CHRIST

EROS AND THE CHRIST

LONGING AND ENVY IN PAUL'S CHRISTOLOGY

DAVID E. FREDRICKSON

Fortress Press
Minneapolis

EROS AND THE CHRIST

Longing and Envy in Paul's Christology

Cover image: Pothos (one of Aphrodite's erotes, and brother of Eros). Parian marble statue, Imperial Roman, 2nd century CE. Museo Archeologico Nazionale, Naples, Italy © Vanni / Art Resource, NY

Cover design: Tory Herman

Library of Congress Cataloging-in-Publication Data is available

Print ISBN: 978-0-8006-9823-2

eBook ISBN: 978-1-4514-2630-4

The paper used in this publication meets the minimum requirements of American National Standard for Information Sciences — Permanence of Paper for Printed Library Materials, ANSI Z329.48-1984.

Manufactured in the U.S.A.

This book was produced using PressBooks.com, and PDF rendering was done by PrinceXML.

CONTENTS

Abbreviations

Ancient Sources

For letters written by ancient authors, the abbreviations *Ep.* (singular *Epistula*) and *Epp.* (plural *Epistulae*) are used. These are not included in the following list. Similarly, many of the works are fragmentary (abbreviated *Frg.*) and are not included in the list.

Achilles Tatius
    Leuc. Clit. *Leucippe et Clitophon*
Aeschylus
    Ag. *Agamemnon*
    Eum. *Eumenides*
    Pers. *Persae*
    Prom. *Prometheus vinctus*
    Suppl. *Supplices*
Apollonius of Rhodes
    Argon. *Argonautica*
Aristophanes
    Av. *Aves*
    Lys. *Lysistrata*
    Plut. *Plutus*
Aristotle
    Eth. Eud. *Ethica Eudemia*
    Eth. nic. *Ethica nicomachea*
    Metaph. *Metaphysica*
    Pol. *Politica*
    Rhet. *Rhetorica*
Artemidorus
    Onir. *Onirocritica*
Athenaeus
    Deip. *Deipnosophistae*
Bion
    Epitaph. Adon. *Epitaphius Adonis*

Callimachus
  Aet. *Aetia*
  Hymn. Apoll. *Hymnus in Apollinem*
Chariton
  Chaer. *De Chaerea et Callirhoe*
Cicero
  Fam. *Epistulae ad familiares*
  Quint. fratr. *Epistulae ad Quintum fratrem*
  Tusc. *Tusculanae disputationes*
Claudius Aelianus
  NA *De natura animalium*
Clement of Alexandria
  Paed. *Paedagogus*
  Protr. *Protrepticus*
  Strom. *Stromata*
Demosthenes
  1 Aristog. *1 In Aristogitonem*
  Cor. *De Corona*
  [Erot.] *Eroticus*
  Lept. *Adversus Leptinem*
Dio Chrysostom
  Conc. Apam *De concordia cum Apamensibus*
  Grat. *Gratitudo*
  Invid. *De invidia*
  Pol. *Politica*
  Rhod. *Rhodiaca*
  2 Tars. *Tarsica altera*
Dionysius of Halicarnassus
  Ant. rom. *Antiquitates romanae*
  [Rhet.] *Ars rhetorica*
Epictetus
  Diatr. *Diatribai*
Euripides
  Alc. *Alcestis*
  El. *Electra*
  Hec. *Hecuba*
  Hel. *Helena*

Heracl. *Heraclidae*

Hipp. *Hippolytus*

Med. *Medea*

Fronto

Ad M. Caes. *Ad M. Caesarem*

Ep. Gr. *Epistulae Graecae*

Heliodorus

Aeth. *Aethiopica*

Herodotus

Hist. *Historiae*

Hesiod

Op *Opera et dies*

[Scut.] *Scutum*

Theog. *Theogonia*

Hippocrates

Aph. *Aphorismata*

Nat. hom. *De natura hominis*

Praec. *Praeceptiones*

Homer

Il *Ilias*

Od. *Odyssea*

Horace

Carm. *Carmina*

Iamblichus

Vit. Pyth. *Vita Pythagorae*

Isocrates

Ad Nic. *Ad Nicoclem*

Antid. *Antidosis*

Demon. *Ad Demonicum*

Evag. *Evagora*

Hel. enc. *Helenae encomium*

Nic. *Nicocles*

Panath. *Panathenaicus*

Phil. *Philippus*

John Chrysostom

Hom. Col. *Homiliae in epistulam ad Colossenses*

Hom. Phil. *Homiliae in epistulam ad Philippenses*

Josephus

A.J. *Antiquitates judaicae*

Longus

Daphn. *Daphnis et Chloe*

Lucian

Abdic. *Abdicatus*

[Am.] *Amores*

Anach. *Anacharsis*

[Asin.] *Asinus*

Cal. *Calumniae non temere credendum*

[Charid.] *Charidemus*

Demon. *Demonax*

Merc. cond. *De mercede conductis*

Nav. *Navigium*

Philops. *Philopseudes*

Pro imag. *Pro imaginibus*

Somn. *Somnium*

Symp. *Symposium*

Tox. *Toxaris*

Ver. hist. *Vera historia*

Menander

Sam. *Samia*

Nonnus

Dion. *Dionysiaca*

Origen

Fr. Ps. *Fragmenta in Psalmos 1–150*

Mart. *Exhortatio ad martyrium*

Ovid

Am. *Amores*

Ars *Ars amatoria*

Her. *Heroides*

Metam. *Metamorphoses*

Papyri

BGU *Berliner Griechische Urkunden*

CEG *Carmina Epigraphica Graeca,* ed. P. A. Hansen, 2 vols. (Berlin: de Gruyter, 1983, 1989).

P. Giess. Griechische Papyri im Museum des ober-hessischen Geschichtsvereins zu Giessen (Leipzig: Teubner, 1910–12).

P. Giss. Michael Kortus, *Briefe des Apollonius-Archives aus der Sammlung Papyri Gissenses:* Edition, Übersetzung und Kommentar, Berichte und Arbeiten aus der Universitätsbibliothek und dem Universitätsarchiv Giessen 49.

P. Gron. Papyri groninganae: griechische Papyri der Universitätsbibliothek zu Groningen, ed. A. G. Roos

P. Lond. Greek Papyri in the British Museum (London: Trustees of the British Museum, 1893–1974).

P. Mich. Michigan Papyri (Ann Arbor: University of Michigan, 1931–).

P. Oxy. Oxyrhynchus Papyri (London: Egypt Exploration Fund, 1898–)

P. S. I. Papyri Greci e Latini, Pubblicazioni della Società italiana per la ricerca dei papiri greci e latini in Egitto (Florence: E. Ariani, 1912–79).

Pausanius

   Descr. Graeciae descriptio

Philo

   Abr. De Abrahamo

   Mos. De vita Mosis

   Praem. De praemiis et poenis

   Somn. De Somniis

Philodemus

   Lib. De libertate dicendi

Philostratus

   Imag. Imagines

   Vit. Apoll. Vita Apollonii

   Vit. soph. Vitae sophistarum

Pindar

   Nem. Nemea

   Ol. Olympia

   Pyth. Pythia

Plato

   Crat. Cratylus

   Gorg. Gorgias

   Phaedr. Phaedrus

   Phileb. Philebus

Symp. Symposium

Plautus

    Cist. Cistellaria

Plotinus

    Enn. Enneades

Plutarch

    Adv. Col. Adversus Colotem

    Amat. Amatorius

    Amic. multi. De amicorum multitudine

    An seni An seni respublica gerenda sit

    Comp. Dem. Cic. Comparatio Demosthenis et Ciceronis

    Conj. praec. Conjugalia praecepta

    [Cons. Apoll.] Consolatio ad Apollonium

    Exil. De exilio

    Fac. De facie in orbe lunae

    Inim. util. De capienda ex inimicis utilitate

    Inv. od. De invidia et odio

    [Lib. ed.] De liberis educandis

    Lyc. Lycurgus

    Prim. frig. De primo frigido

    Quaest. conviv. Quaestiones convivialum

    Rect. rat. aud. De recta ratione audiendi

    Tu. san. De tuenda sanitate praecepta

Seneca

    Ira De ira

    On Tranq. De tranquillitate animi

Sophocles

    Trach. Trachiniae

Stobaeus

    Flor. Florilegium

Strabo

    Geogr. Geographica

Theocritus

    Id. Idylls

Theognis

    Eleg. Elegiae

Theophilus
> *Autol.* *Ad Autolycum*

Virgil
> *Aen.* *Aeneid*

Xenophon
> *Hell.* *Hellenica*
> *Symp.* *Symposium*

SECONDARY WORKS

AB   Anchor Bible
AJP   *American Journal of Philology*
CBQ   *Catholic Biblical Quarterly*
CCCM   Corpus Christianorum: Continuatio mediaevalis (Turnhout: Brepols, 1969–).
CP   *Classical Philology*
CWS   Classics of Western Spirituality
FC   Fathers of the Church
GRBS   *Greek, Roman, and Byzantine Studies*
HSCP   *Harvard Studies in Classical Philology*
HTR   *Harvard Theological Review*
JAC   *Jahrbuch für Antike und Christentum*
JAOS   *Journal of the American Oriental Society*
JFSR   *Journal of Feminist Studies in Religion*
JHS   *Journal of Hellenic Studies*
JRS   *Journal of Roman Studies*
JSNT   *Journal for the Study of the New Testament*
KJV   King James Version
LCL   Loeb Classical Library
LEC   Library of Early Christianity
MD   *Materiale e discussioni per l'analisi dei testi classici*
NASB   New American Standard Bible
NIGTC   New International Greek Testament Commentary
NIV   New International Version
NovTSup   Supplements to *Novum Testamentum*

NPNF   *Nicene and Post-Nicene Fathers*
NRSV New Revised Standard Version
NTS   *New Testament Studies*
PG   *Patrologia cursus completus: Series graeca,* ed. J.-P. Migne, 162 vols. (Paris: J.-P. Migne, 1857–86).
SBLDS   Society of Biblical Literature Dissertation Series
SBLMS   Society of Biblical Literature Monograph Series
SBLSBS   Society of Biblical Literature Sources for Biblical Study
SemeiaSt   Semeia Studies
SVF   *Stoicorum veterum fragmenta,* ed. H. von Arnim, 4 vols. (Leipzig: Teubner, 1903–24).
WW *Word and World*
WZ *Wissenschaftliche Zeitschrift*
ZPE *Zeitschrift für Papyrologie und Epigraphik*

Epigraphy

Werner Peek, *Griechische Vers-Inschriften. Band. 1: Grab-Epigramme.* Berlin: Akademie-Verlag, 1955.

Reinhold Merkelbach and Josef Stauber, *Steinepigramme aus dem griechischen Osten.* 5 vols. Leipzig: B. G. Teubner, 1998; K. G. Saur, 2001–2004.

Translations from the Loeb Classical Library

Aeschylus. *Aeschylus.* Translated by Alan H. Sommerstein. 3 vols. Cambridge, MA: Harvard University Press, 2008.

Anacreontea. Greek Lyric. Translated by David A. Campbell. 4 vols. Cambridge, MA: Harvard University Press; London: Heinemann, 1982–.

Apollonius of Rhodes. *Argonautica.* Translated by William H. Race. Cambridge, MA: Harvard University Press, 2008.

Aristophanes. *Aristophanes.* Translated by Jeffrey Henderson. 5 vols. Cambridge, MA: Harvard University Press, 1998–2007.

Athenaeus. *The Learned Banqueters.* Translated by S. Douglas Olson. 8 vols. Cambridge, MA: Harvard University Press, 2006–2012.

Basil. *Saint Basil: The Letters.* Translated by Roy Deferrari. 4 vols. Cambridge, MA: Harvard University Press; London: Heinemann, 1961–1962.

Catullus. *Catullus*; *Tibullus.* Translated by Francis Warre Cornish; J. P. Postgate. Cambridge, MA: Harvard University Press; London: Heinemann, 1988.

Cicero. *Letters to Atticus.* Translated by D. R. Shackleton Bailey. Cambridge,MA: Harvard University Press, 1999.

———. *Letters to Friends.* Translated by D. R. Shackleton Bailey. Cambridge, MA: Harvard University Press, 2001.

———. *Letters to Quintus and Brutus; Letter Fragments; Letter to Octavian; Invectives; Handbook of Electioneering.* Translated by D. R. Shackleton Bailey. Cambridge, MA: Harvard University Press, 2002.

Dio Chrysostom. *Dio Chrysostom.* Translated by J. W. Cohoon. 5 vols. Cambridge, MA: Harvard University Press; London: Heinemann, 1971–1995.

Dionysius of Halicarnassus. *The Roman Antiquities*. Translated by Earnest Cary. Cambridge, MA: Harvard University Press; London: Heinemann, 1948–1963.

————. *The Critical Essays in Two Volumes*. Stephen Usher. Cambridge,MA: Harvard University Press; London: Heinemann, 1974–1985.

Euripides. *Euripides*. Translated by David Kovacs. 8 vols. Cambridge,MA: Harvard University Press, 1994–2008.

Fronto. *The Correspondence of Marcus Cornelius Fronto*. 2 vols. Translated by C. R. Haines. Cambridge, MA: Harvard University Press; London: Heinemann, 1962–1963.

Greek Anthology. *The Greek Anthology*. Translated by W. R. Paton. 5 vols. Cambridge, MA: Harvard University Press, 1958–1963.

Hesiod. *Hesiod*. Translated by Glenn W. Most. 2 vols. Cambridge, MA: Harvard University Press, 2006.

Herodes. *The Characters of Theophrastus*. Translated by J. M. Edmonds. Cambridge, MA: Harvard University Press; London: Heinemann, 1967.

Hippocrates. *Hippocrates*. Translated by W. H. S. Jones. 9 vols. Cambridge, MA: Harvard University Press; London: Heinemann, 1967–2010.

Homer. *Odyssey*. Translated by A. T. Murray. 2 vols. Cambridge, MA: Harvard University Press, 1998.

Isocrates. *Isocrates*. Translated by George Norlin. 3 vols. Cambridge, MA: Harvard University Press; London: Heinemann, 1980–1982.

Julian. *The Works of the Emperor Julian*. Translated by Wilmer Cave Wright. 3 vols. Cambridge, MA: Harvard University Press; London: Heinemann, 1969–1980.

Lucian. *Lucian*. Translated by A. M. Harmon. 8 vols. Cambridge: Harvard University Press; London: Heinemann, 1990–1996.

Menander. *Menander*. Translated by W. G. Arnott. 3 vols. Cambridge, MA: Harvard University Press, 1996–.

Moschus. *The Greek Bucolic Poets*. Translated by J. M. Edmonds. London: Heinemann; New York: G. P. Putnam's Sons, 1923.

Musaeus. *Aetia, Iambi, Lyric Poems*. Translated by Cedric Whitman. Cambridge: Harvard University Press; London: Heinemann, 1978.

Oppian. *Oppian; Colluthus; Tryphiodorus*. Translated by A. W. Mair. Cambridge, MA: Harvard University Press; London: Heinemann, 1963.

Ovid. *Heroides and Amores*. Translated by Grant Showerman. Cambridge, MA: Harvard University Press; London: Heinemann, 1977.

————. *The Art of Love*. Translated by J. H. Mozley. Cambridge, MA: Harvard University Press; London: Heinemann, 1979.

————. *Metamorphoses*. Translated by Frank Justus Miller. 2 vols. Cambridge, MA: Harvard University Press, 1984.

————. *Tristia; Ex Ponto*. Translated by Arthur Leslie Wheeler. Cambridge, MA: Harvard University Press; London: Heinemann, 1988.

Pindar. *The Odes of Pindar*. John Sandys. London: Heinemann; New York: G. P. Putnam's Sons, 1930.

Plato. *Plato*. Translated by W. R. M. Lamb. 10 vols. Cambridge: Harvard University Press; London: Heinemann, 1953–1962.

Plautus. *Plautus*. Translated by Wolfgang de Melo. Cambridge, MA: Harvard University Press, 2011–.

Plutarch, *Moralia*. Translated by Edward N. O'Neil. 16 volumes. Cambridge, MA: Harvard University Press, 2004.

Polybius. *The Histories*. Translated by W. R. Paton. 6 vols. Cambridge, MA; London: Harvard University Press, 2010–.

Plotinus. *Plotinus*. Translated by A. H. Armstrong. 7 vols. Cambridge: Harvard University Press; London: Heinemann, 1966–1988.

Sappho. Greek Lyric. Translated by David A. Campbell. 4 vols. Cambridge, MA: Harvard University Press; London: Heinemann, 1982–.

Select Papyri, I. Translated by A. S. Hunt and C. C. Edgar. Cambridge, MA: Harvard University Press, 1932.

Seneca. *Ad Lucilium Epistulae Morales*. Translated by Richard M. Gummere. 3 vols. Cambridge, MA: Harvard University Press; London: Heinemann, 1962–1967.

Sophocles. *Sophocles*. Translated by Hugh Lloyd-Jones. 3 vols. Cambridge, MA: Harvard University Press, 1994–1998.

Strabo. *The Geography of Strabo*. Translated by Horace Leonard Jones. 8 vols. London: Heinemann; Cambridge, MA: Harvard University Press, 1968–1983.

Theocritus. *The Greek Bucolic Poets*. J. M. Edmonds. London: Heinemann; New York: Putnam's Sons, 1923.

Tibullus. *Catullus; Tibullus.* Translated by Francis Warre Cornish and J. P. Postgate. Cambridge, MA: Harvard University Press; London: Heinemann, 1988.

Xenophon. *Xenophon*. Translated by Carleton L. Brownson. 7 vols. Cambridge: Harvard University Press; London: Heinemann, 1968–1971.

Introduction

From Homer to Paulus Silentiarius, it melted innards and emptied the liquefied self unto death. It drove the plot of ancient novels from the first century to the eleventh. Famous letter writers like Cicero and John Chrysostom, obscure ones (only from the West's perspective) like Nikephoros Ouranos and Theodoros of Kyzikos, and the forgotten correspondents of Greek papyri—all wrote to allay it, unsuccessfully. Doctors knew it was a disease with no cure save one. This *pathos* transformed desolation into song, gave birth to sculpture one night at a potter's house in Corinth, erected gravestones, and even tilted the great Alexander's head. It was a god—not Eros but his twin brother. Or, it *was* Eros with covered face mourning his beloved. Paul declared it lodged in the innards he shared with Christ. Epaphroditus suffered it, too. The Greeks called this love infused with grief πόθος. The Romans wrote *desiderium*. In English, it is longing.

There once was a time when Paul's letter to the Philippians was read through *pothos*. Longing played an important role in the reception of Philippians among fourth-century Christians and, to a greater extent, authors of the middle and late Byzantine periods and Latin writers including Bernard of Clairvaux, Guerric of Igny, and Gilbert of Hoyland, the last three of whom John of Ford (1140–1214) called "noble friends of the spouse and attendants to the bride."[1] Why did John award these writers such high honors? Each had exposited the biblical poem Song of Songs. Yet it was more than their labor he praised. Each also had discovered an entry to profound theology in that poem's eroticism. Their exegetical training, which John reports took place in a marriage chamber, was an experience too intimate to relate yet powerful and contagious.[2] Unlike modern interpreters, these writers were attentive to Paul's *desiderium* for Christ and the church. They read the Christ Hymn as if it were a narrative of longing, as if the motivation for the incarnation, life, and death of Jesus had been the Son of God's impossible desire for communion with humanity. Now, it must be admitted that the same writers at times portrayed Paul as an authoritarian leader and the Christ Hymn as an exemplary story of humble submission to the will of the sovereign Father. In this respect they anticipated what most scholars today say about Paul and Paul's God. Unlike their modern counterparts, however, these older authors allowed two distinct readings, one ruled by sovereignty and the other by longing, to occupy their minds and sometimes to stand next to each other on the same page. Their openness to love makes plausible the hunch motivating this book that erotic motifs influenced the composition of Philippians and the letter's earliest reception.

Premodern interpreters offer us something quite valuable, since they read Philippians as if it were written poetically. That is to say, they heard motifs from ancient love poetry in Paul's words. They were unafraid to construe the apostle's emotion as the *erōs* of secular literature even though they knew such readings were out of bounds or, in the words of Baldwin of Ford (c. 1125–1190) that such untamed authority was "unworthy and unsuitable." Still, if pagans experienced love, Baldwin reasoned, and if their love poetry illumines Scriptures, they ought to be consulted. Sappho, for example, knew love. Born in the later part of the seventh century B.C.E., she was the first witness of love's violence perpetrated against the lover. Although she was a most unlikely tutor to Christian exegetes, writers in the Middle Ages nevertheless learned from her about the suffering of love, and hers was not the only voice. Puzzling over the conflicting emotions love brings to the soul, Baldwin appeals to Ovid to defend the propriety of the Bride's words "because I am afflicted with love" from Song of Songs:

> Love is an affliction, and the suffering of a soul that is sick. The authority of the poet—even though it seems unworthy and unsuitable— affirms the truth of this, when he says: "Woe to me, for no herb can cure love." But for religious minds, it should be enough that this is the voice of the bride. She states what she feels and says: "I am afflicted with love."[3]

Baldwin recognized in biblical love the quality Sappho called "sweet-bitter."[4] Baldwin writes, "love is obviously an affliction. Someone who loves, burns and yearns and sighs; he does not have what he wants, and if he is kept from the coveted embraces of the bride, he is tormented by this very fact."[5] In order to place the Bride's spiritual illness within Christian faith, Baldwin developed a typology of love far different from the tripartite division invented by Anders Nygren (*erōs*, *philia*, and *agapē*), which would have excluded her erotic suffering from proper Christian theology. Baldwin cites Phil 1:22, 29; 3:8 as further proof that Ovid's lovesickness is biblical and therefore valid as a form of piety.[6] Paul and Ovid, twin authorities!

Ancient poets called the torment of *pothos* lovesickness. Sappho's list of the lover's physical symptoms was famous in antiquity and inspired the poetic *topos* "love as a disease" lasting well into the middle ages.[7] When lover looks upon beloved the tongue is tied, skin burns, eyes and ears fail, cold sweat breaks out and shaking takes control, and the victim of Eros appears to herself as dead.[8]

The ancients feared Eros. Hesiod tells us why. Like Sleep (in a small way) and Death (in a big way), Eros loosens limbs and tosses the mind from the body:

> In truth, first of all Chasm came to be, and then broad-breasted Earth, the ever immovable seat of all the immortals who possess snowy Olympus' peak and murky Tartarus in the depths of the broad-pathed earth, and Eros, who is the most beautiful among the immortal gods, the limb-melter—he overpowers the mind and the thoughtful counsel of all the gods and of all human beings in their breasts.[9]

Eros revealed to the ancients that they were not masters of their lives. Autonomy flies out the window when your beloved, your all in all, your happiness and the host of your wandering soul walks in the door, or worse, threatens to walk out.

This book is not directly about *erōs*. It is about longing, Paul's longing for the church and for Christ and Christ's longing for mortals. Yet, to get at *pothos* in Paul's letters it will be necessary to acknowledge Eros's dual role in the lives of ancient people: the god was maker of communion and frightful menace. Erotic misfortunes fell upon victims in various ways. Often in formulaic terms, ancient funerary inscriptions recorded an obvious cause of longing: the death of a spouse, children, parents, or friends, and as painful as these deaths were, the beloved's disinterest was even worse.[10] Nothing hurt more than to be told no. *Erōs* was drained of presence and transformed into *pothos* in a mightier way still, through separation; travel broke many hearts in an age without cell phones and jets. The letter to the Philippians and the Christology it contains needs to be reimagined through the space separating Paul and the community. We need to learn how to read through longing.

To that end, this book adopts a reading practice similar to that of Baldwin and his contemporaries. Like them, I listen for echoes of ancient poetry in the language of Philippians and acknowledge the influence of Sappho and the tradition she inspired. She was one of the first to mark love's effect on the body of the lover, and when Paul speaks of love he may be speaking of the physical event she so famously described. Love heated, melted, and finally emptied the body even as sickness wastes human flesh. The openness of Byzantine and medieval Christian writers to erotic suffering is a departure from today's approaches to Paul's letters. Modern interpreters not only subordinate love to sovereignty when speaking about God but also prefer philosophy and religion to poetry when they imagine the composition and reception of Pauline texts. While it has become commonplace to grasp a Pauline letter in one hand and the writings of the Hellenistic philosophers, or the documents of ancient Judaism, in the other and read back and forth, the same cannot yet be said in modern scholarship for ancient poetry and Paul.[11] I hope to change that situation in a small way.

It is not just Pauline interpreters' preoccupation with sovereignty that stands in the way of Christology based on longing desire. When it comes to sex and marriage, Paul's own anti-eroticism is well recognized and threatens to stop the present inquiry in its tracks. It might very well be asked why we should seek out erotic allusions in Paul's discourse when we already know that he opposes desire.[12] It is, after all, better to marry than to burn (1 Cor 7:9), not a glowing recommendation of romantic love. Given Paul's reputation in matters of sex, our proposal to interpret his writings in terms of *erōs* appears counterintuitive.

The following distinction, therefore, needs to be made. In Philippians, Paul does not concern himself with the management of bodies, a topic he covered in 1 Thessalonians 4, Romans 1, and 1 Corinthians 6–7 in ways remarkably similar to the anti-erotic writings of Greek and Roman moral philosophers. When it comes to matters of sex and marriage, Paul's writings rehearse philosophic clichés about avoidance of shame through self-control. Philippians, though, is about the relationship *at a distance* that Paul in company with Timothy, Epaphroditus, Euodia, and Syntyche had with a community of persons. This relationship *in absence* opens on to Paul's longing for Christ, Christ's desire for communion with the church and the world, and, finally, God's own loving relatedness to all of creation. The distinction that needs to be made, then, is between personal ethics, with its concern for the management of bodies and a Christology and ecclesiology that take loss and grief seriously. Paul's antipathy for *erōs* in sex is overshadowed by his passion to apply *erōs* to Christ. Not to make this distinction and to reject the possibility of erotic meanings in the letter is to throw out the baby, as Eros often was pictured, with the bathwater.

If it is the case that Paul's dim view of *erōs* reached only to sexual ethics, then we are free to ask about its significance for his Christology. But does Paul's letter to the Philippians in fact contain erotic terminology?[13] This door having been opened, it would be disappointing to discover that we have walked into an empty room. The burden of this book is to show that Paul did indeed take advantage of ancient culture's tumultuous love affair with *erōs*. To make this point, I will situate Paul's words about Christ in the history of longing as it appears in poetry, novels, letters, medical texts, grave inscriptions, and Christian reception of Pauline texts. These are texts usually considered the turf of classicists and experts in the literature of late antiquity and the medieval period and seldom given attention by New Testament scholars. An expert in none of these fields (and painfully aware of it), I nevertheless ask readers to follow the trail of longing wherever it takes us.

Why has *pothos* not drawn the attention of Pauline scholars, who seek as do I to reinterpret Paul by expanding the horizon of his texts? Perhaps it is because of the company *pothos* keeps. As I emphasized above, *pothos* has no existence apart from *erōs*, for only those who exult in the presence of the beloved ache in the time of absence. In the *Cratylus*, Socrates played fast and loose with linguistic data, but his fanciful etymology revealed a widely held belief about longing's connection to erotic desire: "πόθος (yearning) signifies that it pertains not to that which is present, but to that which is elsewhere (ἄλλοθί που) or absent, and therefore the same feeling which is called ἵμερος when its object is present, is called πόθος when it is present."[14] When the beloved is not there, physically or emotionally, *pothos* arises. *Pothos* is linked to *erōs* as a shadow is to its body. Longing and love must be related, but they must also be distinguished, and in both tasks biblical scholars have fallen short.[15]

For this reason, *pothos* has fared only as well as *erōs* has, and lately it has not gone well for *erōs*. Somewhere along the way biblical interpreters and longing have gotten separated. It was Eros's fault. By the mid-twentieth century, Pothos's twin brother had acquired a reputation for carnality pure and simple. Indiscriminate condemnation brought them both down from their celebrated places in earlier periods of the church; many biblical interpreters now would find the suggestion of an erotic Paul, if it ever were offered, unsavory and ludicrous. This is unfortunate. Although *erōs* might feel like an objectifying concept, it need not be. A broad range of human emotions disappear when erotic experience is limited to sex as a targeting behavior. When some classical scholars speak of *erōs*, they are referring to a reality larger than the acquisition of a partner in sex.[16] Writers from the church's past likewise had a broader imagination, recognizing that *erōs* is about communion. Dionysius the Areopagite writes,

> To those listening properly to the divine things the name "love" is used by the sacred writers in divine revelation with the exact same meaning as the term "yearning" (τὸ τῆς ἀγάπης καί τοῦ ἔρωτος

ὄνομα). What is signified is a capacity to effect a unity, an alliance, and a particular commingling in the Beautiful and the Good.[17]

Erōs seeks connection, the sharing of lives, and the knowing and being known face to face. So, if, as this book argues, Paul intensified the literary representation of his loving Christ and Christ's loving the world by expressing their common passion in poetic diction, contemporary scholars do the apostle an injustice by thinking just of sex when he uses words implying *erōs* in its fullest sense.

A permeable border separates *erōs, agapē,* and *philia,* three ancient forms of love that for the past sixty years Christian preachers have been admonished by professors of New Testament, theology, and homiletics to keep apart. *Agape and Eros,* by Anders Nygren, a book whose influence on preaching since the mid-twentieth century has been considerable, drove a wedge between *agapē* on one side and *erōs* and *philia* on the other. To establish his case for the unique status of *agapē,* Nygren mischaracterized *erōs* claiming that it is selfish.[18] *Erōs* simply uses another human being to satisfy the physical and spiritual needs of the lover. Now, there are indeed ancient texts that support Nygren's view, but one need only breeze through Sappho's fragments to realize that there is something wrong with his notion of *erōs* as *only* other-consuming. There is more to the story of love than Nygren imagined. *Erōs* ate away at the soul, burning and piercing the lover's heart; poets in antiquity testify how frighteningly *self-consuming erōs* was. Furthermore, *agapē,* whose sole ownership by Christians it has been many a preacher's proud moment to proclaim in order to belittle lesser loves, turns out to be a fairly reliable synonym for *erōs* after all. As for *philia,* it never was far removed from *erōs,* as Seneca wrote, "Beyond question the feeling of a lover has in it something akin to friendship; one might call it friendship run mad."[19] Nygren's tidy divisions just don't hold up.

In the ancient geography of the human heart, the long and unguarded border between *erōs* and *philia* was difficult to draw even when there was interest to do so. Definitions rarely sparked the creativity of ancient Greek poets. Their interests lay elsewhere. Rather than limiting *erōs* to sex, some wondered whether love might actually explain the nature of the entire universe. Might it be, they wondered in amazement, that what holds the cosmos together is the same force that binds lover to beloved and ties friends fast? In the third century B.C.E., the god Eros invited the entire world to confess him as Lord in an epigram of Simias of Rhodes that adumbrates Paul's celebration of Jesus as Lord in Phil 2:11. Eros speaks:

Look on me, the lord of broad-bosomed Earth, who stablished the Heaven elsewhere, and tremble not if, little though I be, my cheeks are heavy with bushy hair. For I was born when Necessity was ruler, and all creeping things and those that move through the sky yielded to the dire decrees of Earth. But I am called the swift-flying son of Chaos, not of Cypris or of Ares, for in no wise did I rule by force, but by gentle-voiced persuasion, and the earth and the depths of the sea and the brazen heaven yielded to me. I robbed them of their ancient sceptre and gave laws to the gods.[20]

Eros is Lord, yet his reign relies not on violence but persuasion.[21] He makes the world work through attraction rather than necessity and the "dire decrees of Earth."[22] It would be a shame to allow sex, especially the ancient world's subject–object dichotomous version of it, to get all the attention and for this reason bar *erōs* from Pauline meanings. So much would be missed. If Simias is to be believed, the whole world and its Lord.

Notes

1. John of Ford, *Sermon* 24.2. Translation is from *Sermons on the Final Verses of the Song of Songs, II*, trans. Wendy Mary Beckett, Cistercian Fathers Series 39 (Kalamazoo: Cistercian Publications, 1982), 135. Richard of St. Victor is also named, but his work does not play a significant role in the present study.

2. John of Ford, *Sermon* 24.2 (*Sermons on the Final Verses of the Song of Songs, II*, 135–36): "It was in the marriage chamber that they learned to understand the marriage song, and only then did they become able to explain this sacred love to us. Even so, they could hardly expound in words more than the slightest part of the great things they had learned in their hearts. Still I receive them as angels of God, and I listen to them with my whole heart as to Seraphim, a name that is said to mean those who both burn and set others afire."

3. Baldwin of Ford, *Spiritual Tractates* 14. Translation is from *Baldwin of Ford: Spiritual Tractates, II*, trans. David N. Bell, Cistercian Fathers Series 41 (Kalamazoo: Cistercian Publications, 1986), 141. On this passage, see Bernard McGinn, *The Growth of Mysticism: Gregory the Great through the Twelfth Century*, vol. 2 of *The Presence of God: A History of Western Christian Mysticism* (New York: Crossroad, 1994), 303–5. See also Baldwin of Ford, *Spiritual Tractates* 8, where Virgil's description (*Aen.* 4.1–2) of Dido's wounded heart is admired. See also Theocritus, *Id.* 2.84: "some burning disease wiped me out" (μέ τις καπυρὰ νόσος ἐξελάπαξε) (my translation). Lovesickness is a favorite theme of erotic fiction. See especially Xenophon of Ephesus, *Ephesiaca* 1.5–6, on which see Peter Toohey, "Dangerous Ways to Fall in Love: Chariton I 1, 5–10 and VI 9, 4," *Maia* 51 (1999): 259–75. See also Longus, *Daphn.* 1.13–14, 17–18; 2.7–8; Heliodorus, *Aeth.* 3.7; 4.7, 10. For the intersection of poetry and medicine in this matter, see Mirko Grmek, *Diseases in the Ancient Greek World* (Baltimore: Johns Hopkins University Press, 1989), 36–37, 43–44; Mary Frances Wack, *Lovesickness in the Middle Ages: The Viaticum and Its Commentaries*, Middle Ages Series (Philadelphia: University of Pennsylvania Press, 1990), 1–18. For Greek medical texts in Arabic sources, see Hans H. Biesterfeldt and Dimitri Gutas, "The Malady of Love," *JAOS* 104

(1984): 21–55. The most comprehensive study is Donald A. Beecher and Massimo Ciavolella, *A Treatise on Lovesickness: Jacques Ferrand* (Syracuse: Syracuse University Press, 1990).

4. See chapter 2.

5. Baldwin of Ford, *Spiritual Tractates* 14. Bell, *Baldwin of Ford,* 143.

6. See also Baldwin of Ford, *Spiritual Tractates* 3.

7. See note 3 above.

8. Sappho, *Frg.* 31.

9. Hesiod, *Theog.* 116–22. It is telling that Eros's effects on the body were indistinguishable from those of Hades, god of death. See *Greek Anthology* 12.73.

10. Longing was sometimes declared as the motive for erecting gravestones: "*Pothos* has set this work up before the eye" (*Steinepigramme* 16/31/98). For more examples, see *Griechische Vers-Inschriften* 227, 568, 1745, 2035; *Steinepigramme* 9/6/15; 9/9/15; 14/2/8; 14/3/3.

11. For an important exception, see Christopher Smith, "'Ἐκκλεῖσαι' in Galatians 4:17: The Motif of the Excluded Lover as a Metaphor of Manipulation," *CBQ* 58 (1996): 480–99.

12. Dale B. Martin, *Sex and the Single Savior: Gender and Sexuality in Biblical Interpretation* (Louisville: Westminster John Knox, 2006); David E. Fredrickson, "Natural and Unnatural Use in Romans 1:24-27: Paul and the Philosophic Critique of Eros," in *Homosexuality, Science, and the "Plain Sense" of Scripture,* ed. David L. Balch (Grand Rapids: Eerdmans, 2000), 197–222; and idem, "Passionless Sex in 1 Thessalonians 4:4-5," *WW* 23 (2003): 23–30.

13. There is a quick way to answer yes. In the second century C.E., the scholar and rhetorician Julius Pollux did a favor for public speakers who wished to measure up to attic standards. In his *Onomasticon*, Pollux collected classical terminology on a wide range of subjects. Here are selections from the entry for ἐρᾶν (3.68–72): longing (πόθος); to burn with longing (φλέγεσθαι τῷ πόθῳ); to be a slave (δουλεύειν); voluntary slave (ἐθελόδουλος); desire (ἐπιθυμία); one who desires (ἐπιθυμήτης); taking thought for (φροντίζων); to be seized (κατειλῆφθαι); loving (ἀγαπῶν); beloved (ἀγαπώμενος). When this list is compared with the vocabulary of Philippians, the following shared terms may be noted: ἐπιποθῶ (1:8); ἐπιποθῶν (2:26); ἐπιπόθητοι (4:1); δοῦλοι (1:1; 2:7); ἐδούλευσεν (2:22); ἐπιθυμίαν (1:23); φρονεῖν ὑπέρ (1:7; 4:10); ἀγάπη (1:9, 16; 2:1); ἀγαπητοί (2:12; 4:1); καταλάβω, κατελήμφθην, κατειληφέναι (3:12-13).

14. Plato, *Crat.* 420A. Cf. Plutarch, *Amat.* 759B.

15. With notable exceptions; see L. William Countryman, *Love, Human and Divine: Reflections on Love, Sexuality, and Friendship* (Harrisburg, PA: Morehouse, 2005); and David M. Carr, *The Erotic Word: Sexuality, Spirituality, and the Bible* (Oxford: Oxford University Press, 2003).

16. See Claude Calame, *The Poetics of Eros in Ancient Greece*, trans. Janet Lloyd (Princeton: Princeton University Press, 1999).

17. Pseudo-Dionysius, *The Divine Names* 709CD. Translation is from *Pseudo-Dionysius: The Complete Works,* trans. Colm Luibheid, CWS (Mahwah, NJ: 1987), 81. Yet God does not experience *erōs* in the same way as humans do according to the Areopagite. Divine *erōs* becomes love-patriarchalism as it binds "the things of the same order in a mutually regarding union" and moves "the superior to provide for the subordinate, and it stirs the subordinate in a return toward the superior" (709D). Glimmers of passion do survive, however: God "is, as it were, beguiled by goodness, by love, and by yearning and is enticed away from his transcendent dwelling place and comes to abide within all things, and he does so by virtue of his supernatural and ecstatic capacity to remain, nevertheless, with himself" (712B).

18. For a helpful alternative to Nygren's categories, see Bernard McGinn, "God as Eros: Metaphysical Foundations of Christian Mysticism," in *New Perspectives on Historical Theology: Essays in Memory of John Meyendorff,* ed. Bradley Nassif (Grand Rapids: Eerdmans, 1996), 189–209.

19. Seneca, *Ep.* 9.11.

20. *Greek Anthology* 15.24.

21. For other confessions of Eros as Lord, see Menander, *Sam.* 632: "Love, ruler of my heart" (ὁ τῆς ἐμῆς νῦν κύριος γνώμης, Ἔρως). Cf. Plutarch, *Amat.* 768AB: "when Love enters as

sovereign, men are ever after free and released from all other lords and masters and continue throughout their days to be, as it were, slaves of the god." Cf. Xenophon of Ephesus, *Ephesiaca* 1.4; and *Greek Anthology* 12.28. See Neta Zagagi, *Tradition and Originality in Plautus: Studies of the Amatory Motifs in Plautine Comedy,* Hypomnemata 62 (Göttingen: Vandenhoeck & Ruprecht, 1989), 116.

    22. Cf. Aeschylus, *Suppl.* 1034–42.

1

Troubling Presence

. . . the more they show your presence among us, in some sort, the more they make it impossible for us to bear your absence.[1]

WRITING AND CHRISTOLOGY

Despite the different topics this book explores, in effect only one question is pursued throughout its pages: might the momentous sentence "Jesus Christ is Lord" (Phil 2:11) mean something other than what most interpreters take it to mean—that the world is under Jesus' control and at his disposal? Although "Lord" is widely thought to be the final word on Jesus' identity, a different way of reading cannot be excluded: Jesus is the last word on what a lord is. If words are not privileged beings like kings in palaces kept safe from subjects or like masters ruling slaves, perhaps even a mighty word like "Lord" is vulnerable to invasion by "Jesus Christ." What if "Lord" was defined by "Jesus Christ" as much as or even more than "Jesus Christ" is by "Lord"?

There is a good reason to pursue this question about the semantic stability of "Lord." In Phil 2:6-11, narration of Jesus' character precedes confession of his title. Verses 6-8 tell a story with Jesus as the sole actor; his actions give rise to responses in vv. 9-11. This suggests that Jesus can lay claim to an enduring character, and it is the title "Lord" that is enhanced by the narration. Jesus' story elicits a naming response from God, mortals, and other tongues whose common judgment is that the one known through this story is the very definition of a lord. Paul (or a hymn that he quotes) brilliantly set a scene of voices agreeing with God's praise of Jesus and repeating God's own naming of Jesus as *kyrios*. In fact, if one reads v. 11 out loud, at least three groups of confessors speak in

agreement with God's calling Jesus "Lord." Those who first uttered the words
are held in memory, while living readers repeat the words in anticipation of
the day when every tongue will pronounce them. But what is this universal
agreement about? The story that builds up to the confession resists attempts
to subsume Jesus under the category of those who wield absolute power like
Caesar, Zeus, Hades, Eros, or even God, as if Jesus bested them at their own
game of sovereignty. That would be out of character for the Christ Jesus of
2:6-8. The narrated Jesus infects the title Lord with the life he lived or, more
precisely, with the death he died.

These brief remarks on Jesus' lordship foreshadow the aversion to
sovereign power that readers will detect in the following pages and anticipate
my claim that, at least within the limits of the letter to the Philippians,
longing—not control—is the chief characteristic of Pauline Christology,
apostolic ministry, and ecclesiology. The story of Jesus that shapes lordship in
Phil 2:6-11 is repeated in Paul's desire for the church confessed in 1:8: "For
God is my witness, how I long for you all in the innards of Christ Jesus."
Explorations of Paul's Christology customarily do not reckon with the apostle's
confession concerning his interior life, nor do they begin with an investigation
of his letter writing. As I hope to show, however, what we say about Paul's
letters shapes what we look for in him, and what we say about Paul shapes
what we look for in Christ. This principle holds whether it is sovereignty
or longing that we wish to project onto Christ. If, for example, when Paul's
letters are regarded as instruments of control, then it is quite likely we will
picture the apostle directing, educating, and disciplining congregations while
defending his authority against opponents' attacks.[2] And if this is the Paul we
invent on the basis of Philippians, then Christ likely will be the supreme model
of humble submission to God's will. His obedience to the Father earns him,
somewhat inconsistently, the title "Lord," and his model obedience stabilizes
the community's obedience. Paul's letter creates his directing, educating, and
disciplining presence in the community even as he is far distant from it.
Controlling letters yield an authoritarian Paul who promotes an exemplary
Christ submissive to patriarchal divinity.

I have no objection to a flow of influence. Whether Pauline interpreters
admit it or not, we all follow *some* stream of motifs circulating from the letter
in question, through Paul, to Christ and back to the letter again. Christology
is indeed tuned to epistolography via Pauline biography. My concern is that
motifs of control have been so exaggerated in Pauline studies that longing desire
has not been given a chance to organize our knowledge of the letters, Paul's
writing about himself, or his Christology. If, as it is argued below, Philippians

is a complex symbol that delivers Paul's presence and in so doing also takes it away, we are likely to orient our picture of Paul around his confession of longing for the community, an emotion he shares with Christ (Phil 1:8). And if Philippians both opens space for readers to long for Paul and marks Paul by his desire for communion with an absent community, then a Christ who longs for communion with humanity is plausible. Christ's suffering the absence of his beloved stabilizes (if this is possible) Paul's desire for the church and the church's for Paul. Thus, our understanding of letter writing is crucial for appreciating Pauline Christology.

But what do we understand a Pauline epistle to be? Ancient epistolary theory encouraged readers to imagine themselves in the writer's presence hearing his or her voice and thus through the letter gaining access to ideas. As this chapter argues, letter writers in antiquity in fact had a far more nuanced view, since they doubted the stability of presence and voice that their theory promised. Many modern interpreters, however, have taken ancient theory at its word and regard a Pauline letter as a substitute for his presence and voice through which his ideas about Jesus can be ascertained. This approach to reading Philippians has gone hand in hand with a focus on Paul's authority and Christ's obedience to God. That Paul's emotion of *pothos* could invade sovereignty and obedience appears as wrongheaded as the proposition that the meaning of "Lord" in Phil 2:11 depends on the history of Jesus.

Yet, when epistolary presence is shown to be an illusion and thus fragile, and again I want to stress that ancient letters themselves sadly admit writing's failure to guarantee presence, we are left with a letter stubbornly refusing to let us see through it to the author. It instead reminds us of the distance between writer and reader. Writing returns us again and again to Paul's absence and Christ's. Consequently, neither Paul, nor Christ, nor the original readers of the letter are present to assure us that we have settled on the right meanings. But this is a good thing. Without clear ideas to guide the way, we get distracted from our search for concepts about power and control and concentrate more and more on Paul's passion (Phil 1:8), a longing for communion that will not go away even if his ideas could be possessed securely. This is, of course, a body blow to Pauline Christology normally conceived, since Christian teachings, such as "Jesus is Lord," ought not be susceptible to the instability of desire.[3]

This, then, is the danger of beginning a book on Pauline Christology with a consideration of his letter writing: getting sidetracked in emotion. For this reason, if letters must be considered at all, a more conventional approach would have us wait until Paul's ideas about Jesus have first been clarified. At that point, letters may be analyzed as delivery systems for those ideas. Then investigators are free to show how Paul fit his ideas about Jesus both to available language (theology) and to his audience (rhetoric). Paul's letters express his ideas and persuade audiences to believe them, but the mood they create in hearers and the impression they give of the writer's emotions—these are data not directly relevant to the *logos* of Christ. Now it becomes clear why ancient epistolary theory is more attractive to modern scholars than ancient letter writing itself. Theory encourages us to move through and past Paul's writing to the apostle's Christology. The heart of this theory is that a letter substitutes for the writer's presence and speech. A letter is not really writing but oral communication literally accomplished.[4]

This was a stock motif in ancient letters of friendship. For example, Julian's letter to Maximus claims that a letter substitutes for the writer's presence and speech:

> I sleep with your letters as though they were healing drugs of some sort, and I do not cease to read them constantly as though they were newly written and had only just come into my hands. Therefore if you are willing to furnish me with intercourse (ὁμιλίαν) by means of letters, as a semblance of your own society (εἰκόνα τῆν σῆς παρουσίας), write, and do not cease to do so continually.[5]

Or, on August 23, 133 c.e., a man wrote to his brother: "And do not hesitate to write letters, since I rejoiced exceedingly, as if you had come. From the day that you sent me the letter I have been saved."[6] A papyrus letter later in the century makes the same point: "As soon as I reached Antinoöpolis, I received your letter, through which I got the feeling of seeing you (δι' ὧν ἔδοξα σε θεωρεῖν). I therefore beseech you to do the same constantly, for in this way our love will be increased (οὕτως γὰρ αὐξηθήσεται ἡμῶν ἡ φιλία)."[7]

Letter writers imitated the craft of painters.[8] Words paint a portrait of the sender to create an illusion of presence.[9] The Roman philosopher Seneca wrote,

> I thank you for writing to me so often; for you are revealing your real self to me in the only way you can. I never receive a letter from you without being in your company forthwith. If the pictures of our absent friends are pleasing to us, though they only refresh the memory and lighten our longing (*desiderium*) by a solace that is unreal and unsubstantial, how much more pleasant is a letter, which brings us real traces, real evidences, of an absent friend! For that

which is sweetest when we meet face to face is afforded by the impress of a friend's hand upon his letter,—recognition.[10]

Not only painting, but the art of the miniature is mentioned as a suitable comparison to help make this power of representation known. Julian wrote to George, a revenue official: "in your letters I have already seen you and the image of your noble soul, and have received the impression thereof as of an imposing device on a small seal. For it is possible for much to be revealed in a little."[11] In another letter, Julian writes to the high priest Theodorus, "I was filled with serenity and felicity and welcomed the letter as though I beheld in it an image (εἰκόνα), so to speak, of your disposition."[12]

In addition to creating presence, a letter is the voice of the absent friend saying what would have been said had distance not separated writer and recipient. An epigram made the point wistfully: "Nature, loving the duties of friendship, invented instruments by which absent friends can converse, pens, paper, ink, handwriting, tokens of the heart that mourns afar off."[13] One of Ovid's letters written during his exile took theory's promise of a living voice to an extreme. After a few perplexing moments, present-day readers discover that the letter has its own voice and speaks on behalf of Ovid:

> But thee—O, if thou believest me in anything, dearer than all to him—thee he holds constantly in his whole heart. Thee he calls his Menoetiades, thee his Orestes' comrade, thee his Aegides, or his Euryalus. He longs (*desiderat*) not more for his country and the many things with his country whose absence he feels, than for thy face and eyes, O thou who art sweeter than the honey stored in the wax by the Attic bee.[14]

Ovid's overly literal realization of epistolary theory makes a simple point: letters talk. Synesius speaks of the "letter's power to be a solace for unhappy loves, affording as it does in bodily absence the illusion of actual presence, for this missive seems itself to converse, thus fulfilling the soul's desire."[15] But there is trouble; absence comes around the corner just as presence and voice seem established.

THE FRAGILITY OF EPISTOLARY PRESENCE

Paul's striking confession in Phil 1:8 ("For God is my witness, how I long for you all in the innards of Christ"), in which Paul is more pining lover than authoritative guide, has largely gone unobserved in the modern period. Accordingly, his letters have been conceptualized as instruments of admonition, teaching, and self-defense. There are, however, exceptions to this emphasis on apostolic authority among scholars today. Stanley Stowers called attention to 1:7-8 as a possible example of the motif of yearning for the loved one, a commonplace that he correctly observed could be easily documented in letters of friendship.[16] Some years later, he summarized the work of a number of classicists on ancient epistolography and brought their findings to bear on Philippians: "Expressions of affection and longing to be with one's friends were considered appropriate for letters of friendship and manifest themselves in commonplace phraseology and topoi."[17] The significance of Stowers's insight grows when placed in its historical context. In the early 1990s a challenge arose to a widely held view that Paul organized the letter of Philippians around the problem of his authority; friendship, according to a number of scholars, was instead both the letter's topic and the point of its composition.[18] The letter was not simply an instrument of control but a means of preserving and intensifying the shared lives of separated friends. Paul wrote in the language of friendship to increase friendship.[19] Yet, while the categorization of Philippians as a letter of friendship is, I believe, a real advance because it both recognizes philophronetic motifs and paints a less authoritarian picture of Paul, it nevertheless accepts as unproblematic the notion of the letter as a bearer of the writer's presence. So, while affirming Philippians as a friendly letter, I want to challenge the idea that letters delivered presence purely and simply.

Letters are indeed substitutes for the writer's physical presence, but even in that moment when they create an illusion of presence they also remind readers of the author's absence. Letters of friendship simultaneously give comfort and refresh the wounds of separation, and this double effect was even more the case when letter writers enhanced friendly feelings with allusions to *erōs* and *pothos*. Greek letters, beginning in the fourth century, provide numerous examples of eroticized friendship. John Chrysostom, for example, charged his letters with erotic terminology, often characterizing himself as a lover (ἐραστής) both vehement (σφοδρός) and warm (θερμός).[20] In Chrysostom's letters friends are connected by bonds of love and longing.[21] Erotic love furthermore explains the insatiate desire that he and the recipients of his letters have for more and longer epistles.[22] In Philippians, Paul anticipates the epistolary habits of the fourth century and pushes past the limits of friendship into *erōs* by telling his own story and Jesus' in terms of longing desire, but in so doing he problematized the very presence and voice his letter created.

Interpreters have overlooked the shaky hold readers have on the writer's presence, especially when the relationship has been cast in erotic terms. They need to pay greater attention to writers' own admissions of failure to deliver their presence and voice. Basil's letters frequently incorporated erotic motifs, and in the following letter to Theodorus he faces up to the eroticism of his own epistolary practice and hints at the fragility of presence.[23] He writes,

> Some say that those who are seized with the passion of love (τοὺς ἑαλωκότας τῷ πάθει τοῦ ἔρωτος), whenever through some unusually urgent necessity they are parted from the object of their desire (τῶν ποθουμένων), if they can look upon the semblance of the beloved form in a picture, can check the violence of their passion through the pleasure they derive from the sight. [24]

Basil draws a parallel between portraits and letters. Both simulate presence and overcome longing, but equally important is what he fails to say explicitly: the very same literary object that calms longing also reinvigorates it.[25] He does hint at the problem, however, since the letter can only "check the violence of their passion," not eradicate it. Basil has left the door open just a crack.

When separation is the defining moment of a letter, as it was in Philippians as in all friendly letters, and longing the underlying mood, a letter's significance rests on the *illusion* of presence it creates.[26] Reports of lonely lovers kissing letters before, after, and in the middle of reading bring out the illusory character of letters. Note the "as if" or "as though" quality of epistolary presence, which Julian seems to fear could evaporate at any moment:

> . . . how often I held the letter to my lips, as mothers embrace their children, how often I kissed it with those lips as though I were embracing my dearest sweetheart, how often I invoked and kissed and held to my eyes even the superscription which had been signed by your own hand as though by a clear cut seal, and how I clung to the imprint of the letters as I should to the fingers of that sacred right hand of yours![27]

The novelist Chariton describes a similar mode of reception:

> Dionysius went back to his quarters and shut himself in. When he recognized Callirhoe's handwriting, he first kissed the letter, then opened it and clasped it to his breast as if it were Callirhoe present in the flesh. He held it there for a long time, unable to read it for crying.

> After copious tears he began to read it, with difficulty; and the first
> thing he did was to kiss the name "Callirhoe."[28]

Letters are illusory and insubstantial because the writer's presence and voice are
creatures of the *recipient's* fantasy. It is less the skill of the writer and more the
pothos of the recipient that turns a letter into an image. Longing is creative.[29]
Letters stimulate readers' existing capacity for fantasy.[30] More than any writer
in antiquity, John Chrysostom emphasized that the eyes of love empowered by
longing perceive the absent beloved in the letter itself.[31]

Correspondence between Pliny the Younger and his wife, Calpurnia,
reflects the vulnerability of epistolary presence. Since husbands in antiquity
rarely, as far as we know, wrote to their wives in amatory terms, quoted in its
entirety the following letter surprisingly transforms husband and wife into lover
and beloved. It does so with the aid of well-known motifs from Latin poetry:

> You cannot believe how much I miss you (*desiderio tui tenear*). I love
> you so much, and we are not used to separations. So I stay awake
> most of the night thinking of you, and by day I find my feet carrying
> me (a true word, carrying) to your room at the times I usually visited
> you; then finding it empty I depart, as sick and sorrowful as a lover
> locked out. The only time I am free from this misery is when I am
> in court and wearing myself out with my friends' lawsuits. You can
> judge then what a life I am leading, when I find my rest in work and
> a distraction in troubles and anxiety.[32]

Absence, sleeplessness, lovesickness, the excluded lover, torment of the soul,
remedy of love, and comfort for love—Pliny orders all seven erotic motifs to his
purpose of confessing his *desiderium*, a task that any letter of longing must take
on, and that includes Paul's letter to the Philippians. Pliny's epistle is an early
example of hundreds of longing letters in the following centuries that seek to
intensify the emotional bond between the writer and recipient by describing
their relationship in erotic terms. But that enhancement is two-edged. *Erōs*
opens the door to a more intense experience of the beloved's absence in the very
literary medium in which love promised to give greater presence. Pliny found
this out:

> I in turn keep reading your letters, repeatedly fingering them as
> if they had newly arrived. But this fires my longing (*desiderium*)
> all the more, for when someone's letter contains such charm, what

sweetness there is in conversing face to face! Be sure to write as often as you can, even though the delight your letters give me causes me such torture. Farewell.[33]

While Pliny's tactile reception of letters endured well into the tenth century, so did his experience of simultaneous delight and torture.

Perhaps training in longing desire prepared Pliny to understand Calpurnia's rather curious way of receiving his letters. She might well have been the first to put into action what a papyrus letter several decades earlier had encouraged another lonely recipient simply to imagine: "Think that I am near you."[34] Pliny writes,

> You write that my being absent from you causes you no little sadness, and that your one consolation (*solacium*) is to grasp my writings as a substitute for my person, and that you often place them where I lie next to you (*in vestigio meo colloces*). I am happy that you are missing me, and that my books console you as you rest.[35]

Placed in his imprint (*vestigium*) on their bed, the letters stood in for his body and provided comfort. Pliny approves her ingenuity. She had improved upon the widespread practice of lovers keeping close at hand portraits, figurines, and other traces of traveling or deceased loved ones. These physical reminders/remainders were comforting substitutes, but they also kept open the wounds of separation.[36] Everyday phenomena in antiquity such as the shadow, footprints, hair clippings, and traces of the body on bedclothes were experienced with fascination because of their contradictory effects. Absence and presence of the beloved existed in a single object. And Calpurnia doubled the effects by combing two complex symbols, letters and wrinkled sheets.

Before he became emperor, Marcus Aurelius was a master at eroticizing his friendship with his teacher and confidant Marcus Cornelius Fronto.[37] Famous lovers from the past exemplify his feelings for Fronto: "if he was ever away from Socrates, Socrates never felt for Phaedrus a more passionate longing (*desiderium*) than I for the sight of you all these days."[38] Nuptial imagery works its way into his discourse. Writing in 146 C.E. from Naples, Marcus bored with local amusements writes:

> . . . we have passed whole days more or less in the same occupation: the same theatre, the same dislike of it, the same longing (*desiderium*) for you—the same, do I say? nay, one that is daily renewed and

increases and, as Laberius, after his own manner and in his own peculiar style, says of love, "Your love (*amor*) as fast as any onion grows, as firm as any palm." This then is what he says of love (*de amore*), I apply to my longing (*desiderium*) for you.[39]

Laberius likely meant his lines for the praise of bride and groom.[40] Marcus's redeployment of them amplified his friendship with *amor* and transfigured the teacher and friend into his longed-for Fronto.[41]

Fronto, however, took a cooler approach toward Marcus. He used letters to increase friendship to be sure, as epistolary theory required, but he did so without the eroticism of poetic allusion. Preferring philosophy to poetry and reason to emotion, Fronto creates a better *friend*, a figure less romantic than the parted lover Marcus had invented for Fronto.

> I have received your letter, most charmingly expressed, in which you say that the intermission in my letters has caused a longing for them to arise in you. Socrates was right, then, in his opinion that "pleasures are generally linked to pains," when in his imprisonment he held that pain caused by the tightness of his chains was made up for by the pleasure of their removal. Precisely so in our case the fondness which absence stimulates brings as much comfort as the absence itself causes affliction. For fond longing comes from love. Therefore, absence makes the heart grow fonder, and this is far the best thing in friendship.[42]

From Fronto's perspective, then, what the epistolary situation of their separation calls for is philosophic theory about balanced pleasure and pain, not poetically expressed *erōs*.[43] Yet, in their early correspondence, Fronto was swimming against the strong current of Marcus's longing.

Marcus's use of Laberius indicates how important poetry was for the introduction of *erōs* into letters of friendship. While Laberius was a minor player, Sappho's influence on longing letters was immense. The pseudonymous letter of Julian to Iamblichus opens with two Sapphic quotations. The first nicely states the letter's promise of presence: "'Thou hast come! well hast thou done!' You have indeed come, even though absent, by means of your letter. . . ." In the second we see once again the double effect of the letter to comfort and to reinvigorate longing: "'And I was yearning for thee, and thou didst set ablaze my heart, already aflame with longing (καιομέναν πόθῳ) for thee.'"[44] Sappho helped Julian create an amatory narrative within the letter for himself and Iamblichus.[45] Julian takes on Sappho's identity and her plight. Iamblichus in turn becomes the beloved of Sappho's poem, and longing becomes the dominant mood.

Up to this point, only the vulnerability of epistolary presence has been considered. Letters also carry on conversation, it was said, which in partnership with bodily presence constitutes the joy of friendship. But voice also is an epistolary illusion. In a letter to Trebonius, Cicero locates the pain of separation in loss of conversation:

> It was a pleasure to read your letter, and a great pleasure to read your book. But there was a touch of pain too, for, having inflamed my eagerness to increase our intercourse (our *affection* admitted of no addition), you then go away. . . . Missing you as sorely as I do (*meque tanto desiderio adficis*), you leave me only one consolation—that long, frequent letters will mitigate the sense of loss (*desiderium*) we both feel in each other's absence.[46]

The remedy he suggests, more letters, will actually cause more pain if what he has just said about their power to inflame is true. The remedy is the problem, and there is no breaking free from this vicious circle. The question now is whether Paul wrote Philippians in such a way as to mask the circularity of presence and absence thus promoting his authority and Christ's unreconstructed lordship or whether he exploited epistolary conventions that drove home his and Christ's longing for communion. There is much evidence to suggest the latter.

PAUL IN THE COMPANY OF THE PARTED

There comes a point in every extant longing letter—and there were hundreds from the thousand years following Paul's letter to the Philippians—when the emotions of the writer surface, sometimes breathlessly. Various methods of declaring an aching mind and desire for communion were available, from Pliny's shock and disbelief in *Ep.* 7.5 examined above ("You cannot believe how much I miss you") to Synesius's saucy mix of erotic cliché and calendar checking: "Longing and necessity draw me to you. I should like to know, then, whether you will await me if I come to you."[47] Some avowals are downright gushy. In a pseudonymous letter, Julian confesses his feelings for Iamblichus: "Nay, I admit that I am your lover (ἀλλ᾽ ἐραστὴς μὲν εἶναι σός ὁμολογῶ). . . . For even though someone should say that I am unworthy, not even so shall he deprive me of my longing (τοῦ ποθεῖν)."[48] Cicero took the direct approach writing to an ailing friend, "Missing you brings home to us how useful and pleasant it is to have you. But though I long to see you with my every thought . . . ."[49] Or, finally, he wrote to his brother Quintus, "Can I put you out of my mind sometimes, or even think of you without tears? When I miss you (*te desidero*), I do not miss you as a brother only, but as a delightful brother almost of my own age, a son in deference, a father in wisdom. What pleasure did I ever take apart from you or you apart from me?"[50] In Phil 1:8, Paul announces that he has joined the ranks of the lonely: "I long for you all in the innards of Christ Jesus."

Papyri letters declare their writers' longing by echoing Paul's straightforward style, though with varied terminology. There is Paul's term that he shared with hundreds of letter writers: ἐπιποθῶ or simply ποθῶ. It is surprisingly rare in the papyri, an accident of preservation perhaps. In a letter dated 212–217 C.E. a writer declares, "we who are longing (οἱ ποθοῦντες) pray that we enjoy you with our eyes and no longer by means of letters."[51] More often than ποθῶ, papyri letters employ ἐπιθυμεῖν or ἐπιζητεῖν, both of which occur in Philippians (1:23; 4:17). Desiring to see the recipient in the flesh was a popular motif, as this letter of Theanous from the second or third century C.E. to her mother illustrates: "I greet you, mother, wishing to catch sight of you already (ἐπιθυμοῦσα ἤδη θεάσασθαι) through this letter."[52] In the second century a son wrote to his father Herakleides, "Know that we miss you (ἐπιζητοῦμεν σε) daily."[53]

Paul seals his confession with an oath: "For God is my witness" (1:8). Letter writers in the first thousand years of the common era, regardless of religious conviction, spoke as if they had the same god when they confessed their longing. This god was the hope of parted lovers and separated friends.[54] The divine name had a reputation for making communion.[55] By the tenth century, this divinity bore the epithet "who makes into one."[56] This god made the impossibility of communion between parted friends possible through written text: a letter was a "gift of Fate."[57] For Christians, a "gift of God."[58] For Julian, a "manifest saving presence."[59] Not only did they pray to this god but they also called on it as a witness to their longing. Echoing the witness motif of Phil 1:8, Basil writes to Meletius, bishop of Antioch: "The good God, by affording us opportunities of addressing your Honor, assuages the intensity of our longing (τὸ σφοδρὸν τοῦ πόθου παραμυθεῖται). For He Himself is a witness of the desire (μάρτυς γὰρ αὐτὸς τῆς ἐπιθυμίας) which we have to behold your countenance and to enjoy your good and soul-profiting instruction."[60]

As in Phil 1:8 (cf. Rom 1:11-12), a god was invoked to verify the unseen desire of the heart.[61] Greek letters in the first three centuries of the common era employ the motif. One example is the letter of Chairemon to Apollonius dated between 70 and 80 C.E. in which friendship and desire are verified with an oath: [Ὄμνυμι δέ σοι κατά Δ[ιο]σκ[ο]ύρων . . .[62] Another is found in one of the *Socratic Epistles* in which Phaedrus, having fallen in love with philosophy, dreads Plato's departure: "You wrote to me that since you did not wish to cause me grief, you concealed that you are about to move farther away, but by Zeus the Olympian, I am beginning to miss you (καὶ αὐτὸς δὲ ἄρχομαι ποθεῖν σε νὴ τὸν Δία τὸν ᾿Ολύμπιον)."[63] Finally, Julian wrote to Hermogenes, "For, by the gods, I have long desired to see you (θεάσασθαι γὰρ σε πάλαι τε εὔχομαι νὴ τοὺς θεούς), and, now that I have learned to my great joy that you are safe and sound, I bid you come." Swearing upon the other's eyes or upon one's own soul served the same rhetorical purpose.[64]

It is not entirely accurate to say, as I said above, that longing was a secret of the heart that required divine testimony for confirmation. Longing had obvious physical effects; it was a disease heating the body, liquefying its solid parts, and in the end draining it entirely. Its effects were palpable. As I will assert in chapters 2 and 3, this is the story of Christ's body in Phil 2:6-8 into which Paul writes himself in Phil 1:8 (". . . in the innards of Christ Jesus"). Epaphroditus also longed for the church and "for that reason you heard that he fell ill" (Phil 2:26). Just as a god was called upon to witness the truth of the writer's emotion, the body itself gave indisputable evidence. Marcus wrote as follows to Fronto, whose own illness, incidentally, was not of the erotic variety: "So while you are down in bed, my spirits will be down too (*et mihi animus supinus erit*); and when by God's grace you stand on your feet, my spirits also will stand fast, that are now fevered with the most burning longing for you (*qui nunc torretur ardentissimo desiderio tuo*)."[65] Marcus prays to the gods "that in every journey of mine you may be with me, and I be not worn out with so constant, so consuming a desire for you (*desiderio fatiger*)."[66] He tells Fronto about his nightly letter writing routine: "before I turn over and snore, I get my task done and give my dearest of masters an account of the day's doings, and if I could miss (*desiderare*) him more, I would not grudge wasting away a little more."[67] Bodily proof of desire was a malleable enough theme to cover nonsexual relations. Marcus recalls burning for his mother as he reiterates his longing for Fronto:

> Now, if never before, I find what a task it is to round and shape three or five lines and to take time over writing. Farewell, breath of my life. Should I not burn with love of you (*Ego non ardeam tuo amore*), who have written to me as you have! What shall I do? I cannot

refrain. Last year it befell me in this very place, and at this very time, to be consumed with a passionate longing (*desiderio peruri*) for my mother. This year you inflame that my longing (*Id desiderium hoc anno tu mihi accendis*). My Lady greets you.[68]

Marcus's epistolary persona, the wasting away lover, was a one of the most popular motifs in Greek and Latin love poetry and in the romantic novel.[69] Longing for the community in Philippi, Paul and Epaphroditus thus were in good company.

Julian took quite seriously the deadly effects of longing.[70] To Libanius he wrote, "I assure you, in these three days you have worn me out, if indeed the Sicilian poet speaks the truth when he says, 'those who long (ποθοῦντες) grow old in a day.' And if this is true, as in fact it is, you have trebled my age, my good friend."[71] Not only did longing advance the process of aging; it also felt like dying. To another friend he wrote, "While you are away I cannot be said to be alive." And again, "But I might say that I do not exist at all among men so long as I am not with Iamblichus."[72] Papyri letters also emphasized physical suffering as evidence for longing. Writers agonize over the separation and the uncertainties distance creates.[73] Appetite disappears: "I take no pleasure in food and drink. . . . I lay without eating on New Year's Day but my father came and forced me to eat."[74] Thirst never ends: "Or don't you know that we are thirsting for your letters?"[75] Day after day goes by with no sunshine.[76] In short, missing a friend felt just like grief over his or her death.[77] Separation is a kind of dying, as Epaphroditus experienced (Phil 2:26-27) and as this letter from Taus to Apollonius (107 c.e.) shows:

I beg you, my lord, if it please you, to send for me; else I die because I do not behold you daily. Would that I were able to fly and come to you and make obeisance to you; for it distresses me not to behold you. So be friends with me and send for me.[78]

Or, another:

Serenus to his beloved sister Isidora, many greetings. Before all else I pray for your health, and every day and evening I perform the act of veneration on your behalf to Thöeris who loves you. I assure that ever since you left me I have been in mourning, weeping by night and lamenting by day.[79]

Only lament of the dead seemed an appropriate response to the loved one's absence.

Direct declaration was one method of revealing *pothos*, and it was Paul's choice in Phil 1:8. Epithets did the same work. The "I long for you" of a letter's opening often became "my longed-for one" at its close. Again, this was Paul's choice. In Phil 4:1 we read, "My beloved and longed-for brothers and sisters." Communicating *pothos* through terms of affection was an early, widespread epistolary practice. The Roman military camp of Vindolanda near Hadrian's Wall in northern England is the site of letters discovered in the 1980s written on wooden tablets. Preserved today at the British Museum, they originated around 100 C.E. One of them, a letter of Claudia Severa to Sulpicia Lepidina, displays what one scholar has called "erotically tinged language."[80] Claudia brought her letter to a close, "Farewell my sister, my dearest and most longed-for soul (*karissima et anima ma desideratissima*)."[81]

Affectionate forms of address abound in the correspondence of Marcus and Fronto. Marcus sprinkled pet names liberally at letter endings. As he transformed his friend Fronto into a beloved, his "chief joy," the simple act of saying goodbye was elevated to an art form.[82] "Farewell, breath of my life (*Vale, spiritus meus*)."[83] "Farewell, my greatest treasure beneath the sky, my glory (*Vale mihi maxima res sub caelo, gloria mea*)."[84] "Farewell, my Fronto, most beloved and most loving of friends (*Vale mi Fronto carissime et amicissime*)."[85] "Farewell, my Fronto, dearest and beyond all things sweetest to me (*Vale mi Fronto carissime et supra omnes res dulcissime*)"; and "Fare ever well, my sweetest soul (*Valeas semper anima suavissima*)."[86] Marcus even turns longing itself into a pet name: "Farewell, my—what shall I say when whatever I say is inadequate?—farewell my longing, my light, my delight (*vale, meum desiderium, mea lux, mea voluptas*)."[87] Fronto responds a little less enthusiastically: "Dearly do I love you, my Lord, the glory of our age, my chiefest solace (*solacium*)."[88]

Affectionate forms of address close a number of Julian's letters. *Epistle* 52 ends in a typical fourth-century fashion: "Farewell, brother, most dear (ποθεινότατε) and beloved!" Very similar is the closing of *Ep.* 7: "May you continue in health and happiness as long as possible, my well-beloved and most dear brother (ἀδελφὲ ποθεινότατε καὶ φιλικώτατε)." John Chrysostom's readers are addressed as "longed-for ones," though not as often as one might expect.[89] Letter recipients are lovingly addressed as "much longed-for ones" in the salutation of two epistles from Kellis in the early and middle fourth century C.E.: "To my lords sons who are most longed-for (ποθεινοτάτο[ι]ς) and most beloved (ἐρασμιωτάτοι[ς]) by us Pausanius and Pisistratos";[90] and

"To his most honoured and truly longed-for lord brother (ἀληθῶς π[οθ]εινοτάτωι ἀδελφῶι) Psais, Pamouris sends greetings in God. . . ."[91] The superlative form of ποθεινός did yeoman's work from the fourth century on. Even to be called "thrice longed for" was not unusual.[92] Synesius wrote to Asclepiodotus, "The evil spirit whose business it is to hurt me arranged beforehand also that you, always so dear to me, should not be present. Oh best, thrice dear (τριπόθητε) and most loyal of friends, may you yet come!"[93] Finally, Augustine plays with the motif of tripled longing calling Christinus "much desired brother" three times in one short letter.[94]

The final epistolary motif, which both affirms and challenges epistolary presence, is that of holding the absent one in memory or in the heart. [95] Remembrance, it should be stressed, is by no means a simple comfort, although letters often speak as if this were the case. Memory and longing are in reality a single desire differentiated only with respect to past and future; this means that the ache of longing and grief of remembering contradict the reports of joy when the absent one is imagined to be present. Pain is hidden in the metaphors. The imagery of remembering alludes to injury: inscribing the surface of the soul, stamping or molding it, or the soul's bearing of the absent other as if it were a heavy load.[96]

Having mentioned memory (μνεία) in Phil 1:3, Paul goes on to justify his emotional connection to the community: "because I have you in my heart." Since this sentence might also been translated "because you have me in your heart," Paul's meaning is ambiguous, perhaps intentionally so, and suggests a relationship of mutual ecstasy and shared joy and grief.[97] Longing drove the heart out to abide within the beloved; Cato was thought to have "declared that the soul of the lover is ever present in that of the beloved."[98] Conversely, the absent one dwelt within the lover's heart.[99] Ovid was perhaps the first to employ this poetic motif in a letter. His unusual talking epistle mentioned above addresses the recipient: "But thee—O, if thou believest me in anything, dearer than all to him—thee he holds constantly in his whole heart (*in toto pectore semper habet*)."[100] Yet, instead of pure consolation, the heart's reception of the other created pain as well as joy:

> . . . my fatherland is far away, far my dearest wife, and all that after these two was once sweet to me. Yet these things are so present that, though I cannot touch them, all are visible to my mind. Before my eyes flit my home, the city, the outline of places, the events too that happened in each place. Before my eyes is the image of my wife as though she were present. She makes my woes heavier, she makes

them lighter—heavier by her absence, lighter by her gift of love and her steadfast bearing of the burden laid upon her. You too are fast in my heart, my friends . . . know that I am removed from you by vast space, you are ever present to my heart.[101]

The heart alternates roles changing from host to visitant and back again: "All things steal into my mind, yet above all, you, my wife, and you hold more than half my heart (*et plus in nostro pectore parte tenes*). You I address though you are absent, you alone my voice names; no night comes to me without you, no day."[102] But this alternation does not cure the circularity of absence and presence.

It goes to the point of this chapter that the very same spiritual capacity that in Ovid allowed for the interior presence of his wife also made her "heavier" and sparked renewed longing.[103] This dynamic, which I am claiming is true also of Philippians, does not occur in the philosophically shaped soul. Take Seneca, for example. He manages to banish absence from his mind. Seneca makes the paradoxical claim that the most pleasurable conversations are actually to be had when friends are parted. Leave it to a philosopher to strike out the experience of grief etched within the joyful remembrance of the absent other. Amnesia of this sort allows him to claim that the best conversation takes place purely through the mind.

> You may hold converse with your friends when they are absent, and indeed as often as you wish and for as long as you wish. For we enjoy this, the greatest of pleasures, all the more when we are absent from one another. . . . A friend should be retained in the spirit (*animo*); such a friend can never be absent. He can see every day whomsoever he desires to see. I would therefore have you share your studies with me, your meals, and your walks. . . . I see you, my dear Lucilius, and at this very moment I hear you; I am with you to such an extent that I hesitate whether I should not begin to write you notes instead of letters. Farewell.[104]

We can easily imagine Seneca's reaction to Calpurnia's use of Pliny's letters, since, if he conceived of a note as an improvement upon a letter and even favored the eradication of writing itself in favor of spiritual communication, he would also have been dumfounded at the irrationality of Calpurnia's placing Pliny's letters in the place where he had slept. Calpurnia's artifice kept Pliny safe from being turned into an idea. Even though he was absent to Calpurnia—or precisely because he was absent and the letters would not allow her to forget it—Pliny's body was longed for. Seneca, preferring ideas to bodies, provided his dear Lucilius no such protection. And Paul, sticking with letters to house his Christology, reminds his readers of his absence (Phil 1:12) and confesses *pothos*. He will not let Christ or the believers in Philippi suffer Lucilius's fate.

Reading through Pothos

In this chapter I have wondered about the difference longing makes for the reading of Philippians. Hundreds of letters written in the first thousand years of the common era raise intriguing questions, such as the relative value of emotion and reason in our understanding of Pauline Christology. My purpose in reviewing this literature, however, is not to argue that Philippians reflects an established epistolary form called "the letter of longing"; the handbooks do not mention such a type, and categorization for its own sake is uninteresting. Rather, in preparation for the next chapter I wanted to place Paul in the company of those who deepened friendship by confessing *pothos*, who verified this desire with an oath, characterized readers as "longed-for ones," and acknowledged the heart as host, visitant, scripted surface, and space for carrying about the absent beloved. Enhanced friendship came at a cost: when *erōs* is in play separation hurts all the more. Letters bring both delight and torture. How then do we think about Christology when the Jesus we have available for examination and logical exposition is delivered in such an emotionally conflicted medium?

Letters are usually thought simply to convey information. They re-present the writer and simulate his or her voice. It has not been my intention in this chapter to call into question the veracity of either of these two claims, only their completeness, since letters are also objects like photographs or locks of hair that bring loved ones into presence only then to reiterate their absence. In the ancient world, letters were reread, wept over, kissed, and placed in bed in order to soothe the longing desire they never failed to rekindle. Modern scholars, however, have approached Philippians as if the letter were only Paul's παρουσία and ὁμιλία, and they read his writing as only the expression of his ideas or the contents of his commands. This is insufficient, because the very persons some of us want to know (Paul, Euodia, Jesus, Syntyche, Timothy, Epaphroditus, and the Philippian community) are entangled in Philippians' vicious circle of comfort and affliction, in the letter's delivering the writer and abducting this fictive presence.

Notes

1. Augustine, *Ep.* 27. Translation is from *Saint Augustine: Letters,* trans. Sister Wilfrid Parsons, FC (Washington, DC: Catholic University of America Press, 1951), 88.

2. M. Luther Stirewalt Jr. (*Paul the Letter Writer* [Grand Rapids: Eerdmans, 2003], 81) believes that Philippians "like Paul's other letters, is officially apostolic, and not personal." He finds the categorization of Philippians as a friendly letter unconvincing. It is puzzling, then, when he writes, "For Antiochus goodwill (*eunoia*) is secondary, intended for clothing an authoritative decree. For Paul authority is secondary, even incidental, to the expression of affection (*agape*), the major purpose of his writing" (p. 82). John Reumann ("Philippians, Especially Chapter 4, as a 'Letter of Friendship': Observations on a Checkered History of Scholarship," in *Friendship, Flattery, and Frankness of Speech: Studies on Friendship in the New Testament World,* ed. John T. Fitzgerald, NovTSup 82 [Leiden: Brill, 1996], 83–106) doubts that Philippians is a letter of friendship: (1) he is not convinced that a collection of topoi is enough to decide about a letter's form; (2) he wonders whether the handbook definitions may have been "schoolboy exercises" illustrating a classification scheme seldom used and bearing little resemblance to Philippians; and (3) Paul does not use the word φιλία, indicating his discomfort with a human relationship that is too anthropocentric, exclusive, and thus incapable of forming the backbone of his ecclesiology.

3. I am attempting in this chapter a critique of the shared phonocentrism of ancient epistolary theory and modern approaches to Paul's letters. For Jacques Derrida's challenge to the devaluation of writing and the elevation of the voice in Western philosophy, see Jonathan D. Culler, *On Deconstruction: Theory and Criticism after Structuralism* (Ithaca, NY: Cornell University Press, 1982), 89–110. For another application of Derrida's philosophy to Paul's letters, see Stephen Curkpatrick, "Apostrophic Desire and Parousia in the Apostle Paul's Epistles: A Derridean Proposal for Textual Interpretation," *BibInt* 10 (2002): 175–93. He writes, "Paul's apparent desire is to overcome absence with presence, which he seeks to do with either letter or emissary. This parousia to his congregations is inseparable from a desire to be their father," p. 180. This is precisely the point I am arguing against.

4. On this point I am heavily indebted to the following two studies, whose influence reaches deeply into this chapter: Heikki Koskenniemi, *Studien zur Idee und Phraseologie des griechischen Briefes bis 400 n. Chr.,* Suomalaisen Tiedeakatemian toimituksia B, 102.2 (Helsinki: n.p., 1956); and Klaus Thraede, *Grundzüge griechisch-römischer Brieftopik,* Zetemata 48 (Munich: Beck, 1970); see also Nikolaos Tōmadakēs, ΒΥΖΑΝΤΙΝΗ ΕΠΙΣΤΟΛΟΓΡΑΦΙΑ (Thessaloniki, 1993), 113–16. The idea that visual image and written word had the power to create the presence of an absent one was powerful in antiquity. Graves are very much like letters in this regard. Four brothers set up a stele for their dead sister longing once again to see her face; see *Steinepigramme* 14/3/3.

5. Julian, *Ep.* 12.

6. *P. Mich.* 8.482. See *Michigan Papyri,* vol. 8: *Papyri and Ostraca from Karanis,* ed. Herbert C. Youtie and John Garrett Winter (Ann Arbor: University of Michigan Press, 1951), 76. Cf. Procopius, *Ep.* 27; Dionysius, *Ep.* 68; Leon, *Ep.* 52 (Jean Darrouzès, *Épistoliers Byzantins du Xe Siècle,* Archives de l'orient chrétien 6 [Paris: Institut français d'études byzantines, 1960], 204); Anonymous, *Epp.* 19, 20 (Darrouzès, 357–58).

7. *P. Mich.* 241. See Herbert C. Youtie, "P. Mich. Inv. 241: ΕΔΟΞΑ ΣΕ ΘΕΩΡΕΙΝ," *ZPE* 22 (1976): 49–52. Cf. Cyprian, *Ep.* 6: "I, too, long to have the joy of seeing you. . . . But as it is not possible to share in this joy together, I am sending this letter in my stead to be heard by your ears, to be seen by your eyes." Translation is from *The Letters of St. Cyprian of Carthage,* trans. G. W. Clarke, ACW 43 (New York: Newman, 1984), 63.

8. Procopius, *Ep.* 80.

9. John Chrysostom, *Ep.* 178.

10. Seneca, *Ep.* 40.1.

11. Julian, *Ep.* 67.

12. Julian, *Ep.* 16. Cf. Procopius, *Ep.* 148. See Gustav Karlsson, *Idéologie et cérémonial dans l'épistolographie byzantine: Textes du Xe siècle analysés et commentés,* Acta Universitatis Upsaliensis, Studia Graeca Upsaliensia 3 (Uppsala; Almqvist & Wiksell, 1959), 94–96.

13. *Greek Anthology,* 9.401. Cf. Synesius, *Ep.* 138. See Karlsson, *Idéologie et cérémonial,* 24–33, 51–66.

14. Ovid, *Tristia* 5.4.23-30. See Thraede, *Grundzüge griechisch-römischer Brieftopik,* 47–52.

15. Synesius, *Ep.* 138.

16. Stanley K. Stowers, *Letter Writing in Greco-Roman Antiquity,* LEC 5 (Philadelphia: Westminster, 1986), 60.

17. Stanley K. Stowers, "Friends and Enemies in the Politics of Heaven: Reading Theology in Philippians," in *Pauline Theology,* vol. 1: *Thessalonians, Philippians, Galatians, Philemon,* ed. Jouette M. Bassler (Minneapolis: Fortress Press, 1991), 109.

18. Loveday Alexander ("Hellenistic Letter-Forms and the Structure of Philippians," *JSNT* 37 [1989]: 93) offers a compatible characterization of Philippians as a "Verbindungsbrief" (a term she finds in Koskenniemi, *Studien zur Idee und Phraseologie* , 107), in which the "exchange of news and reassurance . . . *is* initially, at least, the letter's real business."

19. L. Michael White, "Morality between Two Worlds: A Paradigm of Friendship in Philippians," in *Greeks, Romans, and Christians: Essays in Honor of Abraham J. Malherbe,* ed. David L. Balch, Everett Ferguson, and Wayne A. Meeks (Minneapolis: Fortress Press, 1990), 201–15; John T. Fitzgerald, "Philippians in the Light of Some Ancient Discussions of Friendship," in idem, *Friendship, Flattery, and Frankness of Speech,* 141–60; and, in the same volume, Ken Berry, "The Function of Friendship Language in Philippians 4:10-20," 107–24; and Abraham J. Malherbe, "Paul's Self-Sufficiency (Philippians 4:11)," 125–39.

20. σφοδρός: John Chrysostom, *Epp.* 50, 55, 56, 80, 82, 172, 175, 223, 225. θερμός: *Ep.* 218. Cf. Procopius, *Ep.* 26; Dionysius, *Ep.* 1.

21. John Chrysostom, *Epp.* 164, 218. See Karlsson, *Idéologie et cérémonial,* 62–78.

22. John Chrysostom, *Epp.* 22, 96, 222, 223.

23. What holds Basil back from enthusiastic agreement with the theory he articulated so well? Perhaps he is aware of the danger that amplification of friendship by *erōs* posed. For the intricacies of accommodating *erōs* to Christian friendship, see Jostein Børtnes, "Eros Transformed: Same-Sex Love and Divine Desire," in *Greek Biography and Panegyric in Late Antiquity,* ed. Tomas Hägg and Philip Rousseau, Transformation of the Classical Heritage 31 (Berkeley: University of California Press, 2000), 180–93.

24. Basil, *Ep.* 124. It is noteworthy that Basil goes on to say that the letter carrier is the image of the sender. Confusion of letter and letter carrier in re-presenting the writer was not uncommon and deserves further study.

25. Basil knew this; see, for example, *Ep.* 342: "nature has caused those delicate thorns to grow upon this flower that they might serve, as do the sundry ticklings which lovers use, to incite gently to a greater desire (μείζονα πόθον) by their pleasant prickings of their stings (εὐπλήκτοις κέντροις)."

26. See Anna De Pretis, "'Insincerity,' 'Facts,' and 'Epistolarity': Approaches to Pliny's *Epistles* to Calpurnia," *Arethusa* 36 (2003): 127–46.

27. Julian, *Ep.* 77. See also *Ep.* 78: "And when I received it I kissed it and held it to my eyes and kept tight hold of it as though I were afraid that while I was in the act of reading your letter the phantom of your image might elude me and fly away." See Theodoros of Kyzikos, *Ep.* 2.

28. Chariton, *Chaer.* 8.5.13. Translation is from *Collected Ancient Greek Novels,* ed. B. P. Reardon (Berkeley: University of California Press, 1989), 119. Braulio of Saragossa (590–651) was encouraged by his bishop, Isidore of Seville, to receive letters from friends in a physical way: "When you receive a letter of a friend, dearest son, you should not delay to embrace it as a friend. For it is a fine consolation among the absent that if one who is loved is not present, a letter may be

embraced instead." Translation is from *The Letters of St. Isidore of Seville,* trans. Gordon B. Ford Jr., 2nd ed. (Amsterdam: Adolf M. Hakkert, 1970), 19.

29. Procopius, *Ep.* 152.

30. John Chrysostom, *Ep.* 108, 222.

31. John Chrysostom, *Epp.* 23, 34, 56, 154, 229. Cf. Julian, *Ep.* 62: "Nay, when did you ever leave me, so that I need to write, or when do I not behold you with the eyes of the soul as though you were here with me? For not only do I seem to be with you continually and to converse with you, but . . . ." For later examples, see Nicolaus, *Ep.* 33 (*PG* 111:220): Nikephoros Ouranos, *Ep.* 7 (Darrouzès, *Épistoliers Byzantins,* 221).

32. Pliny, *Ep.* 7.5. Antonio Ramírez de Verger remarks that the letter is "one whole series of familiar amatory motifs." See his "Erotic Language in Pliny, *Ep.* VII 5," *Glotta* 74 (1999): 114–16. A. N. Sherwin-White (*The Letters of Pliny: A Historical and Social Commentary* [Oxford: Clarendon, 1968], 407) notes that this is the first time in European literature that the roles of lover and husband are fused. Sabine Grebe ("Marriage and Exile: Cicero's Letters to Terentia," *Helios* 30 [2003]: 143) finds an earlier example in Cicero, *Fam.* 14.2.2.

33. Pliny, *Ep.* 6.7.

34. *Columbia Papyri* 8.215. Translation is from Roger S. Bagnall and Raffaella Cribiore, *Women's Letters from Ancient Egypt: 300 BC–AD 800* (Ann Arbor: University of Michigan Press, 2006), 261.

35. Pliny, *Ep.* 6.7. Translation is from *Pliny the Younger: Complete Letters,* trans. P. G. Walsh (Oxford: Oxford University Press, 2006), 137–38. See also Julian, *Ep.* 12; and Peter Damian (*Ep.* 87): "Indeed, I keep it [a letter] always with me in my cell. I often converse with it, and in it I clearly behold the very likeness of your face and the image of your inner self." Translation is from *The Letters of Peter Damian: Letters 61–90,* trans. Owen J. Blum, FC: Medieval Continuation 3 (Washington, DC: Catholic University of America Press, 1989), 299.

36. Maurizio Bettini, *The Portrait of the Lover,* trans. Laura Gibbs (Berkeley: University of California Press, 1999), 4–54. Bettini does not explore letters, perfect illustration of the phenomenon he describes, since they consist of parchment impressed by the beloved's hand and pen ("contact") and pictures of his or her face painted by words ("similarity"). Theodore the Studite (*Ep.* 28 [*PG* 99:1196]) anticipated the kind of reference Bettini calls "contact": "you have connected (συνῆψας) yourself to us through the letter." For other occurrences of συνάπτω in letters, see Karlsson, *Idéologie et cérémonial,* 25.

37. For a new appreciation of the eroticism in these letters, see Amy Richlin, "Fronto Marcus: Love, Friendship, Letters," in *The Boswell Thesis: Essays on Christianity, Social Tolerance, and Homosexuality,* ed. Mathew Kuefler (Chicago: University of Chicago, 2006), 111–29.

38. Fronto, *Ep. Gr.* 7.

39. Fronto, *Ad M. Caes.* 2.6.

40. For vegetal imagery in nuptial contexts, see J. C. B. Petropoulos, *Eroticism in Ancient and Medieval Greek Poetry* (London: Duckworth, 2003), 32–36, 61–73.

41. See also Fronto, *Ad M. Caes.* 2.2.

42. Fronto *Ad M. Ceas.* 4.9; see also 3.6.

43. Fronto's treatise on love (*Ep. Gr. 8*) shows him the doting teacher and not the ἐραστής, but Marcus wasn't buying it (*Ep. Gr.* 7).

44. Julian, *Ep.* 77.

45. Synesius (*Epp.* 123, 158) sought examples in Homer.

46. Cicero, *Fam.* 207.

47. Pliny, *Ep.* 7.5; for the disbelief motif, see also Cicero, *Fam.* 120. Synesius, *Ep.* 39; for ἕλκειν and the compulsion of love, see Theocritus, *Id.* 1.130; 2:17; *Greek Anthology* 5.25, 64, 205.

48. Julian, *Ep.* 79.

49. Cicero, *Fam.* 147; cf. 207.

50. Cicero, *Quint. fratr.* 3. For the poetic origins of Cicero's blurring of familial lines, see G. O. Hutchinson, *Cicero's Correspondence: A Literary Study* (Oxford: Clarendon, 1998), 42–43.

51. *P.S.I.* 1261. Cited in Karlsson, *Idéologie et cérémonial,* 49.

52. *P. Oxy.* 6.963. Translation is from Bagnall and Cribiore, *Women's Letters from Ancient Egypt,* 261, 333. For further examples, see Karlsson, *Idéologie et cérémonial,* 48-49.

53. *P. Yale* 1240. Text and translation are from George M. Parássoglou, "Five Private Letters from Roman Egypt," *Hellenica* 26 (1973): 277–79. See further *Ep.* 9 in the collection entitled *Letters of Medieval Jewish Traders,* trans. S. D. Goitein (Princeton: Princeton University Press, 1973), 63: "I am writing to you out of strong longing." See also ibid., 198.

54. Basil, *Epp.* 1, 145; *P. Giss.* 22 (Michael Kortus, *Briefe des Apollonius-Archives aus der Sammlung Papyri Gissenses: Edition, Übersetzung und Kommentar,* Berichte und Arbeiten aus der Universitätsbibliothek und dem Universitätsarchiv Giessen 49 (Giessen: Universitätsbibliothek, 1999), 72–75; Bärbel Kramer, John C. Shelton, Gerald M. Browne, *Das Archiv des Nepheros und verwandte Texte,* 2 vols. in 1, Aegyptiaca Treverensia 4 (Mainz am Rhein: P. von Zabern, 1987), 65–69; Theodoret, *Ep.* 58; Theodoros of Kyzikos, *Ep.* 3; Symeon Logothetes, *Ep.* 9 (Darrouzès, *Épistoliers Byzantins,* 104); Fronto, *Ad M. Caes.* 3.9; Augustine, *Epp.* 31, 109; Paulinus of Nola, *Epp.* 6.3; 21.6; Braulio of Saragossa, *Epp.* 2, 8.

55. Julian, *Epp.* 12; Theodoret, *Ep.* 24; Synesius, *Epp.* 139, 140; Paulinus of Nola, *Epp.* 19.1; 23.2; 37.1; Ruricius, *Epp.* 2.9, 17, 19, 34, 36, 52; Bernard of Clairvaux, *Ep.* 115.

56. Nikephoros Ouranos, *Ep.* 26 (Darrouzès, *Épistoliers Byzantins,* 229): τῷ ἐνοποιῷ θεῷ; Nicolaus, *Ep.* 63 (*PG* 111:262); Goitein, *Letters of Medieval Jewish Traders,* 53, 63, 113, 139, 187, 198, 203, 209.

57. Dionysius, *Ep.* 35.

58. Ruricius, *Epp* 1.2; 2.10.

59. Julian, *Ep.* 77.

60. Basil, *Ep.* 89. Cf. Theodoros of Kyzikos, *Ep.* 7; Synesius, *Ep.* 123: "I call God to witness, whom philosophy reveres, that I carry with me the image of your sweet and pious nature in my very heart." See also Fronto, *Ad M. Caes.* 4.8; Paulinus of Nola, *Ep.* 6; Augustine, *Ep.* 31.

61. This was also a poetic theme; see Ovid, *Her.* 2.31-44.

62. *BGU* I 248. Bror Olsson, *Papyrusbriefe aus der frühesten Römerzeit* (Uppsala: Almqvist & Wiksell, 1925), 120–25. Cf. *P. Yale* 1239 (George M. Parássoglou, *AJP* 92 [1971]: 653–54): "The god knows how I love and honor you in my soul like a brother (ὁ θεὸς οἶδεν πῶς σε κατὰ ψυχὴν φιλῶ καὶ τιμῶ ὡς ἀδελφόν μου)."

63. *Socratic Epistles* 25. Text and translation are from *The Cynic Epistles,* ed. Abraham J. Malherbe, trans. Stanley Stowers, SBLSBS 12 (Atlanta: Scholars Press, 1977), 278–79.

64. Julian, *Ep.* 13. Cf. *Greek Anthology* 5.9; Cicero, *Fam.* 182.

65. Fronto *Ad M. Caes.* 3.19; see also 4.4 (in which Marcus plays on Cicero, *Tusc.* 2.24.59): "if you do miss me and do love me (*si me desideras atque si me amas*), you will write to me often to console me and cheer me up (*quod mihi 'solacium atque fomentum' sit*). . . . Farewell to the most affectionate, most delightful, most eloquent of men, master most sweet. When you see the fermenting in the cask, let it remind you that my longing (*desiderium*) for you swells up thus and overflows and foams in my breast."

66. Fronto, *Ad M. Caes.* 3.9.

67. Ibid., 4.6.

68. Fronto, *Ep. Gr.* 6.

69. See chapter 3. The motif runs through Ovid's epistolary poems. Dido, for example, in *Her.* 7.23–26 describes her burning and melting for Aeneas: "I am ablaze with love, like torches of wax tipped with sulphur, like pious incense placed on smoking altar-fires. Aeneas my eyes cling to through all my waking hours; Aeneas is in my heart throughout the stillness of the night."

70. Julian, *Epp.* 12, 76.

71. Julian, *Ep.* 52. The "Sicilian" is Theophrastus (see ch. 3 n. 5), whose exaggeration about the aging effect of *pothos* was repeated also by Procopius (*Ep.* 26, 90); cf. Symeon Logothetes, *Ep.* 7: πόθῳ τῷ περί σὲ κάμνουσαν (*PG* 114:233).

72. Julian, *Ep.* 79.

73. John Lee White, *The Form and Function of the Body of the Greek Letter: A Study of the Letter-Body in the Non-Literary Papyri and in Paul the Apostle,* SBLDS 2 (Missoula, MT: Scholars Press, 1972), 16–18, 20–22.

74. *P. Giss.* 19 in Bagnall and Cribiore, *Women's Letters from Ancient Egypt,* 151.

75. *P. Kellis* 57.B in *Greek Papyri from Kellis: I (P. Kell. G.) Nos. 1–90* (ed. K. A. Worp; Oxford: Oxbow Books, 1995), 184–86. Cf. Symeon Logothetes, *Ep.* 16 (Darrouzès, *Épistoliers Byzantins,* 109).

76. See *P. Oxy.* 3059: "Didyme to Apollonius her brother and sun. You must know that I do not view the sun, because you are out of view; for I have no sun but you" (*The Oxyrhynchus Papyri: Volume 42* [ed. P. J. Parsons; Oxford: Oxford University Press, 1974], 148); for a discussion of this letter, see Bagnall and Cribiore, *Women's Letters from Ancient Egypt,* 275.

77. *P. Oxy.* 1676: "I was deeply distressed (ἐλυπήθην) because I did not see you" (*The Oxyrhynchus Papyri: Part 14,* ed. Bernard P. Grenfell and Arthur S. Hunt [London: London Exploration Society, 1920], 134–35). See also *P. Oxy.* 1680 (ibid., 140–41); *P. Gron.* 17 (*Papyri groninganae: griechische Papyri der Universitätsbibliothek zu Groningen,* ed. A. G. Roos (Amsterdam: Noord-Hollandsche Uitgevers-Maatschappij, 1933], 44–45); *P. Mich.* 487 (second century C.E.). Cf. Synesius, *Ep.* 123.

78. *P. Giess.* 17 in *Select Papyri,* 310–11. See also the comments by Bagnall and Cribiore, *Women's Letters from Ancient Egypt,* 149.

79. *P. Oxy.* 528 (*The Oxyrhynchus Papyri, Volume 3,* ed. Bernard P. Grenfell and Arthur S. Hunt [London: Egypt Exploration Fund, 1903], 263–65).

80. Judith P. Hallett, "The Vindolanda Letters from Claudia Severa," in *Women Writing Latin: From Roman Antiquity to Early Modern Europe,* ed. Laurie J. Churchill, Phyllis R. Brown, and Jane E. Jeffrey, 3 vols., Women Writers of the World (New York: Routledge, 2002), 1:95.

81. *Tabula Vindolanda* 2.292. See Alan K. Bowman, *Life and Letters on the Roman Frontier: Vindolanda and Its People* (London: British Museum, 1994), 128. For another instance in correspondence between women, see *P. Bour.* 25 in Bagnall and Cribiore, *Women's Letters from Ancient Egypt,* 260.

82. Fronto, *Ad M. Caes.* 5.59; see also 1.5.

83. Fronto, *Ep. Gr.* 6.

84. Ibid., 7.

85. Fronto, *Ad M. Caes.* 3.2.

86. Ibid., 4.2.

87. Ibid., 4.7

88. Ibid., 1.3.

89. John Chrysostom, *Epp.* 100, 101.

90. *P. Kellis* 87 (Worp, *Greek Papyri from Kellis,* 167–68).

91. *P. Kellis* 57.B (Worp, *Greek Papyri from Kellis,* 184–88).

92. See, for example, Synesius, *Epp.* 86, 138. For earlier examples of the term, see Bion, *Epitaphius Adonis* 58; Moschus, *Epitaphius Bionis* 51.This form of address lasted at least until the tenth century; see Metropolitan of Chone, *Ep.* 6 (Darrouzès, *Épistoliers Byzantins,* 350).

93. Synesius *Ep.* 126. See *The Letters of Synesius of Cyrene* (trans. Augustine FitzGerald; London: Oxford University Press, 1926), 216.

94. Augustine, *Ep.* 256; cf. *Ep.* 258.

95. For unproblematic remembering similar to Phil 1:3, see *P. Lond.* 42 (*Select Papyri, I,* 283); *P. Antinoopolis* 44 (*The Antinoopolis Papyri, Part I* [ed. C. H. Roberts; London: London Exploration Society, 1950], 101–2).

96. A favorite theme of John Chrysostom; see *Epp.* 23, 25, 31, 34, 39, 42, 66, 74, 83, 89, 91, 99, 100, 101, 138, 143, 146, 187, 189, 196, 215, 216, 218. Chrysostom (*Ep.* 93) justifies his use of this motif by pointing to Phil 1:7 and 1 Thess 2:17. Cf. Symeon Logothetes, *Ep.* 13 (Darrouzès, *Épistoliers Byzantins,* 107); Leon, *Ep.* 52 (Darrouzès, 204); Metropolitan of Chone, *Ep.* 37 (Darrouzès, 371); Theodoros of Kyzikos, *Ep.* 9. See *P. Oxy.* 1664 (*Oxyrhynchus Papyri, Volume 14,* p. 119 "not only we but also our ancestral gods themselves hold you in memory (μεμνήμεθά σου) is clear to all; for our whole youth carries you in their hearts (ἐν τοῖς στέρνοις σε περιφέρει)." For inscribing the heart, see John Chrysostom, *Epp.* 31, 39, 42, 66, 74, 100, 101, 138, 187, 196. Cf. Theodore the Studite, *Ep.* 2.97 (*PG* 99:1349).

97. Even though the poets knew that the heart was the seat of emotions, seldom would they keep it from flying away. For the heart as the seat of the emotions, see the early instance of Sappho, *Frg.* 31; see Joel B. Lidov, "The Second Stanza of Sappho 31: Another Look," *AJP* 114 (1993): 525–28; *Greek Anthology* 5.160; *Anacreontea* 25; Musaeus, *Hero et Leander* 86–99, on which see the texts collected in Karlheinz Kost, *Musaios, Hero und Leander: Einleitung, Text, Übersetzung, und Kommentar* (Bonn: Bouvier, 1971), 281, 290. For Latin and Greek sources, see Keith Preston, *Studies in the Diction of the Sermo Amatorius in Roman Comedy* (Menasha, WI: George Banta, 1916), 48–49.

98. Plutarch, *Amat.* 759C. Cf. *Greek Anthology* 5.212: "stamp (τύπος) on my heart"; 5.274: "The image of me that Love stamped in the hot depths of thy heart, thou dost now, alas! as I never dreamt, disown; but I have the picture of thy beauty engraved on my soul." See further *Greek Anthology* 12.57, 130. See also Patricia Rosenmeyer, *The Poetics of Imitation: Anacreon and the Anacreontic Tradition* (Cambridge: Cambridge University Press, 1992), 182.

99. Meleager raised the profile of the heart in love epigram; see Daniel H. Garrison, *Mild Frenzy: A Reading of the Hellenistic Love Epigram,* Hermes Einzelschriften 41 (Wiesbaden: Steiner, 1978), 75. For later sources, see Kost, *Musaios,* 253, 351–52. For Latin examples, see Propertius 2.12.13-16, on which see Rosenmeyer, *Poetics of Imitation,* 205–6; Tibullus 3.1.20; Virgil, *Aen.* 4:1-5. The soul on occasion stood in for the heart: Achilles Tatius, *Leuc. Clit.* 1.6; 5.13; Xenophon of Ephesus, *Ephesiaca* 1.5.

100. Ovid, *Tristia* 5.4.23-30.

101. Ibid., 3.4.53–74; cf. 1.5.9; 3.3.15–16; 3.5.20; *Ex Ponto* 2.4.6–7. See also Patricia Rosenmeyer, "Love Letters in Callimachus, Ovid, and Aristaenetus, or, The Sad Fate of a Mailorder Bride," *MD* 36 (1996): 15.

102. Ovid, *Tristia* 3.3.15–18. For the heart as host and visitant outside of letters, see John Barsby, "Love in Terence," in *Amor, Roma: Love & Latin Literature,* ed. Susanna Morton Braund and Roland Mayer (Cambridge: Cambridge Philosophical Society, 1999), 9–11. See also Catullus 45.20: "heart in heart they live (*mutuis animis amant amantia*)."

103. Ruricius, *Ep.* 2.9. Very interesting is 2.10, where it looks as if Ruricius agrees with Seneca (about no presence being necessary) and then makes a plea for the letter recipient to come. *Ep.* 2.52 is much more like Seneca.

104. Seneca, *Ep.* 55.9–11.

2

Apostolic Sweetness

*Eros once again limb-loosener whirls me
sweetbitter, impossible to fight off, creature
stealing up.[1]*

PAULOLOGY

This chapter continues to explore Pauline Christology, a familiar topic in New Testament studies. The method of investigation is, however, out of the ordinary. Normally, early Christianity's titles for Jesus (Lord, Christ, Son of Man, Son of God, Savior, and so forth) would take center stage. In the previous chapter, only the confession of Jesus as *kyrios* in Phil 2:11 was given consideration, and this only in order to problematize divine sovereignty and promote longing as an alternative christological motif. In this chapter, titles are abandoned altogether. Confession, however, still plays a key role.

Paul's confession of longing for the church in 1:8 ("For God is our witness how we long for you in the innards of Christ Jesus"), which started us thinking about the relationship of letter writing and Christology, directs our attention to Paul's emotions and informs our approach to the Christ Hymn. Philippians 1:8 bundles Paul and Christ together suggesting that a doctrine of Paul has implications for the doctrine of Christ. What is said about Paul's emotions in this chapter will be said of Christ's in the next. Christ longs for humanity in 2:6-8 just as Paul longs for the church in 1:8. Paulology informs Christology, although the apostle would surely have put the relationship the other way around.

This synoptic approach to Paul and Christ rests on a revised understanding of the Greek term τὰ σπλάγχνα in Phil 1:8. The modern translations that speak in abstractions rather than physiological processes would not allow us to draw a parallel between Paul's longing and Christ's.[2] The translation "bowels" of the

Kings James Version aims too low but is on the right track in its anatomical reference. The "innards" (lungs, heart, gall bladder, spleen, and connective tissue), held up by the diaphragm and held in by the breast bone and ribs, were famous in antiquity for hosting the beloved in the lover's memory, hope, and desire. For ancient writers, emotions were physical events similar to burning one's finger or being stabbed by a sword.[3] The melting and emptying of the longing lover's body directly involves the innards:

> O cruel Love, crafty of counsel, of all gods fairest to behold with the eyes, of all most grievous when thou dost vex the heart with unforeseen assault, entering the soul like a storm-wind and breathing the bitter menace of fire, with hurricane of anguish and untempered pain. The shedding of tears is for thee a sweet delight and to hear the deep-wrung groan; to inflame a burning redness in the heart (σπλάγχνοις) [sic] and to blight and wither the bloom upon the cheek, and make the eyes hollow and to wrest all the mind to madness.[4]

Love happens in the innards.[5] That is where *pothos* lodges.[6] The innards were also known to melt away in longing for an absent beloved.[7]

Paul *felt* his emotions in his innards. Emotions are not judgments that precipitate physiological side effects, as some philosophers taught. Nor is longing a feeling produced by reflection on one's status before God, as an influential theologian of the recent past, Karl Barth, has asserted as we see below. Rather, you fall in love, you find yourself bound to the other, the other goes away, and you long for communion in your innards. Then you waste away, naturally.

Denatured Love

Even though Paul invokes God in Phil 1:8 as the witness of his longing and owns Christ as his co-sufferer, modern interpreters have not given their shared passion its due. The image of Paul today is that of Christ's apostle announcing the rule of God to persons who yield to God's (and by implication Paul's) sovereignty in the obedience of faith. Paul pining away like an anxious lover—an attractive and inspiring thought for John of Ford as we will see below—would today be a symptom of diminished apostolic presence. Of course, if Paul suffers on behalf of Christ and the church—that is, if he bears heroically the legal or social consequences of being a Christian in a Christ-resisting world, not to mention his sharing with every believer the goads of an introspective conscience—then modern interpreters, Protestants especially, are quite happy to dwell on his interiority and pain. *That* sort of suffering exemplifies their ideal of the believer's subordination to God's Lordship in Christ. Yet if Paul suffers for Christ by feeling his absence, or suffers for the church by missing his beloved friends—if, in other words, his pain has its origin in a love that seeks but never reaches communion—then modern commentators appear uninterested.[8]

So, while it is commonplace in recent scholarship to acknowledge that Paul did indeed long for the church, his *pothos* has been denatured and reconstituted theologically.[9] That is, to the extent that longing is considered at all in connection with Philippians it has been transformed by the power of a particular, theological idea: a redeemed humanity standing before a sovereign God. The bonds of human affection implied by longing arise in Paul's case, so it is claimed, not from natural feeling but from a lost sinner's consciousness of redemption in Christ. "I long for you" might be paraphrased "I yearn to be together with you because I see that you are in the same condition as I am: a redeemed sinner before God." Although Karl Barth did not invent this de-eroticized longing, he perfected it and implicitly ruled out of bounds attempts like the present one to read Paul's text in light of ancient love poetry.[10] Barth's influential interpretation of Phil 1:8 therefore calls for close examination and critique.

Surprisingly, in his commentary on Philippians, Barth highlights Paul's longing. He refers to it as it as "real human love," indicating an interpretation that he does not in fact pursue. Rather, he commends the apostle for replacing natural, human feeling with what might be called a faith-based emotion to distinguish it from the everyday variety, whose chief characteristic in the eyes of Barth is self-seeking. We will see in a moment that, for Barth, it is a Christian virtue *not* to be bonded directly to another person through natural emotions, tainted as all feelings are by sin. Paul, Barth asserts, speaks of another sort of longing whose "true reason" for existing is not given with the natural lives of humans:

> God can stand witness for Paul's longing because it is his grace that forms directly the bond of the union which is the true reason for that longing. Here we have men in real human love desiring not to be separated but to be together, but that is because as lost creatures they have found themselves together before God in his grace.[11]

Only Christian comrades knowing themselves to be bound together by the grace of God and standing before God in lost creatureliness share in the emotion that Paul names longing in Phil 1:8.

The problem with Barth's approach is that it trivializes the experience of suffering a loved one's absence. Furthermore, it makes Paul's relationship to the church in Philippi intelligible only to those familiar and sympathetic with the erasure of human subjectivity that characterizes neo-orthodox Christianity.[12] Sappho certainly would have had no clue what Barth meant by the word "longing" (as Barth would no doubt point out), though she with Homer's help before her had invented the discourse of desire that Paul in concert with ancient amatory poetry employed. Likely also among the puzzled hearers of Barth's denatured reading of Paul's longing would be the apostle's first readers, whose access to the meaning of the phrase "we long for you" was their own experiences of loss and their reading about it in poetry and on gravestones.

There is more to criticize in Barth's reading of Phil 1:8. He puts Paul's intriguing phrase in the second half of 1:8 about the innards of Christ into the same conceptual framework he used to de-eroticize the first half of the verse. In 1:8, Paul qualifies his longing christologically: ". . . with the innards of Christ Jesus." For Barth this means that for Paul there is only superficial similarity between the emotions of Paul and Christ, on the one side, and the rest of humanity on the other. Why does he rule out natural emotion as a point of access to Paul's emotion and Christ's innards? It is because self-seeking mars every instance of loving in Barth's survey of the unredeemed human heart:

> It is obviously not the strength and intensity of this "affection" that is to be brought out by the addition "of Christ Jesus," but its *uniqueness* and *peculiarity*. Its uniqueness: though it is not ashamed to appear in the form of a genuine human emotion, yet its motive power is the grace of God in Christ as that grace is proclaimed and believed in the community of the holy. Its peculiarity: if like all real love it seeks the presence of the beloved, yet it seeks him as the love of Jesus seeks men, without that self-seeking that seems to cling like a curse to even the most real human love, seeks him for God's sake and thus in the deepest sense for his own sake.[13]

Intersubjectivity, the idea that selves (redeemed or otherwise) are on their way to becoming something (though we do not know what) through equal, mutual, and desiring relationships with other selves—in a word, *erōs*— is lost on Barth, whose theological commitments to the sovereignty of God and to the dogma of sin-infested, self-seeking human love limit his imagination. As a consequence, lost also is love's suffering of the beloved's absence. And finally, lost is the possibility of thinking about God, Christ, the church, and the world from the experience of loss and grief.

One more point. In a transformation inconceivable to ancient poets, denatured longing readily allows itself to be used as an instrument of apostolic control. Interpreters have turned Paul's confession in 1:8 into an indication merely of the apostle's good relations with the Philippians, and these relations in turn facilitate teaching and disciplining, the proper acts of an apostle in their view. Calvin anticipated the modern consensus that Paul's warm relations with the people at Philippi supported his educational designs on them: "It was, too, more especially of advantage, that Paul's affection should be thoroughly made known to the Philippians. For it tends in no small degree to secure credit for the doctrine, when the people are persuaded that they are beloved by the teacher."[14] Updating Calvin's language but not his idea about Paul's strategic deployment of emotion, Stephen E. Fowl asserts that Paul had a moral purpose in his expression of friendly feelings in 1 Corinthians and Romans, and in Philippians more of the same can be detected:

> In all these cases Paul invokes the relationships of love that bind these communities to him as a way of making various moral demands of the congregation. Hence, in addition to reminding us of the cordial relations between Paul and the Philippians, this phrase ["my beloved"] signals that Paul is going to make some demand regarding the conduct of their common life.[15]

Sweet-bitter Love

The despised frailty of longing in one age might fire other generations' theological imaginations. Some Christian writers from the time of the early church to the fourteenth century were receptive to erotic overtones in Paul's words about his devotion to Christ and his love for the church. These writers were in tune with ancient poetry's simultaneous celebration and lamentation of the lover's desire for communion and his or her suffering another's absence. For the poets, longing was not a character defect, and, for the Christians who drew upon poetic motifs, desire for communion was not a carrier of the sin of self-seeking. Rather, it was a way to approach both the mystery of Christ's love for the world and Paul's apostolic bearing toward the Philippians.

John of Ford turned to poetry to account for the quality of sweetness (*dulcido*) he detected in Paul's confession of longing for the community in Phil 1:8. In John's sixteenth sermon on Song of Songs, one portion of an expository project begun by Bernard of Clairvaux and advanced by Gilbert of Hoyland, John stresses the *continuity* between the love that apostles had for God and their love for the humans around them.[16] Unlike Barth, John feels no need to cleanse the human stain from either Christ's love or Christians' love. John's sweetness is unrepentant and unwashed. This is all the more remarkable because the sweetness of love that John embraced did indeed have a questionable reputation among Christians.[17]

But John did not flinch. Desire for communion and suffering over absence characterize love both human and divine. John looked to Paul in Phil 1:8 as the exemplar of this love, this apostolic sweetness:

> If the tenderness of the love is in question, hear what one of them said on behalf of all: "Who is weak, and I am not weak? Who is scandalized, and I am not on fire?" If the sweetness is, then listen to the following: "I take God for my witness, that I yearn after all of you with the affection of Christ Jesus." And again: "So, my brothers, whom I love and long for, my joy and my crown, so stand fast in the Lord, my beloved." And regarding the greatness of this love: "I will most gladly spend and be spent for your souls."[18]

In this passage John associates longing with sweetness, though it is not the straightforward sense of the latter term that he has in mind.[19] "Sweet" and "desirable" had been interchangeable terms in Greek and Latin writings and throughout his sermons on Song of Songs John himself employed the term in this way.[20] But John reserved for Paul's sweetness a rarer and more exquisite form: the unlikely cohabitation of the sweet and the bitter in the soul longing for the presence of the absent or reticent beloved.

Sweetness of this bitter sort had a long history before John spotted it in Paul. In the seventh century B.C.E. Sappho expressed the complexity of love in a single word, γλυκύπικρος:

> Eros once again limb-loosener whirls me
>   sweetbitter, impossible to fight off, creature stealing up.[21]

In this poem, Anne Carson has translated γλυκύπικρος as "sweet-bitter" over against the customary "bittersweet." This rendering de-emphasizes the often-told narrative of a pleasant beginning turning out badly. Instead, the experience of love is itself made complex in the reordering of terms. Carson explains Sappho's neologism:

> She is not recording the history of a love affair but the instant of desire. One moment staggers under pressure of eros; one mental state splits. A simultaneity of pleasure and pain is at issue. The pleasant is named first, we may presume, because it is less surprising. Emphasis is thrown upon the problematic other side of the phenomenon, whose attributes advance in a hail of soft consonants. . . . Desire, then, is neither inhabitant nor ally of the desirer. Foreign to her will, it forces itself irresistibly upon her from without. Eros is an enemy.[22]

Although love's complexity was a poetic topos enduring well into the Middle Ages, the raving madness and outwardly directed violence that issued from the pain of frustrated love was later replaced around the turn of the eras by internalized aggression.[23] In other words, as time wore on disappointed love was less likely to result in the murder of an aloof beloved than in the wasting away of the scorned lover. In the period of the New Testament and Paul's ministry, love's bitterness no longer manifested itself by striking out in anger. Pain stayed within, and the innards were wounded or liquefied.

Bitterness was sweet Eros's constant companion. The popular "sting" of love is featured in the following epigram of Meleager, who wrote around 100 B.C.E.:

> O flower-nurtured bee, why dost thou desert the buds of spring and light on Heliodora's skin? Is it that thou wouldst signify that she hath both sweets and the sting of Love, ill to bear and ever bitter to the heart?[24]

An epitaph praised Meleager for having "linked sweet tearful Love (ὁ τὸν γλυκύδακρυν Ἔρωτα) and the Muses with the merry Graces."[25] One example is sufficient to show the epitaph (a well-planned composition of the poet himself!) did not misrepresent his work: "Pain has begun to touch my heart, for hot Love, as he strayed, scratched it with the tip of his nails, and, smiling, said, 'Again, O unhappy lover, thou shalt have the sweet wound (τὸ γλυκὺ τραῦμα), burnt by biting honey.'"[26]

In the fifth century C.E., the poet Musaeus depicted the inner turmoil of the young Hero when she sees lovely Leander. His beauty stuns her as Sappho herself had once been thunderstruck:

Now she too had felt the Loves' bitter-sweet sting (γλυκύπικρον . . . κέντρον), And the maiden Hero glowed in her heart with sweet fire (γλυκερῷ πυρί) And trembled at the beauty of Leander, quickener of desire.[27]

Sappho's influence on Musaeus may have been mediated by Medea's swoon over Jason described in the third century B.C.E. by Apollonius of Rhodes:

> . . . and the bolt burnt deep down in the maiden's heart, like a flame; and ever she kept darting bright glances straight up at Aeson's son, and within her breast her heart panted fast through anguish, all remembrance left her, and her soul melted with the sweet pain (γλυκερῇ δὲ κατείβετο θυμὸν ἀνίῃ).[28]

Apollonius and Musaeus show that the influence of Sappho's adjective "sweet-bitter" was far reaching. So much so that generations of poets alluded to the suffering side of love simply by calling it sweet. Bitterness hid in sweet love's shadow. The chorus in Euripides' *Hippolytus* reminds us of the love as enemy motif that Carson identified in Sappho. The chorus pleads for love not to inflict pain:

> Eros, Eros, distilling liquid desire upon the eyes (ὁ κατ' ὀμμάτων στάζων πόθον), bringing sweet pleasure to the souls (εἰσάγων γλυκεῖαν ψυχᾶι χάριν) of those you make war against, never may you show yourself to me for my hurt nor ever come but in harmony. For neither the shafts of fire nor stars are more powerful than that of Aphrodite, which Eros, Zeus' son, hurls from his hand.[29]

Heat, eyes melting into tears, pleasure mixed with the inevitability of suffering—these were by then clichés.[30] While this chorus naively hoped the pain of love might be averted, Asclepiades, one of the originators of erotic epigram in the third century B.C.E., gave a more realistic assessment: "Not even Love the honeyed is ever sweet (ἀεὶ γλυκύς), but often he becomes a sweeter (ἥδιον) god to lovers when he torments them."[31]

This review of sweetness in ancient poetry leads back to the question of John of Ford's perception of Paul. When John selected Phil 1:8 as an example of the sweetness of love, what exactly was he assuming about Paul's love for the congregation at Philippi? Was John aware of the Sapphic sweet-bitter motif in ancient poetry, and was this the lens through which he viewed Paul? It is not possible to be certain, but there are several indications that he was familiar with the topos and that he saw Paul as a longing lover who knew the bitter sweetness of love first hand.

First, the concept of complex love captured by Sappho's adjective γλυκύπικρος comes readily to John as he performs one of the major tasks of interpreting Song of Songs, to describe the Bride's feelings for the Bridegroom:

> You may perhaps be saying: why this coupling of charity and myrrh? The one is all overflowing with sweetness (*dulcedine*), and the other is held to be naturally bitter (*amarior*), which is what gives it its efficacy? Nevertheless, though charity may be exceedingly sweet (*dulcissima*), yet it knows very bitter loathings of its sweetness (*dulcedinis amarissima fastidia*). It knows the very sad complaints and heavy delays of interrupted pleasure. It knows with what great anxiety it desires to come to birth, with what difficulty they go forward with their conception, and how wearisome it is to bring them to an issue.[32]

Or, more succinctly: "Any soul, therefore, that longs for the joys of love, must not shrink back from its bitterness (*amara*) if it desires to experience its sweetness (*dulcia*)."[33]

John's sermons also reflect the turn in ancient poetry from bitterness expressed in acts of violence to inwardly experienced pain such as the wounding, piercing, heating, and melting of the body. Not only does the Bride of Song of Songs have a deep love of God and desire for communion with the Bridegroom; she loves those around her in a way reminiscent of the languishing poets around the turn of the era:

> Then there are the expressions of infinite sweetness (*infinitae dulcedinis*) that she uses when she is in company with the daughters of Jerusalem, clear evidence of her praiseworthy love for her neighbor. She generously reveals to them how love has wounded her, not concealing that her soul has melted away under the force of her beloved's words. She sweeps them into partnership with her endeavors, doing her very best to ensure that they too will be quick to follow in her footsteps.[34]

Furthermore, the Bridegroom loves the Bride with the same sweetness that she loves her mates. A sermon on Song of Songs 7:3 describes Jesus as a devoted lover willing to make any sacrifice to commune with the beloved:

Hence you came down from heaven, O Lord, my true Solomon, son of David, and you gave your whole heart to the task of building that was laid on you. You swore a vow to the god of Jacob, that you would not lay your head on your pillow nor go to the bed of your repose, namely, the bosom of the Father, where you were before, until you found 'a place for the Lord, a dwelling for the God of Jacob.' And so, in the rich variety of your holiness and in the sweetness of your love, by which you loved your bride, fashioning and making her lovely through the power and charity of your death, you carved out from your own self and in your own self, the columns of your house.[35]

This line of christological thought imperceptibly slides from sweetness into similar qualities of love—tenderness and greatness—that John believes Paul evinces in Phil 1:8:

Not even Paul himself could give full expression to the greatness of this motherly love of his, but equally, he had not the least wish to present it as other than it was. 'God is my witness', he says, 'how I yearn for you all in the inmost heart of Christ Jesus.' O invaluable tenderness, which he surrendered to God alone to be valued! What but an excessive tenderness could have caused in Paul's heart that great grief and continual sorrow, which he calls upon the spirit to witness is present? So great was this tender love that it wounded Paul's heart and blazed within his inmost depth, so that he could much more truly be considered as mad from too much love than from too much learning! Surely we can only think of it as some kind of madness or insanity when he desired, for the sake of his brother's salvation 'to be anathema to Christ'? . . . On this occasion, completely carried away into ecstatic self-forgetfulness, our Benjamin was too immoderate for our capacity . . . this cry is the cry of a man who is intoxicated or of a soul taken up into ecstasy, not to say that of a madman.[36]

A wounded heart, tenderness, madness, ecstasy, intoxication—and sweetness! These erotic motifs from classical literature describe the vulnerability of the lover to the beloved's welfare and response. The apostle who bears these marks is not the neo-orthodox, Barthian Paul. The Paul of John of Ford was sweet and thoroughly Sapphic.

Thus, Barth's notion of true longing as an emotion experienced by a company of lost creatures standing in faith before the sovereign God plays no role in John's exegesis, nor does John catch a whiff of calculation on Paul's part, as if the apostle's friendship aimed to ensure the success of his teaching or moral directing. This is not to say that the ancient and medieval periods lacked interpretations oriented around divine sovereignty and Paul's control of the church, but readings like John's have not informed modern Pauline scholarship to the extent that they might. In their readiness to associate Paul with the classical motifs of erotic love and longing desire, John of Ford, Baldwin of Ford, Bernard of Clairvaux, and other Christian writers of the West and the East help us to realize how little we have esteemed the discourse of love but also what a powerful vantage point ancient *erōs* might become for interpreting Pauline letters.

Bodies Melting

John of Ford was on to something. His intuition or, more likely, his familiarity with long-established poetic imagery helped him identify longing as the controlling theme of Paul's self-presentation in Philippians. Might Paul's first audiences have regarded 1:8 in the same way? The literary history of longing from Homer to Paulus Silentiarius tempts us to think so. *Pothos*, the emotion Paul conveyed to the church in Phil 1:8, goes to the heart of Greek and Latin love poetry and the romantic novel. Paul evoked love under the pall of absence when in Phil 1:8 he declared, sweetly in John's estimation, that he longed for the church.

The story of Paul's longing began long before the apostle's birth. Odysseus's leaving for Troy and his wandering back home set the stage. Before Paul yearned for the Philippians, Penelope longed for her husband, Odysseus. She did not bear the pain of his absence alone. His mother Antikleia dearly missed him too and wasted away to the point of death.[37] Desperate for home, Odysseus emptied out his "sweet life."[38] They all found themselves wasted and worn away, melted, and poured out. *Pothos* worked "chronic dissolution" on all of its victims.[39]

But Penelope suffered most. Unaware of the true identity of the beggar listening to her words, she confessed an intense longing for (and to) her husband: "in longing for Odysseus I waste my heart away."[40] Soon after comes a tender passage, whose precise words were in all likelihood unknown to Paul and the Philippians, although the sentiment is all too familiar to anyone ever separated from a loved one:

Then he made the many falsehoods of his tale seem like the truth, and as she listened her tears flowed and her face melted (τήκετο). As the snow melts (κατατήκετ᾽) on the lofty mountains, the snow which the East Wind thaws (κατέτηξεν) when the West Wind has poured it down, and as it melts (τηκομένης) the streams of the rivers flow full: so her lovely cheeks melted as she wept and mourned for her husband, who even then was sitting by her side.[41]

First to speak of longing as a physiological event, Homer was not the last. Longing liquefies flesh; this poetic construct endured to the time of Paul and far beyond. Homer and the erotic poetry that followed him created a discourse for Paul to express his emotions to the Philippians and his feelings for Christ. And, as the next chapter argues, Christ longed for the world in the same way. To love an absent one is to melt and flow away.[42]

In Greek and Latin literature *pothos/desiderium* never failed to melt the solid self.[43] Sappho acknowledged longing's power to melt innards: "You have come, and I was longing for you, you cooled my heart which was burning with desire (καιομέναν πόθῳ)."[44] Pindar compared the effect of longing with the surging of the sea; for anyone who "hath seen the rays flashing from the eyes of Theoxenus" it is impossible that his heart not "swell with desire (πόθῳ κυμαίνεται)," unless it is "forged of adamant or of iron."[45] But then he left the sea and returned to Sapphic heat: "But I, for the sake of that Queen of love, like the wax of the holy bees that is melted beneath the heat of the sun, waste away (τάκομαι) when I look at the young limbs of blooming boys."[46]

Representations of *pothos*'s effects on the body multiplied as poets eroticized other poets' non-erotic diction.[47] The loosening of limbs, for example, which Homer attributed to death and sleep, Sappho said to be the handiwork of erotic love.[48] In the middle of the seventh century, Archilochus complained that longing does to him what death does to all other mortals: "But comrade, the limb-loosener (ὁ λυσιμελής) subdues me, desire (πόθος)."[49] Describing the loving looks one choral dancer shoots to another, Alcman bemoans the melting effects of longing: "with limb-loosening desire (λυσιμελεῖ τε πόθωι), more meltingly than sleep or death she glances."[50]

Two more effects of *pothos* can be detected in archaic poetry: organs migrate from the body, and they are made to suffer wounds of several kinds: scrapings, piercings, and even the scratching of writing instruments. The heart especially is susceptible to these attacks, as later poets and novelists would emphasize.[51] Ideas about ecstasy and organs vulnerable to outside forces became very popular by the fourth century B.C.E. and remained so through Paul's day right up the sixth century of the common era.[52] In ecstasy, the body as a whole, or represented by one of its organs, enters into Eros or into the beloved. Sappho tells of a man who fell in love twice: "he came the second time to a longed-for love (πόθεννον εἰς ἔρον)."[53]

More often innards (τὰ σπλάγχνα) stay in the body and love enters them. Eros invades the body, entering through the eyes or piercing the skin. He then inscribes himself on or lodges in the victim's organs. Archilochus experienced Eros's invasion *and* the ecstasy of his wits:

> Such a desire for love rolled up beneath the heart
> poured a thick mist down over the eyes,
> stealing out of the breast the soft wits.[54]

Pothos and *erōs* have the same effect:

> I lie here wretched with desire (πόθῳ)
> Breathless, at the gods' will by bitter pains
> Pierced right through the bones.[55]

Pothos continued to melt innards in the sixth and fifth centuries B.C.E. The chorus in Aeschylus's *Agamemnon* reports on Menelaus's grief at Helen's leaving him in the company of her abductor, Paris:

> . . . and the seers of the house said this, with many a groan: "Alas for the house, alas for the house and its chiefs! Alas for the bed and the traces of a loving wife! One can see the deserted, silent, dishonoured, neither reviling nor praying; because of his longing (πόθῳ) for her who is beyond the sea, a phantom will seem to rule the house. The charm of beautiful statues has become hateful to the husband: because they lack eyes, all their loveliness goes for nothing.[56]

One scholiast believed the phantom to be Helen's ghost, but more likely Menelaus in mourning appears to the courtiers as an insubstantial replica of himself. His hungry eyes, too, tell the morbid tale of *pothos*. They have been emptied through his tears.[57] For Sophocles, also, eyes dissolving into tears represent the entire body wasting away. Deianeira misses her husband, Heracles:

> For I learn that with an ever yearning (ποθουμένα) heart Deianeira,
> she who was fought over, like some sorrowful bird can never lull to

sleep without tears the longing (πόθον) of her eyes, but, nourishing a fear that keeps in mind the absence of her husband, she is worn away on her anxious couch bereft of him, fearing, poor woman, a miserable fate.[58]

Just as longing turned Menelaus into a phantom, so it consumed Deianeira.[59] And just as the Spartan king's eyes were emptied of their capacity for pleasure or pain, her tears put her to sleep. With the weeping comes welcome news that the relief of slumber is at hand, but ancient audiences would not have missed the mixed message. Sleep mirrors the oblivion of Death.

As we saw above, Euripides in his *Hippolytus* also puts the liquefaction of eyes to dramatic use: "Eros, Eros, distilling liquid desire upon the eyes (ὁ κατ' ὀμμάτων στάζων πόθων) . . . ."[60] These lines of Euripides mark an important conceptual shift as much as they testify to established motifs. No longer was it sufficient to think of *pothos* as *erōs* in the circumstance of the beloved's absence. Now, *erōs* distills *pothos*. In other words, *pothos* wastes the lover regardless of whether the beloved is absent. Authors from this point forward will equate *erōs* and *pothos* to acknowledge the fragility of erotic relationships even when they are experienced face to face. The hard truth coming to literary consciousness is that the beloved is mortal.[61] Presence itself points to absence; happy *erōs* masks a grieving *pothos*. Or, in the case of Phaedra's desire for Hippolytus, the beloved before her eyes is impossible to possess because he is her stepson. The neat distinction between *pothos* and *erōs*, though occasionally observed in the coming centuries, was falling apart.

We turn next to two Alexandrian poets of the third century B.C.E., Apollonius of Rhodes and Theocritus. Though working in different genres, each testifies to the physiological effects of *pothos*.[62] The third book of Apollonius's *Argonautica* tells the story of Jason and Medea. The plot hinges on Medea's falling in love with Jason and betraying her father. Book 3 begins with a conversation between Hera and Athena, who was the divine superintendent of Jason's adventure. They ask Aphrodite to prevail upon her son Eros to inflict Medea with *pothos* for Jason.[63] Apollonius's description of Medea's looking upon Jason is an exquisite account of longing's effects on the body:

. . . and speechless amazement seized her heart . . . and the arrow burned deep down in the girl's heart like a flame. She continually cast bright glances straight at Jason, and wise thoughts fluttered from her breast in distress. She could remember nothing else, for her heart was flooding with sweet pain. And as when a woman piles twigs around a flaming brand, a working woman whose task is wool-spinning, so as to furnish light under her roof at night as she sits close by, and the flame rises prodigiously from the small brand and consumes all the twigs together—such was the destructive love that curled beneath her heart and burned in secret. And her tender cheeks turned now pale, now red, in the distraction of her mind.[64]

This passage has no equal in ancient literature for psychological insight, with the exception of Sappho, *Frg.* 31, on which it is believed to have been modeled.[65] Apollonius knew from the poetic tradition that Eros melts inner organs.[66] He also knew the organs' vulnerability: the θυμός is seized and the heart is burned into and coiled under. Medea even experiences a kind of ecstasy when her unguarded mind is left to wander about on its own. When she views Jason later in the story, his face again induces ecstasy: "and the girl, fixing her eyes upon him at an angle, gazed from the shining veil, smoldering with grief in her heart, creeping like a dream, fluttered after his footsteps as he went."[67]

Theocritus turns away from epic vision. Instead, he pictures everyday life among goatherds, farmers, reapers, and the like. Take for example the clichéd association of *pothos* with the absence of the beloved. This bit of erotic common sense occurs in the patter between Bucaeus, who is "ailing" for love of a maiden and acting like a "ewe with a thorn in her foot," and Milon, his fellow worker and disdainful drudge. Milon castigates Bucaeus for sloughing off, but the lovesick slacker excuses himself:

> Bucaeus: Good master early-and-late-wi'-sickle, good Sir chip-o'-the-flint, good Milon, hath it never befallen thee to wish for one that is away (ποθέσαι τινὰ τῶν ἀπεόντων)?
> Milon: Never, i' faith; what has a clown like me to do with wishing (πόθος) where there's no getting?[68]

Common folk lack the glamour of Homeric heroes, but Theocritus teaches that bumpkins fall victim to *erōs* just like anyone else. And they know erotic theory.

In *Idyll* 2, Theocritus again studies *pothos* through the lens of absence. This poem is about the vengeance of a young woman, Simaetha. She has been jilted by Delphis. The poem has two parts. In the first, an act of witchcraft takes place; Simaetha conjures the heat of love to burn Delphis's bones and melt him so he might know in his body what pain he has caused in hers. In the second half, Simaetha tells the story of the *pothos* that she continues to bear.[69] Her present condition is desperate. Love has emptied her: "Woe's me, remorseless love! Why hast clung to me thus, thou muddy leech, and drained my flesh of the red blood every drop?"[70] Even before Delphis betrayed her by chasing after a new *pothos*,[71] she displayed the symptoms of lovesickness: a warming around the θυμός, a melting away of her beautiful face, and a wasting fever.[72] *Pothos* seems to have infected *erōs*.

Not only does *pothos* warm and melt innards, but it lacerates, stings, and pierces them too. *Idyll* 13 culminates with a description of Herakles' crazed *pothos* as he searches for Hylas, his companion abducted by nymphs.[73] Herakles searches wildly but in vain for the drowned youth. In the words of one commentator, "Herakles' madness has close parallels in descriptions of erotic frenzy . . . from both 'high' and 'low' literature."[74]

> When a fawn cries in the hills, some ravening lion will speed from his lair to get him a meal so ready; and even so went Heracles wildly to and fro amid the pathless brake (ἀτρίπτοισιν ἀκάνθαις), and covered much country because of his longing for the child (παῖδα ποθῶν). As lovers know no flinching, so endless was the toil of his wandering by wood and wold, and all Jason's business was but a by-end. . . . But he alas! was running whithersoever his feet might carry him, in a frenzy, the God did rend so cruelly the heart within him.[75]

"Untrodden thorns" is a better translation of the phrase appearing here as "pathless brake." Heracles' thorn-punctured feet hint at his whole body's exposure to Eros's penetrating missiles.[76] The final phrase about Eros's laceration of his heart confirms this point. What the lyric poets knew has not been forgotten; innards are the location of *pothos*'s workings.[77]

Epigrams worked especially well for the expression of erotic ideas, since their brevity presupposed knowledge of past narratives of *erōs*. The widely separated dates of the two major writers of epigrams selected for the present study, Meleager (first century B.C.E.) and Paulus Silentiarius (sixth century C.E.), indicate the durability of the genre. The following epigram by Meleager employs different terminology for longing and love. Note that the neat division between *erōs* and *pothos* breaks down:

> Cypris denies that she gave birth to Love ('Ερώτα) now that she sees Antiochus among the young men, a second Love ("Ιμερον). But, ye young men, love (στέργοιτε) this new Love (Πόθον); for of a truth this boy have proved to be a Love better than Love ("Ερωτος "Ερως).[78]

This poem works only because of the interchangeability of πόθος, ἔρως, and ἵμερος. The playfulness of the poem masks a serious issue. Who will win this definitional tug-of-war? Does *pothos* lose its obsession with absence, death, and the impossibility of union? Or has *erōs* with its happy connotations of union with the beloved been dragged across the line into *pothos*? The contest has no unambiguous result. Nevertheless, since our interest in the history of *pothos* is tied to Paul's letter to the Philippians, where the themes of absence, memory, and the suffering of love take center stage, we end this chapter by examining writings in which *pothos* overtakes *erōs*.

Erotic epigrams lend beauty to suffering, but suffering has an effect on beauty as well. Longing withers the body.[79] The tears of longing are the liquefaction and the flowing away of the innards.[80] There is carnage when beauty smites the lover with *pothos*: "My love is a running sore that ever discharges tears for the wound stancheth not."[81] *Pothos* causes lovesickness with all the symptoms we have seen before: burning, hollow eyes, pale complexion, and dissolution of the body.[82] Reminiscent of Homer, the key term in these poems for *pothos*'s operation on the body is "melting (τήκω)."[83] The heat of *pothos* makes you grow old before your time by emptying you of moisture and vital heat:

> Why find fault with my locks grown grey so early and my eyes wet with tears? These are the pranks my love (πόθων) for thee plays; these are the care-marks of unfulfilled desire (φροντίδες ἀπρήκτοιο πόθου); these are the traces the arrows left; these are the work of many sleepless nights. Yes, and my sides are already wrinkled all before their time, and the skin hangs loose upon my neck. The more fresh and young the flame is, the older grows my body devoured by care.[84]

In the end, if not ended by union, longing kills.[85]

Before it comes to this deadly result, however, *pothos* impresses itself on the innards or, conversely, it causes the heart and mind to travel outside of the body.[86] Beauty throws *pothos* like a flaming ball.[87] When it strikes, you burn.[88] And again, like stone or parchment the heart is a writing surface and receives love's "well-known stamp."[89] But longing might also erase the soul's capacity for perceiving the external world by emptying it of "phantasies," a philosophical term for the powers of perception.[90] Paulus Silentiarius best expresses the simultaneous impressionability of organs and their ecstatic flight: lovers are "longing, if it could be, to enter into each other's hearts (ἐς κραδίην)."[91]

The overall impression that erotic epigrams give is that *pothos* creates an extraordinary form of human relationship: when two are in love but separated each is both host and visitant of the beloved other.[92]

FROM PAULOLOGY TO CHRISTOPATHY

Much is at stake in a doctrine of Paul, but, as the apostle himself would affirm, reflection on him is just a trial run for Christology. Their common innards have given us a chance to practice our skills at inquiry on Paul to discover the assumptions we carry and adjust them, if necessary, before we tackle Paul's doctrine of Christ in the next chapter. Some reassessment seems prudent, since we have confirmed that Paulology is indeed an inappropriate term as readers may already have judged. But it is improper for a reason other than its recent coinage. As John of Ford insisted, the most remarkable feature of Paul was not his *logos* but his *pathos*, his passion of sweet-bitter love for the Philippians. Based on John's reading of Phil 1:8, then, if a replacement term is necessary it ought to be this: Paulopathy. The connotation of physical ailment directs us to the effects of longing worked on the human body in poetry from Homer to Paulus Silentiarius: warming, melting, pouring out, and wasting away. Exploration of Paul's Christopathy, then, is the logical next step.

Notes

1. Sappho, *Frg.* 130. Translation is from Anne Carson, *Eros the Bittersweet: An Essay* (Princeton: Princeton University Press, 1986), 3. Reprinted by permission of Princeton University Press.

2. The New Jerusalem Bible on this verse is an intriguing exception: "For God will testify for me how much I long for you all with the warm longing of Christ Jesus."

3. See Ruth Padel, *In and Out of the Mind: Greek Images of the Tragic Self* (Princeton: Princeton University Press, 1992), 12–48. Two representative modern translations of τὰ σπλάγχνα: NIV: "affection"; NRSV: "compassion."

4. Oppian, *Halieutica* 4.9–18. Cf. Theocritus, *Id.* 1.87.

5. See *Greek Anthology* 12.81: "Love-sick deceivers of your souls, ye who know the flame of lads' love, having tasted the bitter honey, pour about my heart cold water, cold, and quickly, water from new-melted snow. For I have dared to look on Dionysius. But, fellow-slaves, ere it reach my vitals (σπλάγχνων), put the fire in me out." Cf. *Greek Anthology* 5.56; 12.80. Kisses penetrate the innards; see Chariton, *Chaer.* 2.8.1.

6. See *Greek Anthology* 12.160: "Bravely shall I bear the sharp pain in my vitals (ὑπὸ σπλάγχνοισιν) and the bond of the cruel fetters." Cf. Achilles Tatius, *Leuc. Clit.* 2.37.10; Theocritus *Id.* 7. 99; Herodes, *Mime* 1.55-56: "and his harte was stung with passion (ἔρωτι καρδίαν ἀνοιστρηθείς), and his entrayles swollen (ἐκύμηνε τὰ σπλάγχνα)." Moschus, *Eros drapeta* 16–17: Eros is "winged like a bird and flies from one to another, women as well as men, and alights upon their hearts (ἐπὶ σπλάγχνοις δὲ κάθηται)."

7. Padel, *In and Out of the Mind*, 13–18, 48, 73–76, 99–100.

8. Exegetes generally think that Paul's phrase "to suffer for him (τὸ ὑπὲρ αὐτοῦ πάσχειν)" in Phil 1:29 refers to persecution, but there is also reason to believe it speaks of the shared suffering between friends or lovers. See Lucian, *Tox.* 6.2; and Heliodorus, *Aeth.* 8.7.2.

9. Today's interpreters are not the first to downplay Paul's longing. Theodore of Mopsuetia paraphrased Phil 1:8 as follows: "For God is my witness, how I am disposed towards all of you." Text and translation are from *Theodori Episcopi Mopsuesteni in Epistolas B. Pauli Commentarii*, trans. H. B. Swete, 2 vols., (Cambridge: At the University Press, 1880), 204.

10. John Chrysostom's paraphrase (*Hom. Phil.* 2; *PG* 62:189) appears to suggest the distinction between natural and Christian emotions that Barth emphasizes: "'I love you with no natural bowels, but with warmer ones, namely, those of Christ.'" Translation is from *NPNF* 13:188. The theme of warmth, however, might also refer to the erotic tradition. See the next chapter on warmth and melting, pp. 59–63.

11. Karl Barth, *The Epistle to the Philippians: 40th Anniversary Edition*, trans. James W. Leitch; (Louisville: Westminster John Knox, 2002), 19. Stephen E. Fowl (*Philippians*, Two Horizons New Testament Commentary [Grand Rapids: Eerdmans, 2005], 31) does not follow Barth's emphasis on lost creatureliness and grace. Yet, like Barth, he describes Paul's emotion disjunctively: "Paul's longing is not simply a personal yearning. Rather, it reflects the love Christ has for the Philippians."

12. Paul is a religious hero for Barth precisely because the apostle eradicates his own subjectivity in order to let God be the one and only true Subject. See Barth's comments on Phil 3:12 in chapter 6, n. 52.

13. Barth, *Philippians*, 20. Perhaps Barth is simply saying what Calvin had said: "He [Paul] places the *bowels of Christ* in opposition to carnal affection, to intimate that his affection is holy and pious." John Calvin, *Commentaries on the Epistles of Paul the Apostle to the Philippians, Colossians, and Thessalonians*, trans. John Pringle (Grand Rapids: Eerdmans, 1948), 30. Here Calvin repeats the distinction Chrysostom and later Theophylact (*Expositio in epist. ad Philipp.* 1.8 [*PG* 124:1145]) made. I doubt, though, that Barth was given merely to rehearsing earlier views, as the commentary tradition on which he relies often did.

14. Calvin, *Philippians*, 30

15. Fowl, *Philippians*, 118.

16. It was no coincidence that interest in Song of Songs intensified during the flowering of friendship in monastic communities. Gilbert made some headway in the project started by Bernard, but the task would be completed by John of Ford. See Brian Patrick McGuire, *Friendship and Community: The Monastic Experience, 350–1250*, Cistercian Studies Series 95 (Kalamazoo: Cistercian Publications, 1988), 296–338.

17. See Romanus's portrayal of Joseph's seductress in *Canticle* 6.6.5.

18. John of Ford, *Sermon* 16.4. Translation is from *Sermons on the Final Verses of the Song of Songs, II*, trans. Wendy Mary Beckett, Cistercian Fathers Series 39 (Kalamazoo: Cistercian Publications, 1982), 20.

19. For which, see Franz Posset, *Pater Bernhardus: Martin Luther and Bernard of Clairvaux*, Cistercian Studies Series 168 (Kalamazoo: Cistercian Publications, 1999), 247–70.

20. *Sermon* 38 is a remarkable study in the sweetness of Jesus in this simpler sense. Cf. Aelred of Rievaulx, *The Mirror of Charity* 2.6.12. For a connection to ancient literature, one example from Plautus (*Asinarius* 614–15) must suffice: One character says, "Oh, you're sweeter than sweet honey," and the other responds, "Certainly you are sweeter than my life to me."

21. See n. 1 above.

22. Carson, *Eros the Bittersweet*, 4.

23. Peter Toohey, *Melancholy, Love, and Time: Boundaries of the Self in Ancient Literature* (Ann Arbor: University of Michigan Press, 2004), 59–91. I return to Toohey's thesis in chapter 3.

24. *Greek Anthology* 5.163; see also 5.134; 12.153.

25. Ibid., 7.419. In Latin poetry, too, sweetness was laced with bitterness. See Propertius 3.8.29; 2.30B.29-32; Tibullus 3.11.7.

26. *Greek Anthology* 12.126. For other instances in Meleager's epigrams, see *Greek Anthology* 5.212; 12.68, 167.

27. Musaeus, *Hero et Leander* 166–68.

28. Apollonius of Rhodes, *Argon.* 3.285–90; cf. 4.1147, 1168. See also *Greek Anthology* 12.99; Lucian, [*Am.*] 3.

29. Euripides, *Hippolytus* 525–32. Euripides' model is perhaps Alcman, *Frg.* 59, quoted in Athenaeus, *Deip.* 13.600F: "When sweet Eros, at Cypris' bidding, floods my heart and warms it (γλυκὺς κατείβων καρδίαν ἰαίνει)." Euripides in turn became the model for Philodemus, *Epigram* 9.6 (David Sider, *The Epigrams of Philodemus: Introduction, Text, and Commentary* [Oxford: Oxford University Press, 1997], 95) and Philostratus, *Imag.* 2.9. See also Lucretius, *De rerum natura* 4.1058–60.

30. Plato, *Phaedr.* 251B-C.

31. *Greek Anthology* 12.153.

32. John of Ford, *Sermon* 24.4. Translation is from Beckett, *Sermons on the Final Verses of the Song of Songs, II*, 137–38. Text is CCCM 17:204.

33. John of Ford, *Sermon* 24.4–5. Translation is from Beckett, *Sermons on the Final Verses of the Song of Songs, II*, 139. Text is CCCM 17:205.

34. John of Ford, *Sermon* 81.4. Translation is from *Sermons on the Final Verses of the Song of Songs, V*, trans. Wendy Mary Beckett, Cistercian Fathers Series 45 (Kalamazoo: Cistercian Publications, 1983), 236. Text is CCCM 18:20.

35. John of Ford, *Sermon* 33.8. Translation is from *Sermons on the Final Verses of the Song of Songs, III*, trans. Wendy Mary Beckett, Cistercian Fathers Series 43 (Kalamazoo: Cistercian Publications, 1982), 59–60.

36. John of Ford, *Sermon* 72.2–4. Translation is from Beckett, *Sermons on the Final Verses of the Song of Songs, V*, 120–21.

37. Homer, *Od.* 11.197–203. This motif is important in grave inscriptions. See, for example, *Griechische Vers-Inschriften* 1:1985.

38. Homer, *Od.* 5.152. For the figure of Penelope in an epistolary context, see Synesius, *Ep.* 158.

39. Monica Silveira Cyrino, *In Pandora's Jar: Lovesickness in Early Greek Poetry* (Lanham, MD: University Press of America, 1995), 24.

40. Homer, *Od.* 19.136. For Penelope in grave inscriptions, see, for example, *Steinepigramme* 16/31/83.

41. Homer, *Od.* 19.204-209. The father of Theseus suffered similarly: "wasting his longing eyes in constant tear-floods." The notion that tears were liquefied flesh endured; see Catullus 64.242; *Greek Anthology* 5.280. Jon Steffen Bruss, *Hidden Presences: Monuments, Gravesites, and Corpses in Greek Funerary Epigram*, Hellenistica Groningana 10 (Dudley, MA: Peeters, 2005), 56–57.

42. Hesiod was as apprehensive but far less tender than Homer. If longing liquefies internal organs in Homer, in Hesiod bodies are eaten. See Hesiod, *Op.* 66; [*Scut.*] 41.

43. The coastal areas of the southern Peloponnese still knew this in the 1980s. See C. Nadia Seremetakis, *The Last Word: Women, Death and Divination in Inner Mani* (Chicago: University of Chicago Press, 1991), 115, 216.

44. Sappho, *Frg.* 48.

45. Pindar, *Frg.* 123.2–4. See also Herodes, *Mime* 1.56–57; Heliodorus, *Aeth.* 4.4.3.

46. Pindar, *Frg.* 123.8–10. See also *Greek Anthology* 5.210; 12.72.

47. See Leah Rissman, *Love as War: Homeric Allusion in the Poetry of Sappho*, Beiträge zur klassischen Philologie 157 (Königstein/Ts.: Hain, 1983); Charles Rowan Beye, "Jason as Love-hero in Apollonios' *Argonautika*," *GRBS* 10 (1969): 31–55.

48. Emily Vermeule, *Aspects of Death in Early Greek Art and Poetry,* Sather Classical Lectures 46 (Berkeley: University of California Press, 1979), 145–57.

49. Archilochus, *Frg.* 196. Translation is from Cyrino, *In Pandora's Jar,* 75. For discussion of this fragment, see Cyrino, 74–79; and Patricia Rosenmeyer, "Tracing *Medulla* as a *Locus Eroticus,*" *Arethusa* 32 (1999): 22–24.

50. Alcman, *Frg.* 3.61–62. Translation is from Cyrino, *In Pandora's Jar,* 83. Cf. Theognis, 2.1339: ἐκλέλυμαι δὲ πόθου.

51. See Theocritus, *Id.* 11.15; 30.8; Herodes, *Mime* 1.55–56; Bion, *Epitaphius Adonis* 17; Moschus, *Europa* 17, 25; Achilles Tatius *Leuc. Clit.* 2.7.6; Longus, *Daphn.* 1.14.2; 1.17.2; Heliodorus, *Aeth.* 3.5.6; 4.7.4. For a look at the ancient heart from the vantage point of the seventeenth century, see Donald A. Beecher and Massimo Ciavollela, *A Treatise on Lovesickness: Jacques Ferrand* (Syracuse: Syracuse University Press, 1990), 256–57.

52. For Hellenistic epigram, see Claude Calame, *The Poetics of Eros in Ancient Greece,* trans. Janet Lloyd (Princeton: Princeton University Press, 1999), 57–59; J. D. Reed, *Bion of Smyrna, The Fragments and the Adonis,* Cambridge Classical Texts and Commentaries 33 (New York: Cambridge University Press, 1997), 224–25. See also Xenophon of Ephesus, *Ephesiaca* 1.9.6–8; *Greek Anthology* 5.14; 5.78. For the latter epigram, see Walther Ludwig, "Platons Kuss und seine Folgen," *Illinois Classical Studies* 14 (1989): 435–47.

53. Sappho, *Frg.* 15. See further Karlheinz Kost, *Musaios, Hero und Leander: Einleitung, Text, Übersetzung, und Kommentar* (Bonn: Bouvier-Verlag, 1971), 177.

54. Archilochus, *Frg.* 191. Translation is from Cyrino, *In Pandora's Jar,* 77.

55. Archilochus, *Frg.* 193. Translation is from Cyrino, *In Pandora's Jar,* 76.

56. Aeschylus, *Ag.* 408–19. On this passage, see Maurizio Bettini, *The Portrait of the Lover,* trans. Laura Gibbs (Berkeley: University of California Press, 1999), 14–17.

57. The connection between *pothos* and tears is made forcefully in Aeschylus, *Pers.* 133–39.

58. Sophocles, *Trach.* 103–11.

59. For an example of τρύχω and πόθος in the later poets, see *Greek Anthology* 12.143.

60. Euripides, *Hippolytus* 525–26. See n. 29 above.

61. For an unfeeling description of the situation, see Gregory of Nyssa, *On Virginity* 3.

62. Apollonius adapted epic form to express erotic content. Graham Zanker ("The Love Theme in Apollonius Rhodius' Argonautica," *Wiener Studien* 13 [1979]: 72) writes that "the keynote of the new heroism is not traditional individualistic prowess but the willingness to admit to and exploit the power of a more human force, love."

63. Apollonius of Rhodes, *Argon.* 3.33, 86. It is fitting that Medea suffers *pothos,* the emotion that accentuates the beloved's absence, since she often suffered visions of Jason dying and abandoning her. See *Argon.* 3.459–62.

64. Apollonius of Rhodes, *Argon.* 3.284–98. For possible models of Medea's lovesickness in earlier writings, see Malcolm Campbell, *A Commentary on Apollonius Rhodius Argonautica III 1–471,* Mnemosyne 141 (Leiden: Brill, 1994), 256–73.

65. See the introduction above, p. 3.

66. See Apollonius of Rhodes *Argon.* 3.755–65.

67. Apollonius of Rhodes, *Argon.* 3.444–47. For the wandering soul in erotic contexts, see Campbell, *Commentary,* 367–68. Another moment of ecstasy is recorded in *Argon.* 3.962: "Then her heart dropped out of her breast." And yet another in *Argon.* 3.1015–21. See Robert V. Albis, *Poet and Audience in the Argonautica of Apollonius,* Greek Studies: Interdisciplinary Approaches (Lanham, MD: Rowman & Littlefield, 1996), 87–88. For the theme in Greek and Roman comedy, see Netta Zagagi, *Tradition and Originality in Plautus: Studies of the Amatory Motifs in Plautine Comedy,* Hypomnemata 62 (Göttingen: Vandenhoeck & Ruprecht, 1980), 78–79, 134–37.

68. Theocritus, *Id.* 10.7–10.

69. Ibid., 2.164.

70. Ibid., 2.55–56. Love sucks the blood out of its victim. *Pothos* empties the body by feeding on bone marrow. See *Id.* 30.21–22: ὁ πόθος καὶ τὸν ἔσω μύελον ἐσθίει. For such physiological effects, see Rosenmeyer, "Tracing *Medulla,*" 26–27.

71. Theocritus, *Id.* 2.150.

72. Ibid., 2.82–85; see also 2.106–10. Like Sappho and Apollonius, Theocritus regarded *pothos* as a disease. The aging process, thought to be the body's loss of vital heat and drying up is remarkably accelerated by *pothos,* so much so that lovers grow old in a single day (*Id.* 12.2). See Richard Hunter, *Theocritus and the Archaeology of Greek Poetry* (Cambridge: Cambridge University, 1996), 186–95.

73. Theocritus, *Id.* 13.65. For the popularity of this story in the Hellenistic period, see Alison Sharrock, *Seduction and Repetition in Ovid's Ars Amatoria II* (New York: Oxford University Press, 1994), 36–38.

74. Hunter, *Theocritus,* 284. For other examples of *pothos* induced frenzy, see Menander, *Leukadia* 13; Musaeus, *Hero et Leander* 134, 196–97.

75. Theocritus, *Id.* 13.62–73.

76. See Hunter, *Theocritus,* 284.

77. Theocritus, *Id.* 7.99: παιδὸς ὑπὸ σπλάγχνοισιν ἔχει πόθον.

78. *Greek Anthology* 12.54. Scholars have reached a consensus: beginning in the Alexandrian period very little distinguished *pothos* and *erōs.* See Sider, *Epigrams of Philodemus,* 69–70; Kost, *Musaios,* 177; Campbell, *Commentary,* 44.

79. *Greek Anthology* 5.153, on which see Kathryn J. Gutzwiller, *Poetic Garlands: Hellenistic Epigrams in Context,* Hellenistic Culture and Society 28 (Berkeley: University of California Press, 1998), 130–32.

80. *Greek Anthology* 5.211, 212.

81. Ibid., 5.225; 12.160.

82. Ibid., 5.87, 259, 264.

83. Ibid., 12.99, 125, 166. See Daniel H. Garrison, *Mild Frenzy: A Reading of the Hellenistic Epigram,* Hermes Einzelschriften 41 (Wiesbaden: Steiner, 1978), 78. For the melting motif in Christian piety, see *Greek Anthology* 8.159: "I, Maxentius, was born of noble blood; I stood in the Emperor's Court, I was puffed up by vain glory. But when Christ called me, throwing all to the winds, I walked, stimulated by love (πόθοιο) for him, in many ways of life, until I found the steadfast one. I wasted (τῆξα) my body for Christ by many hardships, and now flew up lightly from here."

84. *Greek Anthology* 5.264. For the aging effects of *pothos,* see chapter 3, note 5.

85. *Greek Anthology* 6.71; Aulus Gelius, *Attic Nights* 6.8.7.

86. *Greek Anthology* 12.99, 159; *Anacreonta* 25.7; 31:4–8: "my heart (κραδίη) jumped up all the way to my nose" linked to Homer and Sappho by Patricia Rosenmeyer, *The Poetics of Imitation: Anacreon and the Anacreontic Tradition* (Cambridge: Cambridge University Press, 1992), 103,168.

87. *Greek Anthology* 5.214

88. Ibid., 5.139; Musaeus, *Hero et Leander* 247.

89. *Greek Anthology* 5.212. Cf. Plutarch, *Amat.* 759C.

90. *Greek Anthology* 5.235.

91. Ibid., 5.255. A wish echoing Theocritus, *Id.* 27.62: καὶ τὰν ψυχὰν ἐπιβάλλειν.

92. *Greek Anthology* 5.255. See also Musaeus, *Hero et Leander* 68–72, 155–56.

3

Kenōsis, or As the Snow Melts

*I am on fire, and in my but now vacant
heart Love sits his throne.*[1]

EROTIC KENOTIC

Imagine looking over the shoulder of an industrious poet of the sixth century, Paulus Silentiarius. When not occupied with the duties of a silentiary or composing an epic length poem on the architectural wonders of Agia Sophia, Paulus wrote some of the best erotic verse of his generation. Your curiosity is not directed at the poems he writes, however, but the ones he thumbs through. Were you to read his favorites and see the images that inspired his own writings, your eyes would gaze out over a sea of longing lovers. You would see lover after lover melt like wax, or just plain melt.[2] Lovers sucked dry of blood, emaciated, and dissolved.[3] You would see them dripping, pouring themselves out, overflowing, draining and drained dead.[4] You would see lovers wither, shrivel, and grow old in a single day.[5] How quickly they waste away![6] Blankly they stare with hollow eyes emptied by the shedding of tears.[7] Empty are their hearts, and chasms gape where hearts once beat.[8] Roasted, with only bones and hair left, their marrow and innards burned up, longing has consumed limbs and whole bodies.[9] In a gesture of respect to Hesiod, Sappho, and Alcaeus, Paulus selects their jarring descriptor of love as "limb-gnawing" and tenderly puts it to use in his own poem about the infinite longing of two lovers.[10]

The Christian tradition is familiar with poured-out divinity; the condescension of the second person of the Trinity is standard stuff. Yet few theologians have understood Christ's *kenōsis* in a poetic way.[11] What if Paulus's favorite texts shed light on Paul's Christology and were allowed to inform

Christian doctrine? What if Christ were one of these erotic sufferers? What if Christ's *kenōsis* in Phil 2:7 were the melting away of his body in love?

No doubt it takes a deep bending of the contemporary Christian mind just to listen to these questions, since most interpreters have considered "he emptied himself" emphatically not erotic. *Kenōsis* has rather been a matter of voluntary self-limitation: Christ gave up, constrained, or hid divine power, privilege, and status. Few interpreters think the second person of the Trinity suffered *kenōsis* as a bodily experience, and fewer still believe that Christ's emptying was the physical correlate of his falling in love with humanity. But haven't they missed something? Read the texts Paulus read. From Sappho on, what lovers had in common was the melting of innards.

Though relatively few of these sufferers are described with words having the κεν- root, the notion of emptying is nevertheless there when lovers pour themselves out, waste away, wither, or suffer any other physiological process involving liquefaction of the flesh. A few ancient texts say so explicitly. The fifth-century c.e. lexicographer Hesychius, for example, equated ἐρᾶσαι ("to pour forth," "to vomit," but also "to love") with κενῶσαι.[12] The fact that one and the same verb designates loving and the pouring forth of liquid is not surprising, given the long association of falling in love with the liquefaction and draining away of the lover's organs. A lexicon of the thirteenth century (falsely ascribed to the twelfth-century historian Zonaras) reports that κενῶσαι means "to drain dry (ἀντλῆσαι)" and is equivalent to "to melt (τῆξαι)."[13] Lastly, an eminent classicist of the recent past draws what he believes to be an obvious connection between love and liquid in *eraō*: "No satisfactory etymology has been found for *eraō*. . . . It was, I suggest, in origin just *eraō* 'I pour out (liquid)' . . . *eramai* would thus originally mean 'I pour out myself, emit liquid' (Middle) or 'I am poured out'. . . ."[14]

The evidence so far has been philological. Staying with this approach a little longer, we call attention to a scholium on a passage from the *Argonautica* of Apollonius of Rhodes. In order to depict Medea's love for Jason, Apollonius alluded to standard erotic motifs found in the archaic poets:

> . . . she cast her eyes down and smiled with divine sweetness. Her heart melted within her (χύθη δὲ οἱ ἔνδοθι θυμός) as she was uplifted by his praise, and she raised her eyes and looked into his face; yet she did not know what word to utter first, but was bursting to say everything at once. Casting off all restraint, she took the drug from her fragrant sash, and he received it at once into his hands with joy. And then she would even have drawn out her whole soul from her

breast (πᾶσαν ἀπὸ στηθέων ἀρύσασα ψυχήν) and given it to him, exulting in his need for her—such was the love flashing its sweet flame from Jason's golden head and captivating the bright sparkles of her eyes; and her mind within her warmed (ἰαίνετο) as she melted (τηκομένη) like the dew on roses that melts (τήκεται) when warmed by the rays of the dawn.[15]

A scholiast took an interest in "drawn out (ἀρύσασα)." Apollonius's term certainly touched on an association with liquid; it meant to draw water. This of course fits with Medea's melted θυμός at the beginning of the passage. The scholiast suggests that the poet could have used three other terms in place of ἀρύω, the last of which is of particular interest to readers of the Christ Hymn: ἀφαιρέω, ἀπαντλάω, or ἐκκενόω.[16]

Long before philologists, poets had connected loving with emptying. For the second-century B.C.E. poet Bion of Smyrna *pothos* was a mixture of grief and desire that evacuates mourners. Aphrodite's beloved Adonis has been mortally wounded, and in lamentation she shares her grief with the emptied Erotes: "You are dead, O thrice-desired (τριπόθητε), and desire (πόθος) has flown from me like a dream. Cytherea is widowed; the Loves throughout the palace are bereft (κενοί)."[17] Christian poetry of the fourth century also spoke of emptying. Nonna, the mother of Gregory of Nazianzus, had a great longing for God.[18] The form of her death bears a resemblance to Christ's in Phil 2:6-8, although it is not possible to say whether the author, her son the theologian, alludes to the Christ Hymn. I suspect that his sources are poetic and biblical: "Springing from a pious root I was the flesh of and the mother of a priest. To Christ I brought my body, my life, my tears, emptying out my all (Χριστῷ σῶμα, βίον, δάκρυα, πάντ᾽ ἐκένωσα φέρουσα); and last of all here in the church I Nonna was taken up, leaving my aged body."[19]

It would appear, then, that modern scholars are incorrect when they associate self-emptying with humility and submission to divine will. But if not in the description of self-effacing persons, when did the ancients speak about emptying, apart from these relatively few poetic instances and rather obscure lexicographic entries just discussed?[20] An answer to this question initially leads us away from poetry to medicine. But it soon takes us back.

WHAT DOCTORS AND POETS KNEW

Kenōsis was chiefly a medical term. The rare, reflexive phrase "to empty oneself" which occurs in Phil 2:7 had a meaning quite corporeal and not nearly so voluntary as it has been made out to be. Vomiting, evacuation of the stomach or bowels, bloodletting, and similar medical treatments intended to return sick bodies to a balanced, healthy state were all termed *kenōsis*.[21] In this regard Plato's brief definition of medicine is revealing: "For medicine may be described as the science of what the body loves, or desires, as regards repletion and evacuation (κένωσιν). . . ."[22] The Hippocratic *Nature of Man* contains antiquity's most famous definition of health.[23] Here a crucial problem is addressed: What causes pain? To scientific minds of antiquity the human body was composed of blood, phlegm, and yellow and black bile. These components combined in a balanced way to produce health, but their imbalance leads to the following condition:

> Pain is felt when one of these elements is in defect or excess, or is isolated in the body without being compounded with all the others. For when an element is isolated and stands by itself, not only must the place which it left become diseased, but the place where it stands in a flood must, because of the excess, cause pain and distress. In fact when more of an element flows out of the body than is necessary to get rid of superfluity, the emptying (κένωσιν) causes pain. If, on the other hand, it be to an inward part that there takes place the emptying (κένωσιν), the shifting and the separation from other elements, the man certainly must, according to what has been said, suffer from a double pain, one in the place left, and another in the place flooded.[24]

This passage teaches that *kenōsis* whether within or proceeding from the body is liquid on the move. As internal inundation or outward flowage, *kenōsis* hurts and often is noticeably wet. Running on too long, *kenōsis* kills.

All in all, this is a fairly coherent account of pain if reasoning and imagination rather than hypothesis and experiment guide the process of discovery. Yet there is a piece missing from the account. How, precisely, does liquefaction of the flesh occur? Heat is the key factor, and here is the connection we have been seeking between medicine's *kenōsis* and poetry's *pothos*. Both doctors examining patients and poets accosted by Eros noted the effects of melting. Flowing liquid explained physical and mental experience.[25]

The term that medicine and poetry shared for the origin of pain is "melt" (τήκω). Take medicine first. Pondering the divine provision of human need for food, Plato observes in the *Timaeus*, "And when all the limbs and parts of the mortal living creature had been naturally joined together, it was so that of necessity its life consisted in fire and air; and because of this it wasted away (ἔφθινε) when dissolved (τηκόμενον) by these elements or left empty (κενούμενον) thereby; wherefore the Gods contrived succor for the creature."[26] In a divine design flaw, the vital heat that animates a body also melts it, empties it, and causes it to waste away, but the gods in their providence patched together the remedy of food and drink.

Medical interest in *kenōsis* extended not only to pain and nutrition but also to massage. The therapeutically informed gentleman of antiquity was wary of the physical therapist who did not understand the melting effects of massage, which, if prolonged, could do more harm than good. With the stakes so high, Galen faults an earlier expert on gymnastics, Theon, for his failure to discuss the duration of massage, although Galen acknowledges that Theon pretty much teaches what Hippocrates had earlier taught. If only he had more carefully observed the Hippocratic vocabulary. Galen writes: "Theon, therefore, when he says in his discussion of gentle and prolonged massages that it dissolves and liquefies (τήκειν), if by liquefying (διά τοῦ τήκειν) he means emptying (τὸ κενοῦν), designates nothing more than dissolving."[27] Galen's quibbling hints at a standardized way of speaking about illness and pain shared by physicians, gymnastic trainers, massage therapists, and anyone using their services in a knowledgeable way. Theon's language may not have been precise enough for Galen, but in concert with the broader medical community he intended to say that pain was the result of the body melting and then emptying itself.

Just as emptying attained axiomatic status in medical accounts of pain, nutrition, and massage from the fifth century forward, poetry from the earliest times relied on liquefaction to represent longing's effect on the body.[28] Poems frequently had a lover melting and flowing away in his or her yearning for an absent or unresponsive beloved. This motif began with Penelope's longing for Odysseus.[29] Later poets showed a sense of humor and agreed with Meleager: "Love is an admirable cook of the soul."[30] Recapturing Homeric seriousness with a dash of Sapphic spice, the young male victim of Eros in Longus's erotic novel *Daphnis and Chloe,* who was puzzled by the new emotions he felt and their physical accompaniments, cried out "My breath comes in gasps; my heart leaps out of my breast; my spirit dissolves (τήκεται ἡ ψυχή)—and yet I want to kiss her again. . . . But while the violets and hyacinth flourish, Daphnis wastes away."[31]

There are further indications that Love's melting power was known to a broad audience. Imagine that it is shortly before 79 c.e. The place is Pompeii. As one walked to the Small Theatre through its *graffiti*-covered west entrance, a series of short poems offered for public enjoyment might have attracted attention. One of them in particular borrows its conceits from the Greeks.

Taburtinus's lines tell of a fiery love melting his soul; tears are unable to put out this flame, and the last line is "burn . . . and waste my spirit (*incedunt tabificantque animum*)."[32]

Christians, too, in later years reckoned with the powerful effects on bodies of love's warmth, as the Italian mystic Jacopone da Todi testifies. Like others before him, Jacopone spoke about his relationship with Christ in poetic imagery of lover and beloved:

> At the sight of such beauty I am swept up
> Out of myself to who knows where;
> My heart melts, like wax near fire.
> Christ puts His mark on me, and stripped of myself
> (O wondrous exchange!) I put on Christ.
> Robed in this precious garment,
> Crying out its love,
> The soul drowns in ecstasy![33]

Symeon the New Theologian (949–1022) also felt the ravages of his heated longing for God:

> Oh, what is this reality hidden to all created essence!
> What is this intelligible light, which no one sees
> and what is this abundant wealth, which no one in the world
> has ever been able to discover or posses totally?
> As a matter of fact, it is imperceptible to all,
> the world cannot contain it.
> It is most longed for (ποθεινότατος), more than the entire world;
> It is desirable (ἐπιθυμητός) also, as much as this God surpasses
> visible things created by Him.
> It is in that that I am wounded (τιτρώσκομαι) by His love,
> insofar as I do not see it,
> I dry up in my spirit (ἐκτήκομαι τὰς φρένας),
> my intelligence (τὸν νοῦν) and my heart (τὴν καρδίαν)
> are warmed (φλεγόμενος) and groan.
> I wander and I am on fire (καίομαι), searching here and there,
> and nowhere do I find the Lover
> of my soul (τὸν ἐραστήν . . . τὴν ψυχῆν μου).[34]

In order express love for Christ and Christ's love for them, Jacopone and Symeon repeat erotic motifs of heat and melting originating in the earliest period of Greek poetry and reaching to Paulus Silentiarius and beyond. Might Paul not have done the same?

Problems with *Kenōsis*

Melting innards have not figured into recent kenotic theory. Since the nineteenth century there has been agreement that *kenōsis* ought to be understood as some form of divine self-limitation.[35] Certainly, debates about the Christ Hymn have arisen, but they have centered more on the timing of *kenōsis* in the life of the Word of God and less on the nature of emptying itself. On the one hand, if the agent of the narrative in Phil 2:6-8 is the pre-incarnate Son of God, his kenotic action is thought to be a matter of setting aside privileges, rights, and powers. If, on the other hand, the agent is the earthly Jesus, kenotic action is thought to be Christ's humble subordination to God's will: he gives himself up to God as he gives himself up on behalf of humankind.[36] For those in the thick of this battle between pre- and post-incarnation starting points of *kenōsis*, the stakes are very high. The divinity of the Son and salvation itself rest on getting *kenōsis* right.

Yet in either approach to *kenōsis*, whether pre-incarnation or post, divine sovereignty occupies center stage and drives the plot of the Christ Hymn. In the first case, sovereignty is expressed in God's freedom over physical reality and the height of divine invulnerability from which Christ descended to save humanity by accommodating himself to mortal limitations. In the second scheme, sovereignty is the unchanging and unique character of God, which requires the human obedience that Jesus, emptied of divinity's advantages, perfectly models.

So what are the problems with traditional *kenōsis*? Although these two versions of *kenōsis* as self-limitation are distinct, they share a similar theological shortcoming: the erasure of Christ's body. For the reading beginning with the pre-incarnate Son, the problem is that the "self" in "he emptied himself" is not a body but a cipher for the properties, capacities, or status a very powerful being might have and yet part with in order to accomplish some good. With the other approach, which begins after the moment of the incarnation, the earthly Jesus empties himself in a different sense; he refuses to reproduce in his own story the first Adam's grasping after divine status. In this post-incarnation version of *kenōsis,* it appears that Christ's body is back, a cipher no longer. But if Jesus' action in Phil 2:6-8 is his humble submission to God's will, why would Paul use the term "emptying," a distinctly physical term, as I have shown above? Moreover, since self-emptying as humble submission is more a state of mind and less an action, here again the incarnate Christ's body disappears from view just as in the case when *kenōsis* starts from the position of the pre-incarnate Word. What we are left with is Jesus' exemplary *attitude* of self-abnegation and subservience, an ironic loss of physicality, since it is, after all, with the taking on of human flesh that Christ Jesus begins the story in the first place.

The loss of Christ's body is not the only problem with traditional understandings of *kenōsis* as voluntary self-limitation. There is as well a moral deficiency hiding in the high-sounding language of self-renunciation. Claims about the moral goodness of self-limitation often cloak one-sided power. Feminist critics of *kenōsis* such as Sarah Coakley have described the way elites exercise power even when they proclaim self-limitation to be a virtue.[37] How does this work?

At first glance, the limiting of the self is a fine message and under the right conditions possibly inspiring. Yet the powerful rhetoric of theologians ought not exempt their ideas from criticism. In a likely reference to Phil 2:7, Bernard of Clairvaux, whose praiseworthy insights into the erotic character of Paul's language is featured below, nevertheless wrote "to lose yourself, as if you no longer existed, to cease completely to experience yourself, to reduce yourself to nothing is not a human sentiment but a divine experience."[38] This understanding of spiritual perfection as self-erasure was and still is alluring. Yet calls by Bernard and others for the reduction of the self ought to be approached warily. Why?

The self-emptying imperative is morally acceptable only if it is delivered to those persons who have selves to limit. The point is this: it is immoral for the elite to celebrate Christ's self-limitation as if the call for reduction of the self applied to everyone equally. *Kenōsis* of this kind appeases the bad conscience of the powerful (to the extent that we have one) through compensation in a fantasy world in which gods descend to earth for a while before they return to their former glory. Yet it does nothing for non-elites except to encourage their resignation to low status and exclusion from power. Very much like the Christology of 1 Peter, in which Jesus models acceptance of oppression for slaves and women, this way of thinking replaces justice with ideology.

In short, to praise Christ's selflessness, making it the highest Christian virtue, confuses spiritual aspiration and self-denigration. The interests of the powerful are served when those persons who are struggling to form a self are persuaded that it is the highest expression of Christian faith not to want one in the first place. A compelling reason, then, for the interpretation advanced in this chapter of involuntary *kenōsis* that comes with longing is to break the cycle of elitism and masculine hegemony that self-limitation and humility historically have preserved, even if it feels, mostly to men, as though power *were* being critiqued when Jesus is praised for his humility.

Thus, instead of subjecting traditional *kenōsis* to further refinement with hopes of purging it of these theological and political difficulties, the rest of this chapter finishes the task of placing Christ's emptying into an entirely different web of meaning not dependent on notions of self, privilege, and power but on the wasting effects of love.[39] Building on the insights of ancient doctors and poets, we might now regard emptying as an event befalling the body. Emptying happens when absence falls between lover and beloved. The experts in this kind of *kenōsis*, then, are not the Christian theologians who beautify monarchical power with talk of divine love condescending to mortal station but the poets and novelists of ancient Greece and Rome and a handful of Christian writers from the past. They are experts because they have been educated in the suffering and sweetness of erotic love. The experts are those kenotic sufferers we, with Paulus Silentiarius, saw bobbing in the sea of tears.

SERVITIUM AMORIS

A grammatical point about the participle λαβών ("having taken") in Phil 2:7 supports our claim that *kenōsis* is an event that befalls Christ's body and does not refer to a limitation or concealment of divine substance. Since λαβών is an aorist circumstantial participle, it is quite possible that its action occurs before that of the main verb, ἐκένωσεν ("he emptied himself").[40] Even though word order in 2:7 suggests that Christ first emptied himself and then took on the form of a slave, as this verse is usually understood, it is possible to read the text as if the opposite had taken place. He first took on the form of a slave and then he emptied himself. It is not a god that is emptied but a slave.

This possible grammatical adjustment suggests other questions. To whom was Christ a slave? To whom was he obedient? The hymn itself leaves unnamed the one whom Christ regarded as his master, but a number of commentators think that Jesus rendered perfect obedience to God.[41] In today's theological environment, when sin is often understood as rebellion against God, Paul's words are taken to mean that Christ's obedience reverses the disobedience of Adam in the Fall. Christ sets aside the privileges of divinity and humbly subordinates his will to the Father.[42] Although Christ Jesus possessed all the properties that constitute divinity, he did not grasp them for his own advantage. Instead, he yielded them up or limited his divine powers and privileges. He lowered himself to human status. As the New Adam he demonstrated what God expects from humans and what is now revealed to be humanly possible: voluntary submission to the Father's will.

Like their modern counterparts, Christian authors in late antiquity and the Middle Ages for the most part also thought that the unnamed master to whom Christ rendered obedience was God. It must be emphasized, however, that many of these interpretations were made in a context of spiritual formation of monks and nuns. Context matters. Skeptical about spiritual perfection and freed of its historic disciplines, modern interpreters, Protestants especially, make Jesus' obedience to the Father a demand universally applicable not just for those seeking spiritual perfection and communion with God. Humble submission has come to define the ideal relation of the human to the divine, and Jesus' obedience reveals God's supreme characteristic: sovereignty.

To appreciate the difference that interpretive contexts makes, it is instructive to go back to Symeon the New Theologian, whose view of Christ's obedience was influenced by his monastic context. He explains the spiritual guide's role to young men embarking on a life of holiness. Note how he weaves in elements of the Christ Hymn:

> Those who, in fear and trembling, have laid the good foundation stone of faith and hope in the hall of righteousness, who have planted their feet immovably on the rock of obedience (ὑπακοῆς) to their spiritual father, who listen to his teachings as if they came from the mouth of God, those who with humble souls (ἐν ταπεινώσει ψυχῆς) raise an unshakable edifice on this foundation of obedience (ὑπακοῆς), these will succeed immediately. It is they who succeed in that basic and all-important goal of self-renunciation (τὸ ἑαυτοὺς ἀπαρνήσασθαι). To do another's will instead of one's own leads not only to a denial of one's own life (ἀπάρνησιν τῆς ἰδίας ψυχῆς), but even makes a man dead to the entire world. A man who contradicts his [spiritual] father makes the devils rejoice, but when a man humbles himself even to death (τὸν δὲ μέχρι θανάτου ταπεινούμενον), he makes the angels stand amazed. For this man performs the work of God by imitating the Son of God who was perfect in obedience (τῷ τὴν ὑπακοὴν πεπληρωκότι) to his own father, even to death, death on a cross.[43]

Symeon's emphasis here is on success in spiritual formation, not on the sovereignty of God. Obedience to one's spiritual father aids the renunciation of self and dying to the world.

More akin to present-day emphasis on Christ's obedience to God's sovereign will is a passage from the ninth-century Byzantine writer Nicetas Paphlago. His encomium on the apostle Thomas draws a parallel between the saint's service to Ethiopian rulers and Christ's obedience to the Father. The story goes that Thomas became notable for marvelous works "just as Christ Jesus himself became obedient to his Begetter and took a slavelike form, and having humbled himself on account of the divine economy, demonstrated obedience even to death." Nicetas extols the slavery to God exhibited by Christ and finds in Thomas the Lord's perfect imitator:

> Thus the genuine disciple [Thomas], acquainted with the rank of the Son, looking to the Master's humiliation, did not scorn the pretense of slavery. He did not desist through impatience from selling himself for the ungodly. No call for despair but eagerness. No call for dishonor but honor. No call for shame or grief but glory and good cheer, since he regarded (ἡγούμενος) the enslavement temporary.[44]

Although Christ's subordination to the Father is a model of obedience for all humans, the emphasis here falls on legitimating civil authority, not praising divine sovereignty.

One of the many homiletic interests of Alan of Lille (c. 1116–c. 1202) was to explain how well-worn moral topics such as gluttony, perseverance, and slander ought to be preached to monks. Each chapter of *The Art of Preaching* treats a virtue or a vice in a manner not unlike the moral treatises of the ancient philosophers. But there is an important difference between preacher and philosopher; scriptural passages head the list of texts to which Christian listeners should pay heed. In chapter 16 ("On Obedience"), Alan draws on Phil 2:8. This verse is joined by three others that Alan thinks preachers should use: 1 Sam 15:22; 1 Pet 2:16; and Rom 13:2. Then the preacher ought to move to extrabiblical reasons for obedience:

> From these authorities one must proceed thus: O man, for our sake the son of God was made obedient to the indignity of the Cross; are you not for your part willing to obey the precepts of the Gospel? When an angel obeys God in all things, do you, who are dust and ashes, defy God's law? Inanimate objects obey the Lord. You, who alone are endowed with reason, do you battle against God's will?

> The sun does not deviate from its course. . . . The more quickly, then,
> a man makes his peace with God, the more his pride in his own will
> is suppressed; he sacrifices himself on the sword of the law . . . while
> we humbly submit ourselves to another's orders, we subdue ourselves
> in our own hearts.[45]

Note that Alan shares with Symeon a pastoral idea that obedience is good
for the soul, ridding it of presumption and training it in humility: "This
above all: obedience nourishes humility, tests patience, scrutinizes gentleness."[46]
Moreover, by including Phil 2:8 with 1 Pet 2:16 and Rom 13:2 Alan expands
the range of obedience to include subordination to God in addition to civil
authority. He reads Christ's obedience in parallel with the submission of sun,
stars, and moon to God's sovereign direction, and in this he anticipates modern
readings.

Other writers of roughly the same period departed from the "obedience
to God" model and offer us a radically different way to read the Christ Hymn.
They detected in Christ's slavery a tale of suffering love. Such readings of
the Christ Hymn are found in Cistercian writers of the twelfth century, who
championed the cause of love and friendship in both theology and in their
communal life.[47] For them it was quite possible for Christ to be a slave to
God *and* to humans.[48] Guerric of Igny (1080–1157), an associate of Bernard
of Clairvaux, starts off a Palm Sunday sermon (appointed text: Phil 2:6-8)
amplifying the usual point about humanity's rebellion against God:

> "Let this mind be in you which was in Christ Jesus, who, although
> he was by nature God . . . ." This is for the hearing of the wicked and
> runaway slave, man I mean, who although he was by nature and rank
> a slave and bound to serve, refused to serve and tried to appropriate
> freedom and equality with his Lord. Christ was by nature God;
> equal to God not through robbery but by birth because he shared
> omnipotence, eternity and divinity. He nevertheless dispossessed
> himself (*exinaniens semetipsum*) and not only took the nature of a
> slave, fashioned in the likeness of men, but also carried out the
> ministry of a slave, lowering his own dignity and accepting an
> obedience to the Father which brought him death, death on a cross.

Guerric's opening sentences repeat a familiar mode of treating this passage, but
he turns away from the standard interpretation and asserts, albeit inconsistently,
that Christ's slavery is directed to humanity:

But reckon it as too little for him to have served the Father as a slave although his Son and co-equal unless he also served his own slave as more than a slave. . . . "I will not serve," man says to his Creator. "Then I will serve you," his Creator says to man. "You sit down, I will minister, I will wash your feet. You rest; I will bear your weariness, your infirmities. Use me as you like in all your needs, not only as your slave but also as your beast of burden and as your property."[49]

Guerric returns in another sermon to the point that Christ's obedience was given to humanity: "He has been pierced with so many wounds, his whole body has suffered crucifixion; from where can he draw strength to resist that charity which led him, as if conquered and a prisoner, through every kind of weakness even to death, death on a cross?"[50]

What prompted Guerric to revive this interpretation that Christ enslaved himself to humans? Bernard of Clairvaux may have been his inspiration on this point, since he had written of the "Lord, who under love's inspiration emptied himself." And further: " 'He emptied himself, taking the form of a servant,' and so gave us the pattern of humility. He emptied himself, he humbled himself, not under constraint of an assessment of himself but inspired by love for us. . . . "[51] This is it not love at arms' length. Not pity, nor condescending grace. To describe this love, Guerric used an erotic motif made famous by ancient poetry, "Love conquers all (*vincat omnes Amor*)."[52] Like the lover of Latin elegy, Christ is defenseless against the power of love. It conquers him and makes him a prisoner. The Lord is a slave of love.

Might Guerric have been on to something by reading Phil 2:6-8 through the erotic motif of *servitium amoris*? I believe so. The lover as slave of the beloved (or, lover as slave of Eros) was a popular motif in ancient literature flowering at the time of the Roman elegists, most likely Guerric's ultimate source. But how was the motif available to Greek speakers like Paul and his readers? This is a germane question, since until recently classicists did not believe *servitium amoris* was present in Greek literature with the same vigor or frequency as it was in Latin poetry. Plato's oxymoronic term for the lover, "voluntary slave," had been thought to be the extent of the motif in older Greek writings, and the Hellenistic period offered little more. Paul Murgatroyd has demonstrated, however, that this was not the case, and other scholars have discovered the motif's path from Greek literature to Latin poetry through Roman comedy.[53] Once the popularity of this motif becomes known, it is difficult to see how the earliest audiences of Philippians would not have had the enslaving power of love on their minds, as Guerric had on his, when they read μορφὴν δούλου λαβών.

Servitium amoris ruined the neat opposition of "active" and "passive" that ancient philosophers and eventually Christian theologians would employ in accounts of agency both human and divine. Voluntary slavery, which is the fate of every true lover, is the emotional paradox that nullifies the world divided into subjects and objects. When Eros takes up residence in the lover's innards, the reputable philosophic notions of volition, free will, and intentionality become naïve untruths.[54] It is the precisely the voluntary character of Christ's enslavement that has so engaged the imagination of interpreters through the ages, that and the accompanying notion of willed humility. Yet, without the *servitium amoris* inducing readers to think about the psychosocial effects of longing on the lover (depression and degradation), Christ's slavery has been appropriated to serve a *purpose*: the salvation of humankind. The prevalent interpretation is this: for the sake of fallen, disobedient humanity and with a conscious, uncomplicated act of the will the Son of God took on the form of a slave in order to illustrate humble submission, which is the proper bearing toward God. But *servitium amoris* from Plato forward pointed away from the idea of humility and instead to the humiliated condition of the longing lover whose "extravagant devotion" even to the point of death resulted in behavior and emotional states that from the vantage point of the non-lover appeared slavish.[55] Like the slave (that is, the elite's construction of the slave) the lover lacked self-control and self-respect.[56] The question why anyone in their right mind would choose such inner turmoil prompted widespread reflection on Eros's invasive, seducing power.

Homer, the *Homeric Hymn to Aphrodite*, Hesiod, and the lyric poets contain prototypes of *servitium amoris*. A term from the battlefield, δαμνάζω, was redeployed to describe the humbling power of Eros. It perhaps is a predecessor to ταπεινοφροσύνη and ταπεινόω in Phil 2:3 and 8.[57] The verb "is used in two apparently different semantic fields: those of killing men and raping women. In both areas, the role of the dominated one is marked by unwillingness and ultimate submission to an unwanted fate."[58] Ominous indeed is Hesiod's depiction of Eros, "the fairest of the deathless gods; he unstrings the limbs (λυσιμελής) and subdues (δάμναται) both mind and sensible thought in the breasts of all gods and all men."[59] The *Homeric Hymn to Aphrodite* (1–3) begins: "Sing to me, O Muse, of the works of Aphrodite, the Kyprian, who stirs sweet longing in gods and subdues the races of mortal men." Later in the poem Aphrodite finds herself a victim of love for Anchises, a shameful turnabout for a goddess accustomed to humbling her male conquests:

. . . I mated all immortal gods to mortal women, for my will tamed (δάμνασκε) them all. But now my mouth will not bear to mention this among the immortals because, struck by great madness in a wretched and grave way, and driven out of my mind I mated with a mortal and put a child beneath my girdle.[60]

Anacreon invented an adjective (δαμάλης) whose antecedents discussed above are now familiar and used it as an epithet for Eros.[61] Sappho's plea to Aphrodite: "Petal-clad immortal Aphrodite, child of Zeus, guile weaver, I beg you: do not overwhelm (δάμνα) my heart, lady, with aches and miseries. . . ."[62]

Love Triumphs, Desire Takes Flight, and a God Is Emptied

The present study is not the first time Christ's *kenōsis* has been imagined in terms of *erōs*. Bernard of Clairvaux, Hadewijch of Antwerp, Gilbert of Hoyland, Nicholas Cabasilas, and Jacopone da Todi went down this path when they wrote about the Christ Hymn. Yet none of these authors did so with perfect consistency, and therefore it cannot be claimed that there was an organized rival to the traditional kenotic ideas. But pockets of unease with *kenōsis* as it had come to be taught as a foil for God's condescending rule can be detected. Two classical motifs ("love conquers all" and "wings of desire") helped challenge the usual reading of Phil 2:6-8.

For the writers considered below, *kenōsis* was not simply a matter of Christ's humble submission to God's will or his setting aside of divine prerogatives and powers. Rather, they believed that Christ longed for humans and desired communion with them. For them, the Son of God's passion to be with sinners and to bear the destiny of mortals is at the heart of the Christ Hymn. Shocking ideas now see the light of day. Desire conquered the second person of the Trinity. Love dragged the Word into communion with dying and sinful mortals. Christ the Lord got drunk on love. Admittedly, the following interpretations of *kenōsis* in Phil 2:7 do not fully reflect ancient poetry's obsession with melting innards. But Bernard and other medieval writers made a crucial point about the framework within which Christology ought to be fashioned. They broke away from the pattern of sovereignty and obedience and instead read the story of Christ though *amor* and *desiderium*.

It is fitting to begin with Bernard, who turned a pronoun in a line from Song of Songs 2:15 ("Catch us the foxes") into a profound meditation on the story of Christ, whom, just outside the limits of this quotation, he describes in amatory terms as "so devoted" and "so eager a lover." Bernard writes,

You see how he [Christ] speaks, as though to equals—he who has no equal. He could have said 'me', but he preferred to say 'us', for he delights in companionship. What sweetness! What grace! What mighty love! Can it be that the Highest of all is made one with all? Who has brought this about? Love has brought this about, without regard for its own dignity, strong in affection and efficacious in persuasion. What could be more violent? Love prevails even with God (*Triumphat de Deo amor*). What could be so non-violent? It is love. What force is there, I ask, which advances so violently towards victory, yet is so unresisting to violence? For he emptied himself (*semetipsum exinanivit*), so that you might know that it was the fullness of love outpoured, that his loftiness was laid low and that his unique nature made to be your fellow.[63]

For Bernard, Phil 2:7 is a story of "violent love," off-putting terminology surely for readers today but signifying something quite tender to audiences of the twelfth century. The only victim of violent love from antiquity to the Middle Ages is the one who loves.[64] Love triumphs over all—that is the classic formulation, and Bernard weaves it into the Christ Hymn with the words "Love prevails even with God."[65]

Along similar lines, Hadewijch of Antwerp, a female Flemish mystic and poet of the thirteenth century, associated the Christ Hymn (alluded to in the final line) with the theme *amor vincit omnia:*

What seems to the loved soul the most beautiful encounter
Is that it should love the Beloved so fully
And so gain knowledge of the Beloved with love
That nothing else known by it
Except: "I am conquered by Love"
But he who overcame Love was rather conquered
So that he might in love be brought to nought.
God the lover is victim of love.[66]

For Gilbert of Hoyland, love has wings. This had been a favorite erotic idea for epistolographers of the fourth century. Basil wrote to Libanius,

I should have gone to be with you, having fashioned for myself wings of Icarus. But nevertheless, since it is not possible to entrust wax to the sun, instead of using wings of Icarus I do send you by letter words which prove our friendship. And it is the nature of words to disclose the love that is within the soul.[67]

Love certainly needed this mode of transport, since in Gilbert's view chaos lay as an immeasurable gulf between the human and the divine.[68] Wings are a poetic fiction, of course; what actually transports God from the heights of majesty to human nothingness is longing. *Desiderium* makes the divine nature empty itself:

> In Scripture, a great gulf (*chaos*) is fixed between the divine nature and ours. What kind of gulf, you ask. To be sure, that of our emptiness. . . . Rightly is our substance considered empty, for by assuming it his fullness is said to have emptied itself. What approach then and what nearness can the void have with what is solid, can nothingness have with what is immense? For what reason then does the bride say: 'When I had passed on a little beyond them, I found him whom my soul loves'? Is it perhaps that charity is winged and soars with the swift flight of ardent desire (*pennigera est charitas, et praepeti volatu ardentis desiderii*) over this intervening gulf (*vacuum*) of which we are speaking? Yes, I agree. For to love is already to possess; to love is also to be assimilated and united. But why not, since God is charity?[69]

This passage is full of erotic clichés from the classical world. Chief among them is Eros equipped with wings.[70] He needed feathers, since his duties required him to cross immense distances.[71] Wings showed the longing heart its way.[72] Even on humans' shoulders wings sprout if longing is strong enough, or at least that is what separated lovers in need of comfort fantasized.[73]

This Eros, who traverses chaos so lightly, is not late born Aphrodite's son, the "mischievous infant as painters light-heartedly portray."[74] Rather, he is the primeval Eros of Hesiod and Empedocles, comingling all things and uniting humans with humans, animals and animals, even plants with one another.[75] This Eros was hymned by orators at weddings, and appropriately so since the Greek marriage ritual was considered to be a miniature of cosmic harmony.[76] Gilbert's selection of clichés is not merely the flourish of a well-read preacher. Though writing Latin in the twelfth century, he participated in an intense debate about love going back to the earliest days of Greek literature.[77] The same *erōs* he reaches for in order to explain Christ had inspired Hesiod and all the others who praised love for its desire to make communion.

In the twelfth century, Isaac of Stella came very close to reading Christ's emptying as erotic melting. His topic is Christ's zest for humanity and the necessity that monks love Christ in the same way as they are loved by him. His jumping-off point is the eroticism established by the intersection of several biblical texts, including Song of Songs 2:16 and 5:16 and Phil 2:5-7:

> And your love will find expression in, "He is my intimate friend," and "All mine, my true love, and I all his; he shall lodge in my bosom." This is the purpose conversion should have. It is not for the tepid, not for the half-hearted and lazy; you must be generous, must go at it with zest (*zelo*) and fervor (*fervore*), and yet with an ease past all describing, as you are caught away where the impulse of the Spirit would have you go. Take note of the zest (*zelo*) with which the Son of God crossed over to what, since he could not surpass himself, was beneath him. He crossed over to you, the lowest he might go. He gave all for you so that he could come to this marriage mentioned in our text. Since, brothers, 'yours is to be the mind which Christ Jesus showed,' you must seek to understand from what, why and for what reason he 'dispossessed himself of the prerogatives of God (*exinanivit semetipsum*),' and took on 'the likeness of sinful flesh'."[78]

The cliché of love's heat, which was usually accompanied by melting in the poetic tradition, is communicated in Isaac's choice of *fervor* (heat, ardor, passion), and it is matched by the Son of God's *zelo*.

Authors in the Christian West by no means monopolized *erōs*-based readings of the Christ Hymn. Turning to Orthodox Christianity, we discover the fourteenth-century theologian Nicholas Cabasilas. In *The Life in Christ*, Cabasilas used the Son's *kenōsis* to illustrate that "desire is the origin of all action," an abstract principle but fruitful nonetheless when it comes to the interpretation of God's self-emptying in the Christ Hymn. *Erōs* and *pothos* are the specific forms of desire that Cabasilas had in mind as he touched on several popular themes from ancient love poetry:

> Just as human affection (τὸ φίλτρον), when it abounds, overpowers those who love (τοὺς ἐρῶντας) and causes them to be beside themselves (ἐξίστησι), so God's love for men emptied God (ὁ περὶ τοὺς ἀνθρώπους ἔρως τὸν θεὸν ἐκένωσεν). He does not stay in His own place and call the slave. He seeks him in person by coming down to him. He who is rich reaches the pauper's hovel, and He

displays His love by approaching in person. He seeks love in return and does not withdraw when He is treated with disdain. He is not angry over ill treatment, but even when He has been repulsed He sits by the door and does everything to show us that He loves (τὸν ἐρῶντα), even enduring suffering and death to prove it. Two things reveal him who loves and lead the lover in a triumphal procession (θριαμβεύει ἐράστην)—the one, that in every way possible he does good to the object of his love (τὸν ἐρώμενον); the other, that he is willing, if need be, to endure terrible things for him and endure pain. Of the two, the latter would seem to be a far greater proof of friendship than the former. Yet it was not possible for God since He is incapable of suffering harm. . . . It was necessary, then, that the greatness of His love should not remain hidden, but that He should give the proof of the greatest love and by loving display the utmost measure of love (δεῖξαι τὸν ἔσχατον ἔρων ἔρωτα). So He devised this self-emptying (κένωσιν) and carried it out, and made the instrument . . . by which He might be able to endure terrible things and to suffer pain.[79]

A word appears at the beginning of this passage with two related meanings: τὸ φίλτρον ("human affection"). It might also be rendered "love potion." Cabasilas was not the first to play on the double meaning of the word.[80] It appears that Cabasilas read the Christ Hymn as if erotic magic had been at work on God, creating love for humans and inducing ecstasy. This fits well with the erotic tradition in which love magic propelled victims into erotic ecstasy, a form of madness.[81] Meleager illustrates the love potion's power: "The noise of Love is ever in my ears, and my eyes in silence bring their tribute of sweet tears to Desire (Πόθοις). Nor night nor daylight lays love to rest, and already the spell (ὑπὸ φίλτρων) has set its well-known stamp on my heart."[82]

Cabasilas's language is similar to a sweeping claim about the power of *erōs* in a fragment of Iamblichus's second-century romantic novel *A Babylonian Story*: "Eros causes all to stand outside of themselves (πάντας μὲν ἀνθρώπους ἐξίστησιν ἔρως)."[83] Ancient moralists, of course, thought of ecstasy as quite a bad condition for humans. Yet, in poetry a more positive evaluation prevailed: *erōs* and *pothos* enabled the lover's heart to dwell in the beloved's interior.[84] While some Christian writers embraced ecstasy for the believer's relationship with Christ, Cabasilas's portrait of an ecstatic God is quite rare.

"He sits by the door." To depict God's devotion to humanity, Cabasilas calls upon the pathetic figure of the locked-out lover (τὸ παρακλαυσίθυρον), a motif closely related to another common theme in Greek and Latin poetry, the lover as slave of the beloved (*servitium amoris*) examined above. In this poetic figure, the scorned lover waits outside the entrance of the beloved's house all night in the rain, barred from going in, sleepless, and anxiously awaiting a response to his overtures.[85] Such humiliating behavior often resulted in the lover's death in dejection and melancholy, the ultimate proof of longing desire and an ending familiar to readers of ancient poetry and romantic fiction where the love-hero carries out *servitium amoris* fully.[86] Finally, Cabasilas touches on another erotic motif also closely aligned with the *servitium amoris*: God the lover is led by Eros in triumphal procession: θριαμβεύει τὸν ἐραστήν.[87] Paul himself introduced this striking amatory image into Christian discourse in 2 Cor 2:14, though there God played the role of Eros and Paul the uncertain lover.[88]

An extensive quotation from the later works of the Italian mystic Jacopone da Todi concludes this survey of Christian writers who interpreted *kenōsis* through *erōs*. To be clear, none of these writers said that Christ's self-emptying was a matter of his flesh's melting out of desire for communion with humans, although Isaac of Stella came close. But the ease with which they called upon other erotic motifs other than melting indirectly supports the thesis of this chapter that Christ's *kenōsis* was for Paul not a matter of self-limitation, exemplary humility, or obedience but the bodily manifestation of longing. Jacopone races through the erotic clichés discussed in the previous pages, adds others, and weaves them together with allusions to the Christ Hymn. It is an amazing testimony of wildly erotic love conquering both Jacopone and Christ, to whom he speaks:

> You did not defend Yourself against that Love
> That made You come down from heaven to earth;
> Love, in trodding this earth
> You humbled and humiliated Yourself,
> Demanding neither dwelling place nor possessions
> Taking on such poverty so that we might be enriched!
> In Your life and in Your death You revealed
> The infinite love that burned in your heart.
>
> You went about the world as if you were drunk,
> Led by Love as if You were a slave . . .
>
> You, Wisdom, did not hold Yourself back,
> But poured out your Love in abundance—born of Love

Not of the flesh, out of love for man, to save him!
You rushed to the cross to embrace us;
I think this is why, Love, You did not answer Pilate,
Or defend Yourself before his judgment seat—
You wanted to pay the price of Love
By dying on the cross for us.

Wisdom, I see, hid herself,
Only love could be seen.
Nor did You make a show of Your power—
A great Love it was
That poured itself out,
Love and Love alone, in act and desire,
Binding itself to the cross
And embracing Man

Thus, Jesus, if I am enamored
And drunk with sweetness,
If I lose my senses and mastery of self,
How can You reproach me?
I see that Love has so bound You
As to almost strip You of Your greatness;
How, then could I find the strength to resist,
To refuse to share in its madness?

For the same Love that makes me lose my senses
Seems to have stripped You of wisdom;
That love that makes me weak
Is the love that made You renounce all power.
I cannot delay, nor seek to—
Love's captive, I make no resistance . . .[89]

CONCLUSION

Christian writers of the medieval church, ancient philologists, doctors, and, above all, poets have something to teach us (the latter three groups unwittingly, of course) about Paul's momentous christological sentence "he emptied himself." They help us see that Christ's story is about a lover longing for communion with a beloved. The desire is so strong that enslavement, wasting away, and death in complete solidarity with the beloved are the only possible ending to this passion.

This is an odd reading, since in its long history of interpretation the Christ Hymn has been celebrated as the great condescension of God in Christ, the magnanimous act of humility required if humankind were to be saved. Clement of Alexandria was one of the earliest to comment on Phil 2:7, and his subtle transformation of divine longing for humans to divine longing *to save* humans opened the door to commentators in the ensuing centuries to read the Christ Hymn pragmatically and nonerotically.[90] But pagan instruction in tender feelings proves so persuasive that even stranger than the erotic interpretation of Christ's emptying, which may in fact not be strange at all to ancient ways of thinking, is the distortion performed by recent Christian interpreters of the phrase "he emptied himself." If *kenōsis* afflicts those who long for an absent beloved, then the story of the Christ Hymn does not tell of Jesus, model of humility for a world gone wild with power and self-aggrandizement, but it speaks of Christ's longing for union with mortals and his desire to share with them all that he is and has and all that they are and have, just as lovers long to do.

Notes

1. Ovid, *Am.* 1.1.26.

2. Pindar, *Frg.* 123; Apollonius of Rhodes, *Argon.* 3.724–26; *Greek Anthology* 5.117, 210; 12.72; Callimachus, *Frg.* 75.12–19; *Anacreontea* 11.14–16; Aristaenetus, *Ep.* 1.10.51. See Patricia A. Rosenmeyer, "Love Letters in Callimachus, Ovid, and Aristaenetus, or, the Sad Fate of a Mailorder Bride," *MD* 36 (1996): 27.

3. For sucked dry, see Theocritus, *Id.* 2.55–56; also Patricia A. Rosenmeyer, "Tracing Medulla as a Locus Eroticus," *Arethusa* 32 (1999): 19–47. For emaciated, see Monica Silveira Cyrino, *In Pandora's Jar: Lovesickness in Early Greek Poetry* (Lanham, MD: University Press of America, 1995), 24, 93. For dissolved, see Patricia A. Rosenmeyer, *The Poetics of Imitation: Anacreon and the Anacreontic Tradition* (Cambridge: Cambridge University Press, 1992), 156–59.

4. An early example is Sappho, *Frg.* 112.4. For the archaic poets, see Cyrino, *In Pandora's Jar*, 21–36, 49–52, 81–84, 137–38. For later examples, see Plato, *Crat.* 420A–B; *Phaedr.* 255B–C. Apollonius of Rhodes (*Argon.* 3.287–90, 1015–21) repeats the theme; see Malcolm Campbell, *A Commentary on Apollonius Rhodius Arg. III 1–471,* Mnemosyne 141 (Leiden: Brill, 1994), 262–64. Clayton Zimmerman discusses love's emptying power (*The Pastoral Narcissus: A Study of the First Idyll of Theocritus,* Greek Studies (Lanham MD: Rowman & Littlefield, 1994], 41–70) and draws attention to Plutarch, *Quaest. conviv.* 681A–B: "Vision provides access to the first impulse of love, that most powerful and violent experience of the soul, and causes the lover to melt (ῥεῖν) and be dissolved (λείβεσθαι) when he looks at those who are beautiful, as if he were pouring forth (ἐκχεόμενον) his whole being towards them." Cf. Plutarch, *Conj. praec.* 142F–143A and *Amat.* 767E. Paulus Silentiarius employed the motif in *Greek Anthology* 5.260, where the lover's mind is poured out from the breast. See also *Greek Anthology* 5.249: "souls and languid bodies (ἔκχυτα

σώματα) meet, mingled by the streams of love." See further Philostratus, *Epp.* 32, 33. Betrayed by Aeneas, Dido is said to "pour forth (*effundere*)" her life (Ovid, *Her.* 7.181–90). For the lover drained unto death, see Theocritus, *Id.* 1.140–41 and the comments of Richard Hunter, *Theocritus* (Cambridge: Cambridge University Press, 1999), 66–68).

5. Theocritus, *Id.* 3.17; 12.2; *Greek Anthology* 5.5, 153, 292; 12.166.

6. Longus, *Daphn.* 1.18. Loss of color and wasting away are symptoms of lovesickness: see Ovid, *Her.* 3.141; 11.21–32. See also Donald A. Beecher and Massimo Ciavollela, *A Treatise on Lovesickness: Jacques Ferrand* (Syracuse: Syracuse University Press, 1990), 270–71, 276–77; and Peter Toohey, *Melancholy, Love, and Time: Boundaries of the Self in Ancient Literature* (Ann Arbor: University of Michigan Press, 2004), 73–87.

7. Aeschylus, *Ag.* 408–19; Theocritus, *Id.* 1.37–38, 88–92; *Greek Anthology* 5.87; Achilles Tatius, *Leuc. Clit.* 3.11.1; 5.25.4; Oppian, *Halieutica* 4.16–17; see Eutecnius, *Paraphrasis in Oppiani halieutica.* 4.1.10–30 for a prose version of Oppian's hymn, a treasure trove of erotic clichés. See also Beecher and Ciavollela, *Treatise on Lovesickness,* 276.

8. Anacreon, *Frg.* 363; Heliodorus, *Aeth.* 3.11.1; Ovid, *Am.* 1.1.26: *Uror, et in vacuo pectore regnant Amor.* See also Horace, *Carm.* 9 and *Greek Anthology* 5.278.

9. For roasted, see *Greek Anthology* 12.71. For marrow, innards, and whole bodies eaten, see Sappho, *Frg.* 96.15–17; Theocritus, *Id.* 30.21; *Greek Anthology* 5.239; 5.288; 7.31; Catullus 35.15; 45.16; 64.93; Longus, *Daphn.* 1.32; Musaeus, *Hero et Leander* 87. For limbs consumed, see Hesiod, *Op.* 66; *Greek Anthology* 12.88; 12.143.

10. *Greek Anthology* 5.255.

11. Jürgen Moltmann has touched on the idea; see his "Perichoresis: An Old Magic Word for a New Trinitarian Theology," in *Trinity, Community, and Power: Mapping Trajectories in Wesleyan Theology,* ed. M. Douglas Meeks (Nashville: Kingswood Books, 1990), 115.

12. Hesychius, *Lexicon* E 5630.

13. Ps. Zonaras, *Lexicon* K 1196.

14. Richard Broxton Onians, *The Origins of European Thought about the Body, the Mind, the Soul, the World, Time, and Fate: New Interpretations of Greek, Roman, and Kindred Evidence, Also of Some Basic Jewish and Christian Beliefs,* 2nd ed. (Cambridge: Cambridge University Press, 1954), 202 n. 5. See also Beecher and Ciavollela, *Treatise on Lovesickness,* 232–34.

15. Apollonius of Rhodes, *Argon.* 3.1008–21.

16. *Scholia in Apollonii Rhodii Argonautica* 245. Another scholium (*Scholia on Theocritum* 7.73.2) tells us that Daphnis's girlfriend, Xenea, has a name that means "the empty one (κενεᾶς)" reflecting the wasting death suffered by lovesick Daphnis. See Zimmerman, *Pastoral Narcissus,* 70.

17. Bion, *Epitaphius Adonis* 58–59. Text and translation are from J. D. Reed, *Bion of Smyrna: The Fragments and the Adonis,* Cambridge Classical Texts and Commentaries 33 (New York: Cambridge University Press, 1997), 126–27.

18. For her *pothos,* see *Greek Anthology* 8.29, 32, 52, 77. Gregory composed fifty epigrams commemorating her piety. Cf. Romanos, *Cantica* 21.

19. *Greek Anthology* 8.48.

20. See Athenaeus, *Deip.* 11.67.21; Claudius Aelianus *NA* 5.39.34.

21. Galen, *De praecognitione* 3.15-16. Fainting from an overextended bath had critical theoretical implications. Galen (*De usu respirationis* 4.2) denied the theory of Erasistratus that emptying (τὸ κενούμενον) of the spirit from the body caused fainting. Galen looked instead to the loss of vital heat. See David J. Furley and J. S. Wilkie, *Galen on Respiration and the Arteries* (Princeton: Princeton University Press, 1984), 112–13. For a similar debate about the hazards of vigorous exercise, whether it leaves "our bodies empty (κενόν) and dry," see Lucian, *Anach.* 35. Another scientific use of κένωσις was to explain the waxing and waning of the moon; see Plutarch, *Fac.* passim. With odd results, Maximus of Turin (*Sermons* 30 and 31) explained the Christ Hymn in terms of lunar phases.

22. Plato, *Symp.* 186C. Translation is by Michael Joyce in *The Collected Dialogues of Plato, Including the Letters,* ed. Edith Hamilton and Huntington Cairns, Bollingen Series 71 (Princeton: Princeton University Press, 1961), 539–40. Cf. Plato, *Tim.* 81A–B; Plato, *Phileb.* 36A–B. See also Hippocrates, *Aph.* 2.22: "Diseases caused by repletion (ἀπὸ πλησμονῆς) are cured by depletion (κένωσις); those caused by depletion are cured by repletion." See also *Nat. hom.* 9.

23. Jacques Jouanna, *Hippocrates,* trans. M. B. DeBevoise, Medicine & Culture (Baltimore: Johns Hopkins University Press, 1999), 325–27. See Galen, *De atra bile* 5.120–21. Philosophers borrowed medical ideas about *kenōsis* to explain pleasure and pain. See A. E. Taylor, *A Commentary on Plato's Timaeus* (Oxford: Clarendon, 1928), 447–62.

24. Hippocrates, *Nat. hom.* 4. Cf. Galen, *In Hippocratis de natura hominis commentarii III* 15.63–64.

25. See Ruth Padel, *In and Out of the Mind: Greek Images of the Tragic Self* (Princeton: Princeton University Press, 1992), 81–88.

26. Plato, *Tim.* 77A. Translation is from B. Jowett in Hamilton and Cairns, *Collected Dialogues,* 1198–99. For the continuing importance of *kenōsis* in explanations of hunger, see Plutarch, *Quaest. conviv.* 635B; 688F.

27. Galen, *De sanitate tuenda* 6.102. Translation is from *A Translation of Galen's Hygiene* (*De sanitate tuenda*), trans. Robert Montraville Green (Springfield, IL: Thomas, 1951), 61.

28. See chapter 2, pp. 45–52.

29. See chapter 2, pp. 45–46. The durability of the melting motif is shown in epitaphs; see *Griechische Vers-Inschriften* 1:1166; *Steinepigramme* 16/51/5; Jon Steffen Bruss, *Hidden Presences: Monuments, Gravesites, and Corpses in Greek Funerary Epigram,* Hellenistica Groningana 10 (Dudley, MA: Peeters, 2005), 77.

30. *Greek Anthology* 12.92.

31. Longus, *Daphn.* 1.18.

32. For text, translation, and archaeological context, see David O. Ross, Jr., "Nine Epigrams from Pompeii (*CIL* 4.4966–73)," *Yale Classical Studies* 21 (1969): 127–42.

33. Jacopone da Todi, *Laud* 90. Translation is from *Jacopone da Todi: The Lauds,* trans. Serge and Elizabeth Hughes, CWS (New York: Paulist, 1982), 259. Used with permission of Paulist Press. www.paulistpress.com. Cf. Hadewijch, *Letter* 8.

34. Symeon the New Theologian, *Hymn 16*. Translation is from *Hymns of Divine Love by St. Symeon the New Theologian,* trans. George A. Maloney (Denville, NJ: Dimension, 1975), 58. Text is Athanasios Kambylis, *Symeon Neos Theologos: Hymnen,* Supplementa Byzantina 3 (Berlin: Walter de Gruyter, 1976), 111.

35. For an introduction to kenotic theory, see *God and Incarnation in Mid-Nineteenth Century German Theology: G. Thomasius, I. A. Dorner, and A. E.* Biedermann, ed. Claude Welch, Library of Protestant Theology (New York: Oxford University Press, 1965). For refinements from a feminist pespecive, see Sarah Coakley, *Powers and Submissions: Spirituality, Philosophy and Gender,* Challenges in Contemporary Theology (Oxford: Blackwell, 2002), 3–39.

36. Patristic writers generally thought that the humiliation had to do with the Word's transition from the form of God to the assumption of human nature, but Anastasius of Sinai (*Viae dux* 13.8 [*PG* 89:237]), while granting this, also said that he humbled himself within the status of humiliation: ὅθεν καὶ ἐν αὐτῇ τῇ ταπεινώσει ταπεινοτέρως ἐταπείνωσεν ἑαυτόν.

37. Sarah Coakley, "Kenosis: Theological Meanings and Gender Connotations," in *The Work of Love: Creation as Kenosis,* ed. John Polkinghorne (Grand Rapids: Eerdmans, 2001), 192–210, esp. 204–10. Coakley helpfully maps the complicated ways *kenōsis* has functioned in exegesis and theological systems.

38. Bernard of Clairvaux, *On Loving God* 10.27. Translation is from *Bernard of Clairvaux: On Loving God,* trans. Emero Stiegman, Cistercian Fathers Series 13B (Kalamazoo: Cistercian Publications, 1973), 29. See also Symeon the New Theologian, *Discourses* 27.10; and Baldwin of Ford, *Spiritual Tractates* 12.

39. Coakley's circumspect exploration in *Powers and Submissions* (pp. 32–39) of *kenōsis* as vulnerability and contemplation deserves serious consideration. Rehabilitation of traditional *kenōsis* is a difficult task, however, since a gap exists between the meaning of *kenōsis* in her proposal and the sense of the word in the ancient world.

40. See F. Blass and A. Debrunner, *A Greek Grammar of the New Testament and Other Early Christian Literature,* trans. Robert W. Funk (Chicago: University of Chicago Press, 1961), 174–75. Since the authors indicate that relative past time was not a consistent feature of the aorist participle, its presence in Phil 2:7 is not a certainty.

41. John Reumann (*Philippians: A New Translation with Introduction and Commentary,* Anchor Yale Bible 33B [New Haven: Yale University Press, 2008], 371) dismisses the idea of Jesus giving obedience to God.

42. For a more nuanced division of opinions, including Ernst Käsemann's innovation of bondage to evil forces suffered by all humans, see Peter T. O'Brien, *The Epistle to the Philippians,* NIGTC (Grand Rapids: Eerdmans, 1991), 217–24. Barth's treatment of Christ's slavery anticipated Kasemann's; see Karl Barth, *The Epistle to the Philippians: 40th Anniversary Edition,* trans. James W. Leitch (Louisville: Westminster John Knox, 2002), 63–64. An intriguing exception to the prevalent opinion that the Christ Hymn concerns Jesus' obedience to God is found in L. Michael White's essay "Morality between Two Worlds: A Paradigm of Friendship in Philippians," in *Greeks, Romans, and Christians: Essays in Honor of Abraham J. Malherbe,* ed. David L. Balch, Everett Ferguson, and Wayne Meeks (Minneapolis: Fortress Press, 1990), 201–15. He interprets the Phil 2:5-11 through the ancient notion of friendship, not so very distant from the erotic approach I propose.

43. Symeon, *Capita practica et theologica* 1.61. Translation is from *Symeon the New Theologian, The Practical and Theological Chapters,* trans. Paul McGuckin, Cistercian Studies Series 41 (Kalamazoo: Cistercian Publications, 1982), 48–49. Text is *PG* 120:620–21. For another example of spiritual discipline framing the interpretation of Phil 2:6-8, see Leander of Seville, *The Training of Nuns* 11, 23.

44. Nicetas Paphlago, *PG* 105:140 (my translation). See also Nicetas Pectoratus, *PG* 120:925.

45. Alan of Lille, *The Art of Preaching* 16. Translation is from *Alan of Lille: The Art of Preaching,* trans. Gillian R. Evans, Cistercian Fathers Series 23 (Kalamazoo: Cistercian Publications, 1981), 73.

46. Alan of Lille, *The Art of Preaching* 16 (Evans, *Art of Preaching,* 76). Cf. John of Ford, *Sermon* 82.3; *Sermon* 86.9–10; Archard of St. Victor, *Sermon* 5.

47. See Brian Patrick McGuire, *Friendship and Community: The Monastic Experience 350–1250,* Cistercian Studies Series 95 (Kalamazoo: Cistercian Publications, 1988), 231–38.

48. John of Ford, *Sermon* 73.8.

49. Guerric of Igny, *Sermon* 29.1. Translation is from *Guerric of Igny: Liturgical Sermons,* trans. monks of Mount Saint Bernard Abbey, 2 vols., Cistercian Father Series 8, 32 (Spencer, MA: Cistercian Publications, 1970, 1971), 2:55–56.

50. Guerric of Igny, *Sermon* 41.3. Translation is from *Guerric of Igny: Liturgical Sermons,* 2:55–56. Cf. Baldwin of Ford, *Spiritual Tractates* 12.

51. Bernard of Clairvaux, *On the Song of Songs* 42.7–9. Translation is from *On the Song of Songs II,* trans. Kilian Walsh, Cistercian Fathers Series 7 (Kalamazoo: Cistercian Publications, 1976), 215.

52. See n. 65 for this motif.

53. Paul Murgatroyd, "*Servitium Amoris* and the Roman Elegists," *Latomus* 40 (1980): 589–606. See also Netta Zagagi, *Tradition and Originality in Plautus: Studies in the Amatory Motif in Plautine Comedy,* Hypomnemata 62 (Göttingen: Vandenhoeck & Ruprecht, 1980), 107–17.

54. Menander, *Frg.* 541; Plutarch, *Frg.* 134. See Zagagi, *Tradition and Originality,* 93; G. Luck, "Panaetius and Menander," *AJP* 96 (1975): 257–62.

55. The phrase is Murgatroyd's ("*Servitium Amoris,*" 591). See Xenophon, *Symp.* 4.14: "and I should take more delight in being a slave than being a free man, if Cleinias would deign to be my master." There is immediately after this confession the "unto death" idea. For the lovesick slave of love, see Achilles Tatius, *Leuc. et Clit,* 1.7.2–3.

56. For other examples of the motif between Plato and Paul, in addition to Zagagi above, see Rosenmeyer, *Poetics of Imitation,* 184–85; and *Greek Anthology* 12.81, 169.

57. For the low (τάπεινος) condition of the slave of love, see (possibly) Aeschylus, *Prom.* 907–27; and Isocrates. *Hel. enc.* 59–60. See also *Greek Anthology* 12.158; Luck, "Panaeitius and Menander," 259–60; Plutarch, *Amat.* 753B. Cf. E. J. Bickerman, "Love Story in the Homeric Hymn to Aphrodite," *Athenaeum* 54 (1976): 250.

58. Cyrino, *In Pandora's Jar,* 11–12.

59. Hesiod, *Theog.* 21–22. Translation is from Cyrino, *In Pandora's Jar,* 46. Cf. Archilochus, *Frg.* 196.

60. Translation is from Cyrino, *In Pandora's Jar,* 56, 61.

61. Ibid., 112.

62. Sappho, *Frg.* 1. Translation is from Cyrino, *In Pandora's Jar,* 143. See Karlheinz Kost, *Musaios, Hero und Leander: Einleitung, Text, Übersetzung, und Kommentar* (Bonn: Bouvier-Verlag, 1971), 276–77.

63. Bernard of Clairvaux, *Sermon* 64.10. Translation is from *Bernard of Clairvaux: On the Song of Songs III,* trans. Kilian Walsh and Irene M. Edmonds, Cistercian Fathers Series 31 (Kalamazoo: Cistercian Publications, 1979), 177–78. Text is *PL* 183:1088.

64. For violent love, see the index of Bernard McGinn, *The Flowering of Mysticism: Men and Women in the New Mysticism, 1200–1350* (New York: Crossroad, 1998). *Vehemens* modifies *amor* in Guerric of Igny, *Liturgical Sermons* 27.4: "a love for man so ardent (*vehemens*) that he wills to become man for the sake of man." Translation is from *Guerric of Igny: Liturgical Sermons,* 2:44. Text is *PL* 185:122. For John of Ford, vehemence refers to deepened *desiderium*; see *Sermon* 24.8.

65. Ovid (*Am.* 1.2.19–52) famously depicted Cupid as a victorious general parading a lover through the streets of Rome as a slave. See John F. Miller, "Reading Cupid's Triumph," *Classical Journal* 90 (1995): 287–94. For additional examples of the motif, see Reposianus, *De concubito Martis et Veneris* 7; Ovid, *Am.,* 1.7.35–40; 2.12.1–16; Propertius 2.8.39–40.

66. Hadewijch, *Poems in Stanzas* 8.71–77. Translation is from *Hadewijch: The Complete Works,* trans. Columba Hart, CWS (New York: Paulist, 1980), 151.

67. Basil, *Ep.* 359. See also John Chrysostom, *Ep.* 146; and Bernard of Clairvaux, *Ep.* 176.

68. Cf. Achard of Saint Victor, *Sermon* 12.2.

69. Gilbert of Hoyland, *Sermons on the Song of Songs* 8.6. Translation is from *The Works of Gilbert of Hoyland: Sermons on the Song of Songs, I,* trans. Lawrence C. Braceland, Cistercian Fathers Series 14 (Kalamazoo: Cistercian Publications), 123. Text is *PL* 183:51.

70. Plato, *Phaedr.* 252B; Moschus, *Eros drapeta* 16; *Greek Anthology* 5.57, 268; 12.75–78; 16.103; Propertius 2.12.5–8.

71. Archilochus, *Frg.* 92b (quoted in Plutarch, *Amat.* 750B); Heliodorus, *Aeth.* 4.2.3; 6.7.8; Alciphron, *Ep.* 4.16.5. Ovid, a likely source for medieval writers, also thought that winged Love traveled vast distances; see *Ex Ponto* 3.3.18.

72. *Greek Anthology* 5.179.

73. See Procopius *Epp.* 58, 90. For the lover's wish to change into a creature of flight, see J. C. B. Petropoulos, *Eroticism in Ancient and Medieval Greek Poetry* (London: Duckworth, 2003), 74–88.

74. Lucian *[Am.]* 32.

75. Hesiod, *Theog.* 116–22; Aristophanes, *Av.* 693–701; Oppian, *Halieutica* 4.11–41 (for a prose restatement of this hymn to love, see Eutecnius, *Paraphrasis in Oppiani halieutica* 4.1.20);

Nonnos, *Dion.* 7.110–16. For the early period, see Claude Calame, *The Poetics of Eros in Ancient Greece* (trans. Janet Lloyd; Princeton: Princeton University Press, 1999), 177–79.

76. Menander Rhetor, Περί ἐπιδεικτικῶν 400.29–404.14.

77. At an important point in this debate (third century B.C.E.), Eros, maker of communion, was confessed as Lord. See *Greek Anthology* 15.24. This epigram is a fascinating precursor to Phil 2:5-11. See the introduction above, p. 7.

78. Isaac of Stella, *Sermons on the Christian Year* 10.2. Translation is from *Isaac of Stella: Sermons on the Christian Year,* trans. Hugh McCaffry, Cistercian Fathers Series 11 (Kalamazoo: Cistercian Publications, 1979), 84. Text is *PL* 194:1723.

79. Nicholas Cabasilas, *The Life in Christ* 6.3. Translation is from *The Life in Christ,* trans. Carmino J. deCatanzaro (Crestwood, NY: St. Vladimir's Seminary Press, 1974), 162–63. Text is *PG* 150:644–45. I have slightly modified the translation to bring out more clearly the motif of triumphal procession.

80. See Basil, *Ep.* 220.

81. For τὸ φίλτρον as love potion, see Achilles Tatius, *Leuc. Clit.* 4.15.4; and Reed, *Bion of Smyrna,* 221–22.

82. *Greek Anthology* 5.212.

83. Iamblichus, *Babyloniaca* 96.

84. Zagagi, *Tradition and Originality,* 78–79,134–37. See chapter 1, pp. 26-28.

85. See Christopher Smith, "'Ἐκκλεῖσαι' in Galatians 4:17: The Motif of the Excluded Lover as a Metaphor of Manipulation," *CBQ* 58 (1996): 480–99.

86. For the epic hero as slave of love obedient even to death, see Bickerman, "Love Story in the Homeric Hymn to Aphrodite," 245–50; and Gian Biagio Conte, *Genres and Readers: Lucretius, Love Elegy, Pliny's Encyclopeadia,* trans. Glenn W. Most (Baltimore: Johns Hopkins University Press, 1994), 38. The classic text bringing *servitium amoris* together with death is Xenophon, *Symp.* 4.14; cf. Philostratus, *Ep.* 7. Love-heroism is illustrated (without the slavery motif) in Bion, *Frg.* 12 and discussed by Reed, *Bion of Smyrna,* 175–79. For the lover's dedication unto death in Chariton, see Peter Toohey, "Dangerous Ways to Fall in Love: Chariton I 1,5–10 and VI 9,4," *Maia* 51 (1999): 269; and Alison Sharrock, *Seduction and Repetition in Ovid's Ars Amatoria II* (New York: Oxford University Press, 1994), 58–59. The story of Alcestis's self-sacrifice for Theseus is yet another source of this motif; see Maurizio Bettini, *The Portrait of the Lover,* trans. Laura Gibbs (Berkeley: University of California Press, 1999), 18–25. For the remembrance of her sacrifice, see Plato, *Symp.* 179B–D; Plutarch, *Amat.* 761D–F; *Greek Anthology* 7.691.

87. See n. 65 above.

88. God invents *kenōsis* in order to display longing desire. Note that Cabasilas cannot quite bring himself to say what the motifs he selected were suggesting—that the divine experienced loss of self-control.

89. Jacopone da Todi, *Laud* 90. Translation is from Hughes and Hughes, *Jacopone da Todi: The Lauds,* 262–63. See also *Laud* 65. Used with permission of Paulist Press. www.paulistpress.com.

90. Clement (*Protr.* 1.8.4) is both a help and a hindrance. On the one hand, explaining Christ's emptying he preserves the idea of desire: "longing to save humanity (σῶσαι τὸν ἄνθρωπον γλιχόμενος)." But, more importantly, he does not allow for an immediate, emotional connection between Christ and humans. Instead, he subordinates Christ's desire to a purpose clause. Humankind then becomes the *object* of Christ's saving purpose.

4

Abduction Disregarded

Hades carried her off to wed her . . .[1]

ΑΡΠΑΓΜΟΣ

Although it is impertinent to say so, scholars have misunderstood a crucial word in Phil 2:6-8. If an error has occurred, however, it is entirely understandable, since sensitive minds recoil when ἁρπαγμός, the word in question, appears in one of earliest and most influential christological statements: "he did not regard equality with God a thing to be grasped (οὐκ ἁρπαγμὸν ἡγήσατο τὸ εἶναι ἴσα θεῷ)." The usual translations of ἁρπαγμός ("thing to be grasped" or "thing grasped after") accord with traditional christological doctrine. Yet neither translation is correct. As strange as it may sound, in Paul's day ἁρπαγμός meant "erotic abduction."

There is great theological pressure not to recognize this odd but accurate definition, since many (but not all) past commentators assert and present-day Pauline scholars agree that Phil 2:6-8 tells of Christ's humble obedience to God, not some story about sexual violence. Furthermore, it is often claimed that, by giving up divine attributes and privileges rightfully his own or by not grasping after them in the first place, Christ Jesus illustrates the self-effacement that is required of all humans if they wish to flee Adam's waywardness and live restored lives under the lordship of God. Christ emptied himself to show that his obedience was accomplished with human faculties alone, without the boost provided by flesh infused with divinity. Or, in an alternate narrative, his giving up of divine powers and privileges was itself the perfect illustration of obedience to God. In either interpretation, it is required that ἁρπαγμός in

2:6 be translated "a thing to be grasped" or "a thing grasped after." Divinity is assumed to be a substance that can be retained, let go, or pursued.

Such an interpretation further demands that ἁρπαγμός cover the same linguistic ground as a related term ἁρπαγμά, which without question designates "a thing to be grasped" or "a thing grasped after".[2] The term ἁρπαγμός, which occurs only in Phil 2:6 and a handful of times outside of the New Testament if early Christian commentaries are excluded, is defenseless against the lexical onslaught led by ἁρπαγμά. Beginning in the early church and continuing to the present day, interpreters insist that Paul unquestionably must have meant the more frequently occurring ἁρπαγμά—an understandable claim, given the weirdness of interjecting the topic of erotic abduction into the story of the Son of God's assumption of human flesh.

Just imagine the perplexity of Christian philologists. Tracking down linguistic leads in ancient Greek literature, these researchers had hoped to find a sense of the word ἁρπαγμός that would be appropriate to the conceptual matrix of traditional christological dogma presumed to underlie the Christ Hymn, that is, the metaphysical category of substance and the ethical topics of ruling and subordination. Their investigations took them instead to a treatise on education doubtfully attributed to Plutarch (50–120 C.E.), where ἁρπαγμός refers to a rite of initiation on Crete that through sexual violence guided boys to adulthood. Closest in time to the Christ Hymn, this occurrence of the word has never been brought to bear on the Phil 2:6. Plutarch's treatise takes up a well-worn educational topic, the attention teachers might appropriately show to the lads in their care:

> Now we ought indeed to drive away those whose desire is for mere outward beauty, but to admit without reserve those who are lovers of the soul. And while the sort of love prevailing at Thebes and in Elis is to be avoided, as well as the so-called kidnapping in Crete (ἁρπαγμόν), that which is found in Athens and in Lacedaemon is to be emulated.[3]

Admittedly, a comparison of Plutarch's condemnation of the abduction of young males at Thebes, in Elis, and on Crete with Phil 2:6 is silly if the presupposition of the investigation is a christology oriented to divine sovereignty. But if the task is to reimagine Christology through a longing that moves both Paul and Christ in their innards, then this brief mention of sexual seizure in Crete is intriguing and goes a long way to define what Christ Jesus *did not regard* as a pattern for his own narrative, even if it is not immediately clear what to make of it. We will return to this treatise later in the chapter.

Making Sense of Abduction

If the erotic meaning of ἁρπαγμός in Phil 2:6 is going to be taken seriously, the grammar of οὐχ ἁρπαγμὸν ἡγήσατο τὸ εἶναι ἴσα θεῷ needs to be reconsidered. Mere substitution of the first-century meaning ("abduction") for the erroneous translation ("thing to be grasped") solves nothing. In fact, simply plugging "abduction" into the existing sentence structure creates a rather bizarre statement: "He did not regard equality with God as erotic abduction." A fresh approach guided by grammatical considerations is required in order to place ἁρπαγμός into a meaningful sentence.

This new approach to Phil 2:6 occurs in two stages. First, note that οὐχ ἁρπαγμὸν ἡγήσατο τὸ εἶναι ἴσα θεῷ is an instance of indirect discourse. When indirect discourse is constructed with an infinitive, as it is here, the subject of the clause and the direct object are both in the accusative case, a feature of the Greek language that inevitably introduces ambiguity. Thus, the phrase could be translated either "he did not regard equality with God as erotic abduction" or "he did not regard erotic abduction to be equally with God." Since the second translation follows the Greek word order (which admittedly is not an infallible guide to translation), it has a very slight edge on grammatical grounds. The puzzle is not yet solved, but a new way to read Phil 2:6 is emerging.

The second stage has to do with our recognition of an idiomatic expression in ancient Greek. It is quite true that the phrase "to be equally with God" does not communicate an idea familiar to English speakers. Greek speakers, on the other hand, had something definite in mind. To say that so-and-so existed equally with a god (or the gods) expressed praise for a wonderful quality in that human being. Quite often this excellence was beauty. With great regularity, "I regard (ἡγέομαι)" or its synonyms in combination with "of god," "like god" or "equal to the gods" form a comparison in which someone or something is highly praised. Lucian of Samosata, for example, used this pattern to portray the Cynic philosopher Demonax, who was famous for his gentle treatment of sinners: "He considered (ἡγεῖτο) that it is human to err, divine or all but divine (θεοῦ δὲ ἢ ἀνδρός ἰσοθέου) to set right what has gone amiss."[4] Even closer to the syntactical structure of Phil 2:6, formulaic praise of a person's beauty was quite likely to include an assertion of his or her equality with the divine.[5] In the eyes of the lover the beloved is "equal to god (ἰσόθεος)."[6]

By the time of the New Testament, ancient prose was awash in comparisons to gods for the purpose of praising humans. This rhetorical practice often went over the top. Even so, it was staunchly defended by Lucian in his *Essays in Portraiture Defended*. Here Lucian argues that if such comparisons are not permitted (for fear of impiety he conjectures), then not only would the most famous sculptors be banned, but—and this is unthinkable—Homer himself would have to be struck from the literary canon. Lucian then provides a thesaurus of Homeric phrases, all of which praise human qualities by comparing them to divinity through various terms meaning "equal to" or "like."[7] And what Lucian says of Homer's habit of praising things as equal to the gods could as easily be said of the poetic tradition that imitated Homer's practice. Lucian writes, "this sort of thing is so frequent that there is no part of his poetry which is not well adorned with comparisons of gods."[8] In light of this popularity of "equal to god" in ancient literature, then, an alternative translation of Phil 2:6b now suggests itself: "he did not regard abduction to be worthy of God."

A few comments about the phrase "in the form of God" are in order, since the interpretation I am proposing departs from the common exegetical explanations. Scholars acknowledge perplexity over the word μορφή because of its obvious association with perception and the equally obvious point to them that God does not have a body to be perceived.[9] Convinced that it is inappropriate to visualize God in a human body, most interpreters avert anthropomorphism by transforming μορφή into "nature" or "essence," although with scant lexicographical evidence.[10] Such a philosophically based reading, however, does fit conveniently with the theme of divine sovereignty presupposed by many interpreters. Μορφή as "essence" or "nature" allows the reader to begin the story of the hymn thinking about the divine attributes that Christ Jesus first possessed and then poured out as he manifested himself as a human being obedient to the divine will.

The former interpretation, however, the one that refuses to part with the visual aspect of μορφή, coordinates well with what we have said so far about erotic abduction. First-century audiences might have understood that Paul begins the narrative of Christ's career with a comment about the god's beauty. That the narrative would begin with the visual aspect of its main actor would not have been unexpected, since many stories involving gods and goddesses used beauty to explore profoundly religious themes of ceaseless youth and immortal life.[11] Not only in myth does this hold true. It was a cliché in poetry from Homer onward and in imperial erotic fiction: a beautiful person exists in the divine form.[12] Erotic epigram was especially fond of this idea.[13]

Furthermore, and this is particularly germane to Phil 2:6, anyone in the divine form, whether mortal or immortal, has an insuperable advantage over the less lovely.[14] The epitaph of one of the most famous beauties in antiquity illustrates the dominating power of good looks: "Boastful Greece, unconquered by force, was once enslaved by this godlike beauty, by Laïs, whom Eros begot and Corinth brought up."[15] The "god-shaped (θεόμορφε)" Lycinus masters an enthralled lover's eyes. The wretch cannot look at Lycinus face to face.[16] The god's beauty is power; divine shapeliness is a weapon. It seizes, enslaves, overwhelms, and abducts mortals.[17] Thus, the theological significance of insisting on a literal interpretation of μορφή is great: though he was in the form of God and thus in the position to overwhelm mortals, Christ Jesus did not regard such seizing to be worthy of divinity.[18] He was better than he looked.

RAPTURE CULTURE

So far, the reasons offered for reading erotic abduction into Phil 2:6 have been grammatical and philological. An interesting question remains: what *religious* sense does it make to begin Christ's story with his rejection of abduction, his refusal to see beauty's brute force as divine? In order to get at this question I will pursue once again the philological method adopted by scholars when they wished to find an equivalent term for ἁρπαγμός. Instead of the traditional solution of equating it with ἁπαργμά, however, I urge a careful look at another cognate, ἁρπαγή, whose occurrences numbered in the hundreds in ancient literature. It meant "abduction for erotic purpose."[19]

A passage from the second-century c.e. astrological treatise of Vettius Valens is illuminating, since it employs ἁρπαγή and ἁρπαγμός as synonyms, the very point I wish to make.[20] The horoscopes in this section of Valens's work deal with the erotic destinies of women. Depending on the particular configuration of the planets at the moment of her conception or birth, a woman's marriage will be steady and entered into in the customary way or it will be accomplished by abduction (ἁρπαγή), war, or captivity. Also dependent on the positions of the heavenly bodies is whether a woman will be promiscuous, standing around in brothels, and the like, and if married whether the marriage will be of the abduction type (ἁρπαγμός ὁ γάμος ἔσται), whether she will be seized, or whether her marriage will be by custom.[21]

Before Constantine put the matter to rest with a prohibition in 320 c.e., it is difficult to ascertain the legal status of marriage by abduction.[22] All that is certain is that attitudes toward a marriage accomplished though seizure differed greatly over time and from place to place. From Athenaeus we learn that in ancient Athens Theseus, quite unlike Constantine much later, accepted the practice and did what he could to add to its reputation. He himself was said to have taken a wife in three ways: through love (ἐξ ἔρωτος), by abduction (ἐξ ἁρπαγῆς), and through lawful wedlock (ἐξ νομίμων γάμων).[23] A trace of disapproval can be detected in the pragmatic Seven Sages (sixth century b.c.e.), who called for a fine on the abductor and left it at that.[24] Relating the early history of the Romans, Dionysius of Halicarnassus has Romulus assure the former virgins of Rome's neighbors that abduction "was an ancient Greek custom and that of all methods of contracting marriages for women it was the most illustrious."[25] A character in Achilles Tatius's novel *Leucippe et Clitophon* assumes and acts on "a Byzantine law, to the effect that if a man kidnapped a maiden and made her his wife before he was caught, his only penalty was to stay married to her."[26] This brings us to Basil, whose strongly worded condemnation contrasts with the foregoing permissive attitudes. For Basil, "this wicked custom" of abduction is "an unlawful outrage," "an insult to free men," and even "tyranny against life itself."[27]

Marriage was not the only context of erotic abduction, since the ancients seem to have been obsessed with stories of seizure, and not just those of young men looking for wives. What conception of θεός, then, did these stories of sexual violence bring with them? The point of abduction it appears was that gods can do whatever they damn well please.[28] In the words of Emily Vermeule, "To take Greek myth at face value . . . is to learn that the gods have only two easy ways of communicating with men: by killing them or raping them."[29] Abductions occur in poetry, too, as well as in stories about national origins and in figural art.[30] While it might be thought that the abduction motif is simply about sex and gender, it is more accurate to say that the ancients expressed their deepest anxieties about love, death, the social order, and sex and gender through stories of erotic abduction.[31] For this reason, we must thoroughly familiarize ourselves with this powerful symbol. Only then we can appreciate the theological significance of Christ's *disregard* for it.[32] His refusal to abduct humans emphasizes by means of contrast what the story implies was his real interest, his longing for humanity.

A good place to start is Plutarch's remarks about the educational practices on the island of Crete. Although civic-minded promoters of local culture throughout the Mediterranean boasted that such and such god seized so and so mortal here, no location in the ancient world was more closely identified with erotic abduction than Crete, in part because Crete was the destination of Zeus when, in the form of a bull, he seized the Phoenician princess Europa and transported her on his back across the sea.[33] Abducting a young woman symbolizes the way continents are civilized, it was thought; Greece's complex relationship with Africa was imagined through this myth. Yet, as illuminating as the Europa myth is, the educational practice on Crete to which Plutarch alludes, the so-called kidnappings, reveals the pervasive significance of sexual violence in ancient culture. The historian Ephorus (405–330 B.C.E.) gives a thick description of the practice:

> They [Cretans] have a peculiar custom in regard to love affairs (τοὺς ἔρωτας), for they win the objects of their love, not by persuasion, but by abduction (ἁρπαγῇ); the lover tells the friends of the boy three or four days beforehand that he is going to make the abduction (τὴν ἁρπαγήν) . . . and when they meet, if the abductor (ὁ ἁρπάζων) is the boy's equal or superior in rank or other respects, the friends pursue him and lay hold of him, though only in a very gentle way, thus satisfying the custom; and after that they cheerfully turn the boy over to him to lead him away. . . . And the pursuit does not end until the boy is taken to the "Andreium" of his abductor. They regard as a worthy object of love, not the boy who is exceptionally handsome, but the boy who is exceptionally manly and decorous. After giving the boy presents, the abductor takes him away to any place in the country he wishes. . . . The boy is released after receiving as presents a military habit, an ox, and a drinking-cup (these are the gifts required by law). . . . Now the boy sacrifices the ox to Zeus and feasts those who returned with him; and he makes known the facts about his intimacy with his lover, whether, perchance, it has pleased him or not, the law allowing him this privilege in order that, if any force (βία) was applied to him at the time of the abduction (κατὰ τὴν ἁρπαγήν), he might be able at this feast to avenge himself and be rid of the lover. It is disgraceful for those who are handsome in appearance or descendants of illustrious ancestors to fail to obtain lovers, the presumption being that their character is responsible for such a fate. But the parastathentes (for thus they call those who have been abducted [τοὺς ἁρπαγέντας]) receive honours; for in both the dances and the races they have the positions of highest honor, and are allowed to dress in better clothes than the rest, that is, in the habit given them by their lovers; and not then only, but even after they have grown to manhood, they wear a distinctive dress, which is intended to make known the fact that each wearer has

become "kleinos," for they call the loved one "kleinos" and the lover "philetor."[34]

This passage describes the Cretan way of ritualizing the transition from youth to manhood for aristocratic boys. In Ephorus's account is a set of assumptions that help us understand what ancient readers might have made of Christ's rejection of abduction in Phil 2:6.

First, it should be noted Ephorus situates abduction between persuasion and violence (βία).[35] On the one hand, Ephorus believed that the customs surrounding abduction provided gentle enough treatment of the boy. Friends as the lover's agents in the hunt play an important role mitigating violence. Likewise, tradition granted the youth the opportunity of removing himself from the lover if the whole affair did not please him, that is, if undue force were applied to him by the abductor. On the other hand, in spite of these accommodations to the boy (he was, after all, an upper-class male who in all likelihood would grow up to do his own abducting one day), the youth was raped. He was ripped from his family, taken to the countryside for two months, and subjected through sex to a power outside of himself. Abduction was an ominous event, and even though Ephorus seeks to reassure his readers that it was benign, the youth's experience has deep resonance with the way death itself was conceptualized throughout the entire Mediterranean world.[36]

Gifts, the second of Ephorus' themes, hint at anxiety surrounding the abduction of the young.[37] What was the function of these gifts? On the one hand, they might have compensated the family for their loss when they discover that a son has been "disappeared."[38] On the other hand, the boy himself loses something valuable, his boyhood.[39] Numerous gifts went some distance to make these losses right. Furthermore, in the eyes of the community, the gifts also marked the transition to adulthood, since the ox afforded the abducted-youth-turned-adult the opportunity to host a banquet and the military costume symbolized his newly acquired age status. The honors, including the epithet "famous," granted him a high status for the rest of his life.

A final point deserves to be mentioned. Both Ephorus and Plutarch classify abduction as *just one kind* of erōs. This alerts us to the possibility that some ancient writers imagined an alternate, nonviolent way of loving.[40] If abduction is only one kind of erōs, might there not be another? What would it look like? Might another way of loving have been communicated to readers by Christ's disregard of abduction? Might it be the case that Christology began with an explicit rejection of the sexual violence contained in abduction tales and the broader patterns of social relations they enacted and justified? I believe this was the case. Paul's Christology in Philippians refuses to legitimate abduction and rejects it as a founding myth. Christ might not have been the first human to reject erotic seizure, as we will see below, but he was one of the very few *gods* ever to do so.[41] This must have been a theological wonder to the first readers of the Christ Hymn, confronted as they were daily by the overwhelming power of love, death, and especially the political regimes that eagerly sponsored abduction scenes in public art.[42]

Did no one question the justice of erotic abduction? Poets sometimes lodged a complaint against the rapacious Zeus. When he snatches a beautiful youth, Zeus enters the field of competition for sexual conquests with an undue advantage and depletes the pool of targets for adult male desire.[43] This is a frivolous complaint, of course, expressed for humorous effect. It does nothing to rid *erōs* of the targeting behavior it had acquired and to substitute reciprocal love and fidelity. Nor did the frequent lament of the lover that *his* heart had been snatched by the boy, the girl, or by Eros himself advance the cause of mutuality in matters of love.[44] This latter scenario is a classic case of the person with power justifying the violence of his erotic pursuit by claiming that it is he who is the victim. He, poor unfortunate, is the one who has been abducted.

Meaningful criticism of abduction had to wait until the novelist Achilles Tatius. His novel *Leucippe et Clitophon* challenges abduction, though not from a moralist's point of view or the religious rationalist's offense at the gods' misbehavior, or even from the perspective of the lover pretending to suffer. Rather, abduction is made to look bad from the conviction that there is a better way of loving. Readers are clued in right away about the story's dim view of abduction. Hinting at the deeper meanings the plot will eventually lay bare, the novel begins with a description of a painting of Zeus' abduction of Europa.[45] In cooperation with a playful Eros, raptured Europa gets the upper hand over the bull:

> The maiden sat on his back, not astride but sidesaddle, with her feet together towards the right, and on the left her hand holding the horn as a charioteer would hold the reins. And the bull in fact had turned his head somewhat in the direction of the pressure of her guiding hand. . . . And Eros was leading the bull: Eros, a tiny child, with wings spread, quiver dangling, torch in hand. He had turned to look at Zeus with a sly smile, as if in mockery that he had, for Love's sake, become a bull.[46]

This scene is prophetic, since the rest of the narrative strips legitimacy from erotic seizure; the novel tells the story of equality, mutuality, and fidelity between Leucippe and Clitophon. There is no violence between them, only the longing that comes from separation. (And, yes, there is a happy ending.) This better way of loving suffers the beloved's absence for a time rather than possessing the beloved in the moment through violence.

PROTEST FROM THE GRAVE

Christ's refusal to abduct mortals comes into clearer view against the background of ancient funerary epigrams. As early as the fifth century b.c.e., grave inscriptions depict Hades and other divinities seizing mortals and leading them off to the underworld.[47] Rapture is recorded on steles in cemeteries or standing alongside roads from Italy through Greece and Asia Minor down through Syria, Palestine, and Egypt and extending to the eastern limits of Alexander's conquests and northern limits of Greek colonization. The geographical spread and diachronic durability of the abduction motif suggests that Christ's disregard in Phil 2:6 might well have been understood as a protest against divinity's arbitrary use of power.

Yet the case for widespread protest is not quite as straightforward as inscriptions complaining of divine violence might indicate, since a question arises whether some inscriptions express resignation. For example, was Hades' epithet ὁ πανδαμάτωρ ("The One Who Subdues All") a charge angrily flung against death or did it humbly honor the one whose dictates could not be altered?[48] Other notable abductors (Fate, Time, and Envy) also bore the title, and the question arises in each case whether it communicated accusation or submission.[49] Resignation comes across unambiguously when the dead remind the living that death comes to all without exception, so why dwell on loss or complain about mortality?[50] Other inscriptions plainly exhort the living to cease mourning and to conform to Fate, "for there is nothing more," as an inscription from Larissa gloomily concludes.[51] Nevertheless, the majority of texts are far feistier than these latter examples. Harsh adjectives leave little doubt how the deceased felt about being separated from the living or that survivors experienced grief and anger. The abducting god was called bitter, pitiless, unjust, rejoicing in tears, murky, life-depriving, and insatiable.[52]

Most incisive was the criticism that the gods of death begrudged human happiness and divine envy drove them to snatch the living, often in childhood or in marriageable years.[53] The male divinity Hades was not the only perpetrator. Moira, the goddess of fate, snatched the living and carried them off to Hades' realm.[54] There were yet other abductors: Fate, The Demon, a demon, Death, Nature, Charon, disease, heat of the sun, and nymphs.[55] One more abductor, whose presence in Philippians the next chapter will detect in the opponents to Paul's ministry, stalked friends, lovers, and the praiseworthy: "O Envy, you are the worst and most burdensome of the death-gods."[56] It is crucial to keep in mind that ancient envy (ὁ φθόνος) differs in an important way from modern envy. It is not simply that the envious person wants what others have. Coveting was not the problem;[57] resentment was.[58] Greeks were convinced that gods begrudge humans their happiness, and for this reason abduct (kill) them.

In fairness to the gods it must be acknowledged that some inscriptions put a charitable construction on the death divinities' intentions.[59] On rare occasions the gods preserve mortals by snatching them from evil circumstances. Just as Zeus snatched Ganymede to heaven so that he might serve the gods forever, so also a god might pluck a child from the miseries of life in order to bring it to a far happier place.[60] On a Phrygian grave altar, Markos mourns his son Agathon, whom "Zeus carried away ([ἀφ]ήρπασεν) since he loved him, so that he might abide with him in the air."[61] An inscription from the same region calls the dead lad Antonius "a new Phrygian Ganymede" whom Zeus has led off ([ἐξαγαγ]ών)."[62] In an inscription from Thyateira, Melitine's daughter who was struck by lightning is said to have been abducted by Zeus, who then placed her in the starry sky.[63] Such optimistic use of the abduction motif crossed religious as well as regional borders. The Christian god "snatched (ἥρπασε)" young Diomedes who was "pure and not yet experienced in love matters" and a "friend of Christ" and placed him in paradise before the evil world could lead him astray.[64] An opening, then, existed within the abduction motif for the consolation of mourners.

This opening is important for our coming to terms with 1 Thess 4:17. From Phil 2:6 we have learned that Jesus refused to behave as if he were either one of the sexually violent gods of Greek mythology or an impatient and lawless bridegroom hunting down a bride. Paul's Christ, we thought, scorned the bad habit of abduction. Yet a passage in 1 Thessalonians appears to contradict this crucial christological claim. The dramatic scene in 1 Thess 4:16-17 of Christ's future descent from heaven, the resurrection of the dead, and the meeting of the Lord in the air depends on erotic abduction: "Then we who are alive, who are left, will be caught up (ἁρπαγησόμεθα) in the clouds together with them to meet the Lord in the air; and so we will be with the Lord forever." While it is true that the passive voice of the verb ("we will be abducted") obscures the identity of the agent so that it cannot be said for certain whether God or Christ abducts, Christ nevertheless is complicit. He is there at the abduction and plays

out his role in relation to it. Since abduction is a key part of the final scene of
history, then, it appears that the Christ of 1 Thess 4:17, the one who snatches
humans (or countenances their rapture), undermines the Christ of Philippians 2,
who melts and empties himself to the point of death in longing for communion
with mortals.

Is there a way out of this problem? Perhaps in 1 Thessalonians Paul, not
unlike Markos, Melitine, and the parents of Diomedes, crafted an opening
in the abduction motif along the lines of Zeus's well-intentioned seizure of
Ganymede. This is not to say that Paul read the Ganymede inscriptions cited
above. It is to say there was a complex literary history of the abduction motif
available to Paul and his audiences in various genres, including funerary
inscriptions in which abduction pointed to the reunification of absent loved
ones and family members rather than reiterating separation.[65]

This proposal gains plausibility when it is recognized that in 1 Thess
4:13—5:11 Paul alludes to no fewer than fourteen other popular motifs found
on grave markers.[66] In a sepulchral tour de force Paul situates the reader in
an imaginary cemetery and manipulates the diction of grave epigram to speak
unexpectedly of reunion and lasting human connection. Chief among these
rehabilitated terms is the verb ἄγω ("I lead"), which in 4:14 he links with the
preposition σύν ("with"), stressing union with Christ 4:14 (cf. 5:10). Inscriptions
frequently depicted the dead led away or led down to the underworld.[67] This
dreadful leading was protested in similar terms to the condemnations the gods
received for abduction.[68] Moreover, like ἁρπάζω, ἄγω carried both nuptial
and sepulchral connotations, and this more than anything else explains how it is
that Paul could manipulate the dread it evoked into hope for reunion.[69]

Envy Made Them Do It

These examples of benign rapture ought not to mislead us. As this chapter
comes to a close, a tour of ancient cemeteries and roadside grave steles reminds
us once again of divine abductors' uncharitable intentions and Christ's
disregard, even his protest, of divine power. Envy, the antipode of longing
and the next chapter's topic, was universally recognized as the chief vice of
the gods and goddesses of death: "Ah, mortals have a lowly heart. Know your
betters. Hades begrudges good things [or good people]."[70] Another inscription
complains, "The judge of life for all mortals, himself not subject to judgment,
bitter Hades, who casts an evil eye (βασκαίνει) on all things noble, abducted
(ἀναρπάσας) Apollodoron from his house, hid him in the grave, and left
laments to his parents. Violently he sent him from a chorus of cohorts into
tearful Hades."[71] Given the prevalence of ritual mourning and gravesite visits in

everyday life in antiquity, it is difficult to imagine that Paul's early readers could ignore Christ's stunning disregard of erotic abduction in Phil 2:6. Silently, he protests the malicious abduction of all the dead.

Divine envy ruins everything. The dead did not receive eternal youth and companionship with the gods; instead they were subjected to the underworld, where perception of self and others was destroyed, familial relationships splintered, and mourners liquefied and poured out.[72] The gods were inimical and malicious, since they begrudged mortals the happiness that comes from living in one another's presence.[73] Envy blocks the lasting possession of all that mortals hold dear, whether beauty, youth, marriage, hopes for children, or duties of grace toward parents. Fame or progress in a career provoked abduction.[74] Envy is the divine antagonist of physical beauty and good morals.[75] Young men such as twenty-five-year-old Zenobius of Aphrodisias were taken away by envious Persephone on account of beauty.[76] Young women, too, were snatched—not to sate desire merely but out of resentment of another's good looks.[77]

Overtones of sexual violence were seldom lacking when envy took hold: Hades got himself a new bride when one girl, a very promising poet, died:

> As Erinna, the maiden honey-bee, the new singer in the poets' quire, was gathering the flowers of the Muses, Hades carried her off (ἀνάρπασεν) to wed her. That was a true word, indeed, the girl spoke when she lived: "Hades thou art an envious (βάσκανος) god."[78]

Nor could Envy keep its hand off beautiful children. He seized the child Mēnophilos, who had the lovely form of the threefold Graces.[79] The abduction of youth, from infants up to the age of marriage, was often compared to the plucking of a flower or the breaking of a tender branch in an attempt at consolation still offered today.[80] Hades rejoiced in the death of children and young people.[81] An inscription from the first or second century c.e. in Rome succinctly reveals his evil pleasure: "Barabarianos, child of Pontianos lies here, whom Amastris once buried. The demon seized (ἥρπαξεν) the youth."[82] Youth were abducted before coming into the knowledge of good and evil.[83] To paraphrase this common complaint: "What's the hurry? Since all eventually will fall under your sway, why go after children?"[84]

Inscriptions express outrage at the violation of familial bonds presently enjoyed and those hoped for in the future. Children were snatched from their mothers' breasts and from the innards (ἀπὸ σπλάγχνων) of their parents.[85]

When children were taken from life they could no longer return thanks to their parents for bringing them into the world and raising them.[86] The death of a seven-year-old elicits parental regret of what would never come to pass.[87] Hades enjoyed abducting a spouse as much as seizing a child: "O tearful Hades, why didst thou divorce the bridegroom and bride, thou who thyself takest delight in ravishment (ἁρπαγίμοις)?"[88] After recovering from the shock of his wife's abduction, Prisca's husband counters Moira's deceit with the promise that when he dies he will lie once again with his wife.[89] Again, as in the case of children, resentment drives Moira, Hades, or the other death divinities to abduct spouses: "See, friend, on this grave with eternal letters how malicious (β[άσ]κανος) Hades snatched Aurelia Tateis from her husband. Envy did not wish her to have the enjoyment of her husband."[90] The grave instead of a bridal chamber and mourning songs for nuptial hymns—these are the cruel abductor's wedding gifts.[91]

Two abducted virgins lie in the same grave, and the text above them upbraids the death god: "O demon, who kills out of envy . . ."[92] That same vice of begrudging another's happiness moved Paul's rivals in Philippi to preach Christ. It is to them and Paul's colleagues in ministry that we turn.

Notes

1. *Greek Anthology* 7.13.

2. This paragraph oversimplifies a complex exegetical situation in Philippians, and I ask for patience, especially from those scholars who have benefitted as I have from the sterling work of Roy Hoover ("The Harpagmos Enigma: A Philological Solution," *HTR* 64 [1971]: 95–119). It is not his method I dispute but his conclusions.

3. Plutarch, *[Lib. ed.]* 11F.

4. Lucian, *Demon.* 7. Statements praising friendship took this form. See Euripides, *El.* 67; Iamblichus, *Vit. Pyth.* 35.259. A particular way of life is praised in this way (Antipater, *Frg.* 63.48) as well as honoring parents (*Gnomologium Vaticanum* 545). See also Lucian, *Anach.* 10: "and the one [athletic victor] among them who succeeds in winning counted equal to the gods (ἰσόθεον νομιζόμενον)." See further Apollonius of Tyana, *Ep.* 44: "Other men regard me as the equal of the gods (ἰσόθεον ἡγουμένων), and some of them even as a god."

5. See the collection of texts in Karlheinz Kost, *Musaios, Hero und Leander: Einleitung, Text, Übersetzung, und Kommentar* (Bonn: Bouvier, 1971), 326–38. For the topic, see Peter Green, *The Argonautika*, Hellenistic Culture and Society 25 (Berkeley: University of California Press, 1997), 286–87; Malcolm Campbell, *A Commentary on Apollonius Rhodius Argonautica III 1–471*, Mnemosyne 141 (Leiden: Brill, 1994), 111. For the motif in imperial prose fiction, see Patricia Rosenmeyer, *The Poetics of Imitation: Anacreon and the Anacreontic Tradition* (Cambridge: Cambridge University Press, 1992), 223; Froma I. Zeitlin, "Living Portraits and Sculpted Bodies in Chariton's Theater of Romance," in *The Ancient Novel and Beyond*, ed. Stelios Panayotakis, Maaike Zimmerman, and Wytse Keulen, Mnemosyne 241 (Leiden: Brill, 2003): 71–83.

6. Plato, *Phaedr.* 255A.

7. Lucian, *Pro imag.* 23–29. For the "equal to god" theme in Homer, see Leah Rissman, *Love as War: Homeric Allusion in the Poetry of Sappho,* Beiträge zur klassischen Philologie 157 (Königstein/Ts.; Hain, 1983), 69–87.

8. Lucian, *Pro imag.* 26.

9. Gerald Hawthorne, "In the Form of God and Equal with God," in *Where Christology Began: Essays on Philippians 2,* ed. Ralph P. Martin and Brian J. Dodd (Louisville: Westminster John Knox, 1998), 97–101. For examples of μορφή as beauty, see Ibycus, *Frg.* 1a 45; Theocritus, *Id.* 23.2; *Greek Anthology* 5.260; 12.127; Bion, *Frg.* 14.5; *Epitaphius Adonis* 31.

10. The so-called Aristotelian interpretation has rightfully met with skepticism. See Hawthorne, "In the Form of God," 98–99.

11. Greek mythology had a favorite story: gorgeous mortal, snatched by divine being, lives with the gods undying and forever young. See Mary K. Lefkowitz, "Seduction and Rape in Greek Myth," in *Consent and Coercion to Sex and Marriage in Ancient and Medieval Societies,* ed. Angeliki E. Laiou (Washington, DC: Dumbarton Oaks Research Library and Collection, 1993), 17–37. See Homer, *Il.* 20.232–35; Lucian, *Charid.* 7; *Greek Anthology* 12.20.

12. And not only in poetry and fiction: see Demosthenes, *[Erot.]* 11: "which in human form possesses a natural beauty worthy of the gods (τὴν τῶν θεῶν ἀξίαν)."

13. *Greek Anthology* 5.15; 12.76. See Daniel H. Garrison, *Mild Frenzy: A Reading of Hellenistic Love Epigram,* Hermes Einzelschriften 41 (Wiesbaden: Steiner, 1978), 37.

14. The centrality of the visual is treated by Nancy Worman in "The Body as Argument: Helen in Four Greek Texts," *Classical Antiquity* 16 (1997): 151–203. See also Simon Goldhill, "The Erotic Experience of Looking," in *The Sleep of Reason: Erotic Experience and Sexual Ethics in Ancient Greece and Rome,* ed. Martha C. Nussbaum and Juha Sihvola (Chicago: University of Chicago Press, 2002), 374–399.

15. Athenaeus, *Deip.* 13.589B.

16. *Greek Anthology* 12.196.

17. For the power of the beautiful Homeric hero, see Rissman, *Love as War,* 69–104. For this theme in the Homeric Hymns, see Ann L. T. Bergren, "The Homeric Hymn to Aphrodite: Tradition and Rhetoric, Praise and Blame," *Classical Antiquity* 8 (1989): 1–41. See further A. W. Bulloch, *Callimachus: The Fifth Hymn,* Cambridge Classical Texts and Commentaries 26 (Cambridge: Cambridge University Press, 1985), 190–91. In addition, see Ovid, *Her.* 4.64: "your beauty has captured my heart (*me tua forma capit*)." Cf. *Greek Anthology* 5.62: "Ah! how many hearts did that once god-like beauty burn to ashes." Heliodorus (*Aeth.* 1.4.3) said it well: "Thus may nobility of appearance and beauty of countenance vanquish even a brigand heart and triumph over the harshest of natures." For divine form as a weapon in later poets, see the texts collected at Kost, *Musaios,* 283.

18. Bernard of Clairvaux (*On the Song of Songs* 45.9) would later exclaim on the basis of Phil 2:6-7: "How beautiful you appear to the angels, Lord Jesus, in the form of God, eternal, begotten before the daystar amid the splendors of heaven, 'the radiant light of God's glory and the perfect copy of his nature,' the unchanging and untarnished brightness of the eternal life? How beautiful you are to me, my Lord even in the very discarding of your beauty" (*On the Song of Songs, II,* trans. Kilian Walsh, Cistercian Fathers Series 7 [Kalamazoo: Cistercian Publications, 1976], 239). Bernard's thought was not entirely new. See, for example, Dioscorus of Aphrodito's praise of a bride: "Longing has marked your loveliness (Πόθος ἤλασε μορφήν)" (*Frg.* 24.8). Text and translation are from Leslie S. B. MacCoull, *Dioscorus of Aphrodito: His Work and World,* Transformation of the Classical Heritage 16 (Berkeley: University of California Press, 1988), 81–82. For other examples, see ibid., 83. Dioscoros possibly is dependent on Sappho, *Frg.* 112.

19. The Modern Greek Version replaces ἁρπαγμός with ἁρπαγή, but it is doubtful that contemporary Greek readers understand here a reference to erotic abduction.

20. Hoover ("Harpagmos Enigma," 112–14) agrees, but it appears not to have occurred to him how neatly this solves the problem.

21. Vettius Valens, *Anthologiarum libri ix* 2.38. The marital destiny of women was a popular topic for the prognostic sciences. In the third century B.C.E., Melampus (Περὶ παλμῶν, 83) studied indications of future events provided by twitches; if a widow's right thumb were thus affected she should expect abduction.

22. See Judith Evans-Grubbs, "Abduction Marriage in Antiquity: A Law of Constantine (*CTh* ix.24.1) and Its Social Context," *JRS* 79 (1989): 59–83.

23. Athenaeus, *Deip.* 13.557A–B.

24. *Apophthegmata* 2.51.

25. Dionysius of Halicarnassus, *Ant. rom.* 2.30.5.

26. Achilles Tatius, *Leuc. Clit.* 2.13.3. Evans-Grubbs ("Abduction Marriage," 70) is doubtful. See *Greek Anthology* 15.19. For the absence of criminality in Hellenistic comedy perhaps as a reflection of social practice, see Daniel H. Garrison, *Sexual Culture in Ancient Greece,* Oklahoma Series in Classical Culture 24 (Norman: University of Oklahoma Press, 2000), 233–36.

27. Basil, *Ep.* 270.

28. See Ovid, *Ars* 1.561, where Bacchus points out to Ariadne the futility of her refusing his advances: "[E]asy it is for a god to be all-powerful (*in facile est omnia posse deo*)."

29. Emily Vermeule, *Aspects of Death in Early Greek Art and Poetry,* Sather Classical Lectures 46 (Berkeley: University of California, 1979), 163–64.

30. Two famous abduction stories are told through the visual arts in Vergina at the tomb of Philipp II, where a wall painting depicts Hades in a chariot snatching Persephone. The second is a necklace featuring Zeus's abduction of Ganymede. Elsewhere in Greece, Pausanius reports abduction scenes in public art; see, for example, *Descr.* 1.3.1; 3.17.3; 3.18.15; 5.10.8. For the popularity of the theme on vases, see Christiane Sourvinou-Inwood, "Erotic Pursuits: Images and Meanings," *JHS* 107 (1987) 131–53; Andrew Stewart, "Rape?" in Ellen D. Reeder, *Pandora: Women in Classical Greece* (Princeton: Trustees of the Walters Art Gallery/Princeton University, 1995), 74–90; H. A. Shapiro, "Eros in Love: Pederasty and Pornography in Greece," in *Pornography and Representation in Greece and Rome,* ed. Amy Richlin (New York: Oxford University Press, 1992), 53–72.

31. See Mary K. Lefkowitz, "'Predatory' Goddesses," *Hesperia* 71 (2002): 325–44.

32. The reader is no doubt wondering about 2 Cor 12:2, 4, where abduction is the originating event of Paul's ministry and clearly not to be disregarded. A similar problem arises in the case of 1 Thess 5:17, which will be treated at some length below. A few remarks about Paul's strange experience must suffice. The abduction scene in 2 Cor 12:1-10 is replete with erotic allusions: a garden, wordless words that are not permitted to be repeated, and most of all there is the thorn (σκόλοψ), which from Artemidorus (*Onir.* 33.1) we learn has erotic signification. Further exploration of this text might take its cues from later Christian writers who thought of the abduction as a moment of inexpressible intimacy that Paul longs to recapture. From this perspective, his weakness might be understood as the effects on his body of longing. This approach accords with the contrast he draws between himself and the "super-apostles": they employ harsh treatments, while he exhibits the traits of the longing lover, which Paul redirects to the Corinthian community.

33. Herodotus (*Hist.* 1.1-5) demythologizes the Cretan abduction and other legendary snatchings by exposing them as feuds over stolen women between ethnic groups. His approach did not catch on. For abduction in ancient Greek and Roman foundation myths, see Philip Hardie, "Another Look at Virgil's Ganymede," in *Classics in Progress: Essays on Ancient Greece and Rome,* ed. T. P. Wiseman, British Academy Centenary Monographs (Oxford: Oxford University Press, 2002), 333–61, esp. 347–50.

34. Strabo, *Geogr.* 10.4.21.

35. Sexual violence appears as mock abduction in the rituals of legitimate weddings. See John H. Oakley and Rebecca H. Sinos, *The Wedding in Ancient Athens,* Wisconsin Studies in Classics (Madison: University of Wisconsin Press, 1993), 32–35.

36. Cretan abduction has no downside for the boy in Athenaeus, *Deip.* 11.782C: "Favorite boys among the Cretans are called 'illustrious.' Eager zeal possessed them to carry off boys; and so, in the eyes of the fair among them, it is a disgrace not to get a lover. Those who have been carried off are said to be 'won over'. They give to the boy thus carried off a cloak, an ox, and a cup; they wear the cloak even when they have grown older, to show that they were once 'illustrious.'"

37. For evidence of a compensatory gift in ancient Gortyna, see Athenaeus, *Deip.* 11.502B. Gifts to Ganymede's father mended the damage, and the young man himself was granted immortality. See *Homeric Hymn to Aphrodite* 202–17. A collection of texts on Zeus's abduction of Ganymede can be found in Campbell, *Commentary on Apollonius Rhodius Argonautica III 1–471,* 102–4.

38. The abducted one is ripped from human society and becomes invisible; see Pindar, *Ol.* 1.45. As a result of abduction, the boy never has an opportunity to make a reputation for himself; see Dio Chrysostom, *Oration* 29.17.

39. For girls, abduction marriage means loss of maidenhood. See Aphrodite Avagianou, *Sacred Marriage in the Rituals of Greek Religion,* European University Studies: Series XV, Classics 54 (Bern: Peter Lang, 1991), 115–43. Negative effects on the young women of Sparta are undetectable in Plutarch's account (*Lyc.* 15.3–5).

40. They would have been indebted to Sappho. For her rejection of erotic seizure in favor of mutuality, see Eva Stehle, *Performance and Gender in Ancient Greece: Nondramatic Poetry in Its Setting* (Princeton: Princeton University Press, 1997), 288–98. Classicists have begun to appreciate the alternative way of loving that Sappho introduced to the tradition. See Ellen Greene, "Subjects, Objects, and Erotic Symmetry in Sappho's Fragments," in *Among Women: From the Homosocial to the Homoerotic in the Ancient World,* ed. Nancy Sorkin Rabinowitz and Lisa Auanger (Austin: University of Texas Press, 2002), 82–105. For evidence of mutuality in love after Sappho, see in the forenamed volume Nancy Sorkin Rabinowitz, "Excavating Women's Homoeroticism in Ancient Greece: The Evidence from Attic Vase Painting," 106–66; and Lisa Auanger, "Glimpses through a Window: An Approach to Roman Female Homoeroticism through Art Historical and Literary Evidence," 211–55.

41. Antonio Corso ("Love as Suffering: The Eros of Thespiae of Praxiteles," *Bulletin of the Institute of Classical Studies* 42 [1997–98]: 63–91) argues that "the depiction of Eros as suffering must have been fashionable in Athens during the first decades of the fourth century bc (65)."

42. Rationalist opponents of superstition, of course, opposed the very idea of divine involvement in so mean an act as abduction. Dionysius of Halicarnassus (*Ant. rom.* 2.19.2), for example, praised Romulus for not allowing the people such foolishness as "the disappearance of deities, such as the Greeks perform in commemorating the rape (ἁρπαγήν) of Persephonê. . . ."

43. *Greek Anthology* 12.64–70, 194; Longus, *Daphn.* 4.17.

44. See Claude Calame, *The Poetics of Eros in Ancient Greece,* trans. Janet Lloyd (Princeton: Princeton University Press, 1999), 21; Monica Silveira Cyrino, *In Pandora's Jar: Lovesickness in Early Greek Poetry* (Lanham, MD: University Press of America, 1995), 3, 10, 57; E. K. Borthwick, ΦΥΛΛΑΣΩ or ΛΑΦΥΣΣΩ? A Note on Two Emendations," *Eranos* 77 (1979): 79–83. See also *Greek Anthology* 12.167, 181. For the lover as victim of abduction, see Paul Murgatroyd, "Amatory Hunting, Fishing and Fowling," *Latomus* 43 (1984): 362–68.

45. Some literary works, including the novels of Longus and Achilles Tatius, begin with description (ἔκφρασις) of a scene or object of art that contains clues for the story's development and ending. See *The Verbal and the Visual: Cultures of Ekphrasis in Antiquity,* ed. Jaś Elsner, *Ramus* 31 (2002).

46. Achilles Tatius, *Leuc. Clit.* 1.1. Translation is by John J. Winkler in *Collected Ancient Greek Novels,* ed. B. P. Reardon (Berkeley: University of California Press, 1989), 176–77.

47. See, for example, CEG 84.

48. Callimachus (*Greek Anthology* 7.80) mourned the death of a friend whose literary works were the one thing "which Hades who seizeth all (ὁ πάντων ἁρπακτής) shall not lay his hand." See further *Griechische Vers-Inschriften* 1:850, 916.

49. *Griechische Vers-Inschriften* 1:810, 1809, 1811.

50. Ibid., 1:372, 872, 93; *Steinepigramme* 16/54/1.

51. *Griechische Vers-Inschriften* 1:965.

52. Bitter: *Griechische Vers-Inschriften* 1:847, 1547; *Steinepigramme* 3/7/9; 16/54/1; 18/18/1. Pitiless: *Griechische Vers-Inschriften* 1:957, 1054. Unjust: *Griechische Vers-Inschriften* 1:126. Rejoicing in tears: *Griechische Vers-Inschriften* 1:1154. Murky: *Griechische Vers-Inschriften* 1:123. Life depriving: *Griechische Vers-Inschriften* 1:845. Insatiable: *Griechische Vers-Inschriften* 1:975.

53. *Griechische Vers-Inschriften* 1:293, 645, 856, 962. For the envious Hades, see Richmond Lattimore, *Themes in Greek and Latin Epitaphs* (Urbana: University of Illinois Press, 1962), 147, 276.

54. *Griechische Vers-Inschriften* 1:659, 780, 885, 1402; *Greek Anthology* 7.557.

55. Fate: *Griechische Vers-Inschriften* 1:1815; The Demon: *Griechische Vers-Inschriften* 1:362, 1439, 2029, 2034 (here identified as Moira); a demon: *Griechische Vers-Inschriften* 1:650, 729, 1883, 1938; Disease: *Griechische Vers-Inschriften* 1:241, 704, 1099, 1467; *Steinepigramme* 1.56; *Greek Anthology* 7.711; Death: *Griechische Vers-Inschriften* 1:856, 1547; *Steinepigramme* 3.322; Nature: *Griechische Vers-Inschriften* 1:1011; Charon: *Greek Anthology* 7.603; 7.671; Heat of the sun: *Griechische Vers-Inschriften* 1:1703; Nymphs (that is, death by drowning) *Griechische Vers-Inschriften* 1:952, 1595, 1897; *Greek Anthology* 7.518. See Judith M. Barringer, *Divine Escorts: Nereids in Archaic and Classical Greek Art* (Ann Arbor: University of Michigan Press, 1995), 95–109.

56. *Steinepigramme* 20/15/2. See also *Griechische Vers-Inschriften* 1:583, 705, 858. Cf. *Greek Anthology* 8.100: "Listen Alexandria, Philagrius has lost his beauty, a beauty not inferior to his rational soul, and envy hath carried off Caesarius yet in his youth." For Moira and Envy together, see *Griechische Vers-Inschriften* 1:783. For Τύχη as envious, see *Griechische Vers-Inschriften* 1:899. See Lattimore, *Themes in Greek and Latin Epitaphs*, 51, 145–48.

57. Aristotle, *Eth. nic.* 2.7.15; *Eth. Eud.* 3.7.1; Basil, *Homilia de invidia* 31.373.

58. Katherine M. D. Dunbabin and M. W. Dickie, "*Invida Rumpantur Pectora*: The Iconography of *Phthonos/Invidia* in Graeco-Roman Art," *JAC* 26 (1983): 10: "The terms *phthonos* and *baskania*, with their Latin counterparts *invidia* and *livor*, refer essentially to a state best characterized as one of grudging. . . . The wish to see the other deprived of these goods is implicit in the notion of grudging; the *phthoneros* therefore looks with ill-will upon the object of his *phthonos*. He is therefore regularly thought of and spoken of as malicious, and having a bent for evil."

59. See, for example, *Griechische Vers-Inschriften* 1:1282: "If Moira snatched him, she did not subdue him (εἰ δέ ἑ Μοῖρα ἥρπασεν, οὐκ ἐδάμασσε)" (my translation).

60. In the rare instance when an older person is saved by abduction, allusion to Ganymede is avoided. See, for example, *Griechische Vers-Inschriften* 1:1486.

61. *Steinepigramme* 16/46/1 (my translation). Cf. *Griechische Vers-Inschriften* 1:1765. Public speakers learned to comfort the family of youth who died suddenly. Like Ganymede and other abductees of old, the deceased was "loved by the gods." See Dionysius of Halicarnassus, *[Rhet.]* 6.5. For the popularity of the Ganymede abduction in Roman funerary art, see Hardie, "Another Look at Virgil's Ganymede," 341–42.

62. *Griechische Vers-Inschriften* 1:1318. For Ganymede in other inscriptions, see the references at *Steinepigramme* 16/23/6.

63. *Griechische Vers-Inschriften* 1:1993.

64. *Steinepigramme* 14/2/4 (my translation).

65. This is essentially Abraham Malherbe's proposal, although he does not look to inscriptional evidence; see his *The Letters to the Thessalonians: A New Translation with Introduction and Commentary*, AB 32B (New York: Doubleday, 2000), 276–77. The same approach might be

taken to the verb ἄγω (and its cognates), which occurs frequently on grave markers, underscoring the deceased's separation from the living. The dead are led away: *Griechische Vers-Inschriften* 1:846, 981, 1013, 1122, 1975; or, they are led away to Hades: *Griechische Vers-Inschriften* 1:114, 554, 635. The dead are abducted *and* led away: *Griechische Vers-Inschriften*: 1:1159, 2034. Complaints echo those made against abduction: *Griechische Vers-Inschriften* 1:729, 815, 1470. In 1 Thess 4:13—5:11, Paul uses ἄγω three times (4:14, 17; 5:10), in each instance combining it with a word signifying personal connection, perhaps against the grain of its sepulchral connotation.

66. Sleep (τῶν κοιμωμένων, 4:13): *Griechische Vers-Inschriften* 1:235, 455, 647, 1120, 1332, 1360, 2029. Exhortation to cease grieving (ἵνα μὴ λυπῆσθε, 4:13): *Griechische Vers-Inschriften* 1:1002; 1157; 1275; 2003. Left behind (οἱ λοιποί, 4:13; 5:6 and οἱ περιλοιπόμενοι, 4:15, 17): *Griechische Vers-Inschriften* 1:822, 978, 1164, 1209, 1212, 1950, 2029. Dashed hopes (οἱ μὴ ἔχοντες ἐλπίδα, 4:13): *Griechische Vers-Inschriften* 1:774, 775, 1629. The living (οἱ ζῶντες, 4:15): *Griechische Vers-Inschriften* 1:1600, 1804, 1921. To go first, that is, die before another family member (οὐ μὴ φθάσωμεν, 4:15): *Greek Anthology* 7.378. Air (εἰς ἀέρα, 4:14): *Griechische Vers-Inschriften* 1:11, 881, 1031, 1169. Safety (ἀσφάλεια, 5:3) *Griechische Vers-Inschriften* 1:1699, 1539, 1918. Suddenly (αἰφνίδιος, 5:3): *Griechische Vers-Inschriften* 1:851, 853, 858, 1130, 1165. Destruction (ὄλεθρος, 5:3): *Griechische Vers-Inschriften* 1:10, 17, 36, 42, 53, 73, 217. Pain (ὠδίν, 5:3): *Griechische Vers-Inschriften* 1:684, 846, 873, 1024. Impossible to flee (οὐ μὴ ἐκφύγωσιν, 5:3): *Griechische Vers-Inschriften* 1:29, 556, 624, 688, 851. A divinity's anger (εἰς ὀργήν): *Griechische Vers-Inschriften* 1:965, 1040, 1154, 1275.

67. *Griechische Vers-Inschriften* 1:846, 854, 981, 1013, 1122, 1975; *Steinepigramme* 2/9/33; 3/2/67; 11/8/3.

68. *Griechische Vers-Inschriften* 1:729, 815, 817, 1159, 1470, 1590, 1683, 2034.

69. See *Griechische Vers-Inschriften* 1:935, an inscription possibly of the first century C.E. found in Thessaloniki. See also *Griechische Vers-Inschriften* 1:804, 947, 1470, 1553, 1824. Also having both nuptial and funereal connotations is "meeting" (ἀπάντησιν, 1 Thess 4.14); see *Greek Anthology* 7.188; *Griechische Vers-Inschriften* 1:1431; *Steinepigramme* 3/2/66. For the deceased encountering the insuperable power of a death god, see *Griechische Vers-Inschriften* 1:1476, 1585.

70. *Griechische Vers-Inschriften* 1:636. See also *Griechische Vers-Inschriften* 1:955: "The demon envious of life . . . ."

71. *Griechische Vers-Inschriften* 1:847 (my translation).

72. *Griechische Vers-Inschriften* 1:949; 1418, 2028; *Steinepigramme* 1/1/11.

73. For the envy motif in grave inscriptions, see the literature collected at *Steinepigramme* 9/2/1.

74. *Griechische Vers-Inschriften* 1:1114, 1165, 1941, 1969, 2021.

75. *Steinepigramme* 10/3/3.

76. Ibid., 2/9/33; see also 2/6/18; 4/12/6; 16/23/10; *Griechische Vers-Inschriften* 1:1900; *Greek Anthology* 7.343.

77. *Griechische Vers-Inschriften* 1:1648, 1925.

78. *Greek Anthology* 7.13. Cf. *Griechische Vers-Inschriften* 1:1483.

79. *Griechische Vers-Inschriften* 1:583.

80. Ibid., 1:401, 1038, 1238, 1245; *Steinepigramme* 4/2/11; *Greek Anthology* 7.557.

81. *Steinepigramme* 1/12/15.

82. *Griechische Vers-Inschriften* 1:362 (my translation). Equally brief is *Steinepigramme* 9/5/89; see also 4/16/3, 9/5/42. Cf. *Greek Anthology* 7.308, 389, 481.

83. *Griechische Vers-Inschriften* 1:975.

84. Ibid., 1:1071, 1587, 1588, 1589; 1590, 1591; *Steinepigramme* 11/7/10.

85. *Griechische Vers-Inschriften* 1:1598; *Steinepigramme* 2/14/12; *Greek Anthology* 7.371.

86. *Griechische Vers-Inschriften* 1:780, 953; *Steinepigramme* 4/8/2.

87. *Steinepigramme* 4/7/5.

88. *Griechische Vers-Inschriften* 1:1799; *Steinepigramme* 1/12/13; 16/31/75.

89. *Griechische Vers-Inschriften* 1:1592.

90. *Steinepigramme* 16/45/11; see further 4/11/1; 16/43/3; 16/45/5.

91. *Griechische Vers-Inschriften* 1:856, 947, 1130, 2038; *Steinepigramme* 16/23/12. One of the most popular themes was "grave instead of bridal chamber": see *Steinepigramme* 2/14/12; 16/23/4; *Griechische Vers-Inschriften* 1:966, 1470, 1991; *Greek Anthology* 7.568.

92. *Griechische Vers-Inschriften* 1:1944.

5

Not Eaters of the People

Beware the dogs.[1]

POLITICS

There was something about four of Paul's co-workers that won his respect and earned his endorsement. "Help them," Paul writes in Phil 4:2 concerning Euodia and Syntyche. On behalf of Epaphroditus in 2:29 he asks the church to "accept him in the Lord with all joy." In the same verse, the phrase "hold such ones as these in honor" commends both Epaphroditus and Timothy. Philippians 3:17 looks back to these two men and anticipates Euodia and Syntyche: "Brothers and sisters, join in imitating me, and observe those who live according to the example you have in us." Evidently, Paul was keenly interested in the community's selection of leaders.

The aim of this chapter is to discover what might have qualified these individuals, whose social status markers were very likely quite low, for ministry in the church. Paul's own credentials also were questionable: readers encounter him as a metaphorical slave (1:1), a prisoner (1:7, 13-14), and under threat of suffering shame (1:20).[2] In this chapter and the next, my thesis is that the apostle's longing for the community (1:8), which mirrored Christ's longing for the world (2:6-8), determined the quality he desired the Philippian church to seek in its leaders. In Paul's politics, it will be suggested, longing for communion legitimated leaders, even in the face of low social status and power. Love and politics mingle in the community's selection of leaders.

Philippians is full of political terms from the history of ancient democracy that interact with the erotic motifs identified in the previous chapters to produce a vision of leadership whose chief characteristic is longing for communion. One term is especially significant in this regard. In Phil 1:27, Paul exhorts his readers to "act politically (πολιτεύεσθε) worthily of the gospel of Christ."[3]

Unfortunately, translations of πολιτεύεσθε such as "live your life" (NRSV), or "conduct yourselves" (NASB and NIV) do not make available to readers of English texts Paul's portrayal of the church as a community of political actors.[4] The King James Version (following Tyndale's translation, which was itself working with the Vulgate's *conversamini*) is superior: "Only let your conversation be as it becometh the gospel of Christ." Πολιτεύεσθαι might therefore be paraphrased "to participate in the formation of the city's policies and plans through speaking and listening." The background for this term is the practice of citizen action in the assembly (ἐκκλησία), the deliberative and legislative body of ancient democracies.[5] Such political participation was a contested topic in the philosophical schools, and this debate liberates πολιτεύεσθε from modern translations' narrowed focus on the moral formation of the individual.[6] Nevertheless, it only partially explains use of the term in 1:27.

So, in 1:27 Paul makes a special point of orienting his audience toward a political self-understanding: what goes on in the church at Philippi is to be imagined in analogy to the highly participatory workings of the popular assemblies of democratic governments. But it is even more noteworthy that Paul's exhortation has to do with the *manner* of the community's political engagement, as the adverbial phrase "worthily of the gospel of Christ" indicates.[7] Paul directs his hearers to evaluate their interaction from a particular perspective, that of the "gospel of Jesus Christ." Presumably, the "gospel of Jesus Christ" in 1:27 refers to Christ's refusal to abduct humans and his desire for communion with them as narrated in 2:6-11.[8] If "the gospel" is shorthand for the story of Christ's longing, then the Christ Hymn is a political supplement to the erotic interpretation I offered earlier in chapter 4.[9] In these verses, the longing Christ is the model of political leadership for the church as he takes on the form of a slave and then empties himself in desire for his beloved.

The Christ Hymn's political relevance is strongly suggested by ἡγέομαι in 2:7, which is usually, and quite correctly, translated "regard." But it also meant "go before" or "lead the way." Indeed, the noun form (ὁ ἡγεμών) meant "leader." The topic of leadership is also suggested in v. 7, where Christ, in his imitation of human appearance and form, looks very much like the figure of the demagogue, or popular leader, whose identification with the masses and whose efforts to broaden enfranchisement earned him the affection of the people and condemnation by the elites in ancient cities.[10] In 2:11, the topic of leadership is raised yet again in the confession of Jesus as *kyrios*, a title full of social power in everyday speech but so radically redefined, as I suggested in chapter 1, in its application to Jesus, whose death from desire for communion prompts all voices, even God's, to acknowledge him as Lord.[11]

In light of the politics of longing hinted at in 1:27 and narrated in 2:6-11, the significance of "father" (significantly, the *last word* of the Hymn) requires comment. Like "Lord," it quite rightly raises suspicion that Paul used the story of Christ to support patriarchal authority both at the theological level and in his own ministry. Regrettably, that is, in fact, the way the church, with some very important exceptions, has interpreted Phil 2:6-11: as a story of Jesus' humility and obedience to the sovereign Father whose right to command issues from his status as creator of the universe. But the error of this dominant interpretation is nowhere more apparent than in the ending of the Christ Hymn where sovereign power is transferred to Jesus along with the name "Lord." Jesus' narrative of longing desire from that moment on controls the title. Similarly, the agreement among "the tongues" that Jesus is Lord controls what "father" means in 2:11. That is, God's reputation (δόξα, 2:11) as father depends on universal acknowledgement that Jesus' longing for communion is constitutive of lordship: to love an absent other *is* sovereign power. In the circumstance of the father's dependence on the son, then, the usual notion of ruling power disappears (that is, patri*archy* dies), and "father" refers only to the other great complex of ideas gathered under that name in antiquity: the one who in death gives an inheritance yet lives past death in the future of offspring. Significantly, the Philippians are named "children of God (τέκνα τοῦ θεοῦ)" in 2:15.

ENVY AND LONGING

In addition to Paul's weaving *erōs* and politics together, there is another intriguing pattern in Philippians: Paul consistently praises some leaders while offering only opprobrium for others. In Phil 1:15, we read of leaders who were of quite a different stripe than those persons Paul promotes: "Some proclaim Christ from envy and rivalry, but others from goodwill." Beginning with that verse Paul exhorts the church to reject the rivals and dwells on their negative characteristics (3:2, 18-19). He does this, I believe, to emphasize the positive aspects of those whom he recommends. And what is the chief fault of the rivals? What Paul says about them first, that their preaching Christ is motivated by envy (διὰ φθόνον, 1:15), he reiterates throughout the letter and ends with a vituperative flourish in his infamous phrase "enemies of the cross of Christ" (3:19).

It should be acknowledged, however, that Pauline interpreters have not connected the enmity motif in 3:18 with the rivals' envy in 1:15, as I am proposing. They explain enmity toward the cross in a way unrelated to the motif of resentment; instead, they appeal to Protestant theology's touchstone doctrine of sovereign grace. In other words, the opponents of Paul are enemies of Christ's cross because they refuse to be the humble object of God's freely given salvation. Karl Barth writes:

> And "the cross of Christ" is . . . the strongest expression for the radical opposition of Christian truth, not so much to moral license and the pursuit of earthly, sensual pleasure, as rather to the religious and ethical presumptuousness that seeks to achieve what man is utterly incapable of achieving, what can only be given to him in faith. Those who would seek to get around this barrier, who resist the power of Christ's resurrection that seeks to drive them into fellowship of his sufferings, who will *not* walk the way of poverty described in verses 4-14, the way of being for Christ's sake *not* holy, *not* righteous, *not* perfect—these are 'enemies of the cross of Christ'.[12]

Barth's cross reveals God's condemnation of human desire for self-transcendence and illustrates what life could and should be—voluntary submission to God. For Barth, whose influence on New Testament exegetes has been great, the cross in Pauline thought is a "barrier" that its enemies seek to "get around."[13]

My proposal runs counter to Barth's reading. While I too think that the "cross of Christ" in Phil 3:18 looks backward to the Christ Hymn (2:8; cf. 3:10), I have suggested that 2:6-11 is a story of Christ's longing for communion with humanity. His cross signifies a passion that empties him unto death, as *pothos* did to so many others in ancient poetry. Thus, to be an enemy of the cross is to oppose Christ's longing and to make war against the political implications of this emotion in the church. Specifically, it is to oppose Paul and his colleagues, whose sole qualification for leadership is their imitation of Christ's emptying. Unnamed and in the shadows, at first tolerated by Paul (1:15-18) but finally excoriated (3:2 and 3:18-19), the opponents are outwardly similar to Paul and his colleagues, since they preach Christ. Nevertheless, they begrudge the community its benefits in Christ and oppose longing as a trait of church leaders and the ethos of the community. They are therefore identical to Paul and his colleagues as missionary workers yet radically opposed to them with respect to their emotions. Erstwhile friends, the Greek tradition forcefully taught, make the worst enemies.

There is an even deeper level of complexity in the letter's broken parallel between Paul and his opponents, since the emotions of envy and longing were themselves both similar and dissimilar to one another. Both *phthonos* and *pothos* originated in *erōs* and thus bore a likeness to one another.[14] And like *pothos*, *phthonos* is therefore a kind of grief.[15] Most importantly, the grief coursing through each emotion melted innards and wasted bodies.[16] Just as tears, for example, were thought to be the liquefaction of the mourner's face, watery eyes revealed to those trained in such matters, the physiognomists, an envious disposition.[17] Church writers harvested these insights into envy's imitation of longing as this passage of Gregory of Nyssa illustrates:

> The secret sickness is evidenced, even while it appears to be hidden, by manifest signs about the face. The deadly effects of the things denied often become the marks of one shriveled up by reason of envy; eyes withered, sunk in the hollow of shrunken eyelids, knitted eyebrows, the shape of bones shewing through the flesh.[18]

Ocular melting, whose result was known as "hollow eye," signaled envy but also lovesickness and longing.[19] Thus, it is plausible that the similarity of envy and longing owing to their common origin in *erōs* accounts for the likeness of the Christ-preaching rivals to Paul and his co-workers in 1:15-18.[20]

So what was the rhetorical advantage of the sameness and difference of envy and longing? In Philippians, envy functions as a foil. Paul contrasts the envy of the rivals with his and his co-workers' positive regard for the church. This strategy cohered with the way opponents were often conceptualized in the agonistic culture in which he and his readers lived.[21] Envy had been a popular topic ever since Pindar complained of the resentment of rival speakers ruining not only the renown of the athletes he lauded but his own reputation for praise poetry. Later, Attic orators labored to call attention to their accomplishments in and for the city without provoking resentment.[22] In architectural contexts, mosaics near houses or inscriptions on columns warned off envious persons from casting the evil eye on owners.[23] And envy even moved the gods and goddesses of death to snatch mortals to the underworld, as we saw in the last chapter.[24] In short, envy was everywhere aiming to ruin every good thing, and everyone knew it.[25] To promote himself and his co-workers in the estimation of the Philippian church, Paul took full advantage of envy's omnipresence and omnipotence.

If we are fully to appreciate Paul's rhetorical strategy, however, we must observe that ancient *phthonos* differs from modern envy in two ways. First, readers will recall from the previous chapter that resentment rather than mere coveting was at the heart of ancient envy.[26] It was not only that you have what I want and so I envy you. Rather, it is also the case that I don't want you to have what you have. I begrudge your prosperity, fame, happiness, and so on. The second difference is that envy was conceptualized as a disease of friendship arising only among those who are similar to each other.[27] Envy was a fault of familiarity. This commonplace idea helped Paul negotiate the difficulty that the objects of his scorn in Philippians were in fact his fellow missionaries, who were, at least outwardly, very much like himself and those colleagues he recommends to the church. Paul asks his readers to think of the opponents as competitors, workers (ἐργάται) of the same craft in pursuit of public recognition.[28] Paul's invention of a milieu of resentment accounts for the letter's athletic imagery (1:27, 30; 3:13-14; 4:3), which in Greek society reflects competition for recognition. It also explains why Paul writes in the language of honors sought and honors bestowed (1:10-11, 20, 26; 2:9-11, 13, 15; 3:3-6, 19-21; 4:1, 3, 8-9, 19-20). Finally, the backdrop of envy clarifies the letter's emphasis on progress (1:12, 25; 3:12), the very thing that was most certain to provoke resentment in less successful competitors.[29]

It must be said Paul does nothing innovative when he portrays his rivals as envious, and even when he labels them "enemies." Ancient authors often quoted or alluded to Hesiod's observation about rivalry, how it plagued those of the same profession: "potter at potter doth rage."[30] Hesiod's line reveals that enmity and friendship are not dichotomous.[31] The enmity that envy inevitably generated arises not between strangers but between close relations or workers in the same craft. Professionals in various fields were encouraged to resist Hesiod's dismal pronouncement about rage against co-workers. Hippocrates, for example, whose term for coworker (συνεργός) was the same as Paul's in Phil 2:25 and 4:3, urged doctors to resist envying one another: "Physicians who meet in consultation must never quarrel, or jeer at one another. For I will assert upon oath, a physician's reasoning should never be jealous (φθονήσειεν) of another."[32] Less optimistic, Plutarch doesn't waste his breath on politicians who, without exception, begrudge the success of others: "a government which has not had to bear with envy (φθόνον) or jealous rivalry (ζῆλον) or contention (φιλονεικίαν)—emotions most productive of enmity (ἔχθρας γονιμώτατα πάθη)—has not hitherto existed."[33] What provoked such envious feelings among workers in the same field? The answer is not surprising: success, public recognition, and praise.[34] Lucian said it well: "Generally speaking, slander is most often directed against a man who is in favour (ὁ τιμώμενος) and on this account is viewed with envy (ἐπίθονος) by those he has put behind him."[35] The envy motif thus served Paul very well, since it was widely accepted as an explanation of conflict and opposition among those who, outwardly at least, were very similar. This frequently expressed idea is important to keep in mind when we examine Paul's characterization of his missionary rivals as "enemies of the cross of Christ" in 3:18.

A further advantage of claiming to be the slandered victim of envy was the cover it provided for self-praise or encomiastic speeches for clients.[36] There was a conflicted attitude toward envy: if one is envied it is good, but if one envies it is bad.[37] Like others in the history of oratory, Paul inoffensively praises himself and those whom he recommends (Timothy, Epaphroditus, Euodia, and Synthyche) by alluding to their status as victims of envy.[38] The idea here is this: the fact that my foes envy and speak ill of me is proof of my own success and worth. To be envied is a sign of good fortune.[39] Or, as Pindar put it, "on every man falleth the burden of envy for his merit."[40]

So envy imitated longing in its wasting effects on the body. It was a disease of friendship and a perennial problem among workers of the same craft, and ancient audiences were accustomed to hearing orators contrasting themselves with envious rivals. Keeping these observations about ancient envy in mind, we turn to Phil 1:15-18, where Paul introduces the reader to two types of leaders. They differ with regard to their contrasting motivations for ministry: "on the one hand some on account of envy and strife (διὰ φθόνον καὶ ἔριν), on the other hand some on account of positive regard (δι' εὐδοκίαν) preach Christ." Envy paired with strife had a long history within political communities, and it is in this discourse that Paul situates the opponents.[41]

The motivation of the second group of missionaries was quite different. Instead of resentment they display εὐδοκία, one of several antonyms of envy that occur in the letter. The word meant something like "well-regarding" or "respect."[42] In addition to respect, love characterizes the motivations of the second group. An interesting feature of this love is its relationship to the recognition of Paul as a legitimate leader: to love Paul seems to be a matter of perceiving that he has been "placed for the defense of the gospel."[43] Even more intriguing is the double meaning of κεῖμαι. It generally meant "I am placed, set, or appointed," but it might also have a sepulchral sense, since it was one of the most common words in grave inscriptions: "here I lie."[44] Based on the double meaning of κεῖμαι, there are two ways of reading 1:16. Either one regards, as the envious missionaries do, Paul's imprisonment and enforced silence as metaphorical death, if not in fact an impending execution, or one sees his placement by God as a preacher even though and precisely because his body has been laid out for burial. In other words, either he is good as dead and therefore useless as a proclaimer or, as those on his side perceive through their love of him, his dying body proclaims Christ.

These two ways of reading Paul are transferred to two differing ways of preaching in 1:18, where Christ is said to be proclaimed either "in pretense" or in "truth." Envious persons were noted for the use of deceptive, hypocritical speech.[45] The vice list in Rom 1:29, for example, links envy and insincere speech in a typical fashion.[46] Moreover, in 1:17 Paul exposes the rival's mockery of his imprisonment. There the Greek text (οἰόμενοι θλῖψιν ἐγείρειν τοῖς δεσμοῖς μου) has nuances very difficult to bring into English. First, the diphthong that begins and ends οἰόμενοι is one of the vocalizations employed with disturbing repetition in traditional laments for the dead.[47] Another nuance also pertains to ritualized mourning; the verb ἐγείρειν indicates the purpose of lament—to arouse or to stimulate in the soul of the living emotions commensurate with the destruction of a loved one. In other words, when taken together οἱ and ἐγείρειν add up to keening. It would appear, then, that Paul's opponents are far too eager to lament his death.[48] How does their premature mourning relate to envy? We know from Plutarch that the envious had just such a predilection for lamenting successful people at their demise.[49] Paul returned the insult in 3:18 (κλαίων) calling attention once again to the opponents' envy-motivated speech.

TIMOTHY, EPAPHRODITUS, AND ENVIOUS RIVALS

So, either Paul was a walking corpse signifying nothing or, even as a dying, mute body, he emboldened the preaching of others (1:14) and without words magnified Christ (1:20). Yet Paul was not the only leader in Philippians with ambiguous credentials. Timothy and Epaphroditus were missionaries as unlikely as the fettered and silenced apostle himself. Admittedly, reconstruction of their social status requires a bit of the "mirror reading" that I will criticize below in connection Euodia and Syntyche, but it is very tempting to think that Paul's exhortation in 2:29 that the church "hold such ones as these in honor" suggests that both Timothy and Epaphroditus bore markers indicating low social status.

Timothy's status is the more difficult of the two to determine. In 1 Cor 16:11, Paul warns the community not to "count [Timothy] as a nothing (ἐξουθενήσῃ)." The upper classes employed this term to demean persons of lower social and economic status.[50] It might have been Timothy's age that threatened his exercise of leadership in the Corinthian church, since an allusion to his youth can be detected in Phil 2:22: "you know his character, for as a child with his father he served (ἐδούλευσεν) with me for the gospel." Note also that Paul and Timothy are both pictured as slaves, and their common servitude mitigates the impression of subordination implied by a father–son relationship. If this is the case, Timothy's youth, if that is the problem, has been surpassed by a more serious objection to his leadership: slavery. Servitude normally was incompatible with leadership.[51] Here, however, Paul turns it into a legitimating factor, since the young, metaphorical slave Timothy in his ministry reproduces the story of Christ's leadership in Phil 2:6-11. Also, Timothy is ἰσόψυχος (2:20) with Paul; this adjective is reminiscent of Paul's common innards with Christ in 1:8. If Paul shares emotions with Christ, and Timothy is "equally souled" with Paul, then Timothy and Christ too have a common disposition. Finally, Paul says that Timothy does not seek his own things but the things of Christ; this sounds much like "have this mind among you" as does also "he is genuinely concerned" (2:21).

Epaphroditus's social standing at first seems clear: he is a described as a slave (λειτουργός) provided by the Philippians for Paul's need, or possibly his use depending on the translation of χρεία in 2:25. Yet, because Paul had applied the *metaphor* of slavery to himself and Timothy in 1:1 and just before in 2:22, it is possible that he does the same with respect to Epaphroditus. That Epaphroditus seems to be functioning as Paul's slave, not Christ's, speak against the metaphorical interpretation, however. In either case, the slavery motif still links Epaphroditus to the Christ Hymn just as it had Timothy.

Christ and Epaphroditus share something else: weakness, or sickness. The four verses (2:26-28, 30) characterizing the latter's illness and its consequences give a puzzling emphasis to the matter, which might be explained if Epaphroditus's weakness is seen from the community's perspective. They, after all, sent him to work—not to fall ill. In these verses Paul hints at what some in the community might have asserted, that Epaphroditus was a failure.

The exact nature of the illness requires further investigation, since there is lexical evidence that Epaphroditus's longing for the Philippians played a key role in its onset. Modern translations make it seem as if the illness was one thing and Epaphroditus's longing for the church and distress over his separation from the community was quite another. Thus, the NRSV translates 2:26 as "for he was longing for all of you, and has been distressed because you heard that he was ill." Yet the grammatical construction of ἐπειδή paired with διότι requires a different reading. The verse in Greek is this: ἐπειδὴ ἐπιποθῶν ἦν πάντας ὑμᾶς καὶ ἀδημονῶν, διότι ἠκούσατε ὅτι ἠσθένησεν. A better translation would be "since (ἐπειδή) he was longing for you all and deeply distressed, for that reason (διότι) you heard that he had fallen ill."[52] It was not the case, as the NRSV indicates, that Epaphroditus became distressed because the community heard that he was ill. Rather, in Paul's account, which of course served his rhetorical purposes, Epaphroditus longed for the church at Philippi and was distressed over his separation from it. These emotions, which took a toll on his body, stand behind the news the community received that Epaphroditus had fallen ill.

This revised translation has the additional benefit of relating the two participles ἐπιποθῶν and ἀδημονῶν to each other. The first term "longing" has been extensively treated in earlier chapters and will not be commented on here except to remind the reader once again of its association with lovesickness and its unseen presence in the narrative of the Christ Hymn.[53] The second participle, ἀδημονῶν, indicates that Paul characterizes Epaphroditus's illness as homesickness, a form of longing.[54] Failing to obtain what one longs for gives rise to ἀδημονία.[55] This is especially the case in erotic contexts.[56] Although an emotion, it was also a physical ailment.[57] The symptoms of ἀδημονία include depression, grief, silence, listlessness, indifference, perplexity, and insomnia.[58] Most importantly, ἀδημονία was associated with dissolution of the flesh.[59] These glosses on ἀδημονία suggest that Paul folds Epaphroditus's story (which outwardly looks like a failure) into the narrative of the Christ Hymn, as well as into his own ministry, since the ἐπιποθῶν of 2:26 repeats the ἐπιποθῶ in Phil 1:8. And there is another feature of the Christ Hymn in Epaphroditus's story: both his illness close to death (παραπλήσιον θανάτῳ, 2:27) and his coming to the point of death (μέχρι θανάτου, 2:30) imitate Christ's obedience to the point of death in 2:8.[60] Just as Christ and Paul long for communion, so does Epaphroditus, even at the cost of their lives.

Not only does Paul recommend Timothy and Epaphroditus in erotic language reminiscent of the Christ Hymn and its surrounding exhortations; in 1:28-30 he also reintroduces the rivals as examples of envious behavior. In 1:28, he applies athletic imagery to the rivals; the community is not to be frightened by "those who lay against (τῶν ἀντικειμένων)." The envious were often cast in the role of antagonists, whose aim was to spoil others' success, happiness, and reputation or, as in 1:29, to ruin the reception of a gift (ὑμῖν ἐχαρίσθη) from God.[61] Athletic imagery occurs again in 1:30, where Paul informs the church that the community shares in his struggle (τὸν αὐτὸν ἀγῶνα ἔχοντες).

What was this gift to the community that the opponents resented? It is expressed in the substantive phrase τὸ ὑπὲρ Χριστοῦ, which might woodenly be translated "the being for Christ."[62] It is not entirely clear what this "being for Christ" was. As if he were aware of the opacity of such an expression,

Paul illumines this phrase with two articular infinitives. The first ("to believe in him") is relatively unproblematic and requires no further comment. The second (τὸ ὑπὲρ αὐτοῦ πάσχειν) is more difficult to understand. Interpreters have assumed that Paul refers here to persecution for the preaching of Christ or for being a Christian. There is reason to believe, however, that this phrase refers to the community's longing for communion with Christ (cf. ἀπεκδεχόμεθα in 3:20).[63] If this is the case, then Paul's point in 1:28-30 comes into sharper focus. Here he characterizes belief in Christ and longing for him as God's gift of salvation (understood as preservation of political community), which the opponents begrudge and seek to diminish by calling "destruction."[64]

Envy subtly makes itself known again in the exhortations of 2:1-4. Although Pindar thought that envy was a better emotion than pity, others after him regarded the two opposed to one another in moral value.[65] Envy's opposition to pity suggests that the former is a tacit emotion in 2:1 (εἴ τις σπλάγχνα καὶ οἰκτιρμοί). In 2:3, we find ἐριθεία, which Paul had already associated with φθόνος and ἔρις in 1:15-17. Employing the next term κενοδοξία was a clever move on Paul's part, since the κεν of κενοδοξία anticipates the ἐκένωσεν of the Christ Hymn (2:7). Early in Greek literature, it was recognized that the envious person has an empty mind.[66] As for the δόξα half of κενοδοξία, Plutarch brings out the connection between envy and the desire for glory:

> Now the presence of envy, attended by malice and hostility (φθόνος τοίνυν μετὰ βασκανίας καὶ δυσμενείας), is not a good thing for any undertaking, but it stands in the way of all that is honourable; and it is the very worst associate and counsellor for one that would listen to a lecture, inasmuch as it makes what is profitable to be vexatious, unpleasing, and unacceptable, because envious persons (τοὺς φθονοῦντας) are pleased with anything rather than with the good points of a discourse. Now the man that is stung by the wealth, or repute, or beauty possessed by another, is merely envious (φθονερός); for he is depressed by the good fortune of others; but one who feels discontentment at an excellent discourse is vexed by what is for his own good. . . . Now while envy in other matters is engendered by certain untrained and evil dispositions of a man, the envy that is directed against a speaker is the offspring of an unseasonable desire for repute (φιλοδοξίας) and a dishonest ambition (φιλοτιμίας ἀδίκου).[67]

Finally, 2:4 speaks of selfish behavior (τὰ ἑαυτῶν ἕκαστος σκοποῦντες), one of envy's most vicious companions since the days of Pindar.[68] In 2:21, Paul reiterates this motif to highlight why the Philippian church ought to receive Timothy. His character is very different.

Allusions to envy occur also after the Christ Hymn in 2:14-15. Isocrates notes how envious persons grumble, carp, and find fault with those who are fortunate and successful.[69] The term μῶμος ("censure") is especially important in articulating this aspect of envy, for, as one scholar has aptly remarked, "μῶμος is the voice of φθόνος."[70] Philippians 2:15 attempts to insulate the Philippians from envy's bite by describing them as τέκνα θεοῦ ἄμωμα ("blameless children of God"). It also alludes to the physical consequences of envy on the body in the phrase "twisted and perverse (σκολιᾶς καὶ διαστρεμμένης) generation."[71] It was widely believed that envy contorted the human body.[72] Physiognomists refined this bit of common wisdom into a diagnostic tool: "If you see the shoulders droop and adhere to the chest, judge for the owner envy, wicked deeds and evil."[73] Lucian describes a painting by Apelles of Ephesus of the female figure of slander: "She is conducted by a pale ugly man (ὠχρὸς καὶ ἄμορφος) who has a piercing eye and looks as if he had wasted away in long illness; he may be supposed to be Envy."[74] Dio Chrysostom describes Hesiod's craftsmen, their rivalries, and how the *sophos* is unlike them: "still, not even so will he behave like the potters and joiners and bards, nor will he ever be warped (καμφθήσεται) through want or dishonor or change his own character, becoming a toady and cheat instead of noble and truthful."[75]

To sum up, in Phil 1:27—2:18 Paul strings together attitudes, behaviors, and even physical deformities to portray envy. This passage is a tour de force in which Epaphroditus and Timothy come to be known as much for what they are not as for what they are. They are not: antagonistic, resentful of God's gift, divisive, vainglorious, selfish, full of blame, or twisted. Like Paul, they long for the Philippians as Christ longed for the world.

EUDODIA, SYNTYCHE, AND THE ENVIOUS RIVALS

Most Pauline scholars have thought of Phil 4:2-3, the only access we have to the ministry of Euodia and Syntyche, as theological backwater. Supposedly, as he closes the letter, Paul takes the opportunity to tie off a few loose ends. One of his unfinished tasks is to express gratitude for the gift he had received from the Philippian community (4:10-20). The other, it is frequently said, is to resolve a spat between Euodia and Syntyche. Although there is little evidence to support this view, the scholarly consensus is this: the two women were at odds with each other.[76]

Yet the argument for a disagreement between them is weak. It rests on questionable readings of the phrase τὸ αὐτὸ φρόνειν in 4:2 and the term συλλαμβάνου in 4:3. The latter does not mean "reconcile," as sometimes it is asserted, but simply "help." In the case of τὸ αὐτὸ φρόνειν, it has often been assumed that if Paul exhorts the two women to be of the same mind then they must have been in conflict. About this point John Calvin was rightfully dubious:

> It is an almost universally received opinion that Paul wanted to settle
> a quarrel of some sort between these two women. While I am not
> inclined to argue against this, Paul's words are not definite enough
> for such a conjecture to satisfy us that it really was so. It appears, from
> the testimony he gives them, that they were very excellent women;
> for he assigns them so much honour as to call them fellow-soldiers in
> the Gospel. Hence, as their agreement was a matter of great moment,
> and there was great danger in their disagreement, he stirs them up
> particularly to concord.[77]

Unfortunately, the vast majority of interpreters have ignored Calvin's sensible words.

Scholars have instead reconstructed the occasion of the exhortations by assuming that the behavior of those exhorted must be the opposite of the behavior desired by the writer, a procedure sometimes referred to as "mirror reading." Studies in Greco-Roman moral exhortation have shown, however, that readers or audiences were often encouraged to do what they were in fact already doing.[78] In this case, it could just as easily be concluded that Euodia and Syntyche already agreed in the Lord and that Paul encouraged them to continue to do so. Furthermore, it is noteworthy that some of the same commentators who detect dissension when Paul applies τὸ αὐτὸ φρόνειν to women in 4:2 find none in 2:2 (ἵνα τὸ αὐτὸ φρονῆτε), where gender is apparently not an issue. One wishes not to think that this inconsistency originates in interpreters' unexamined view that women veer toward conflict when not under the tutelage of men, yet an explicit reason for the difference is rarely given. In any case, the repetition of τὸ αὐτὸ φρόνειν in 4:2 casts Euodia and Syntyche into a favorable light by connecting them to longing, the central theme of the Christ Hymn, just as other leaders, Timothy and Epaphroditus, were earlier linked to Christ's passion through slavery and other motifs.

If Euodia's and Syntyche's reconciliation is not the point of 4:2-3, then what is? These verses make good sense as a commendation of the two women to the church at Philippi tucked within the larger context of 3:1—4:8. Coming toward the end of the epistle, this abbreviated letter of recommendation is not unlike 1 Cor 16:10-12 and Rom 16:1-2. Paul asks the Philippian church to support Euodia and Syntyche in the same manner that it had supported him and for which he is grateful (4:10-20).[79] The assistance Paul requests for the two women, then, is financial. Support for this view comes first of all from the form of address Paul applies to the church: γνήσιε σύζυγε. The yoke in ancient literature generally signified companionship, marriage, and for some early Christians it designated the cooperation of wandering preachers like Paul with urban-dwelling followers of Jesus.[80] By naming the church his "genuine yokemate" Paul implies the sort of relationship, one of divided but cooperative labor, that the community ought to enter into with Euodia and Syntyche. Moreover, by naming them in the company of his "co-workers (συνεργῶν)" Paul underscores the equal status they share with him, Clement, and the rest, "whose names are written in the book of life."

The success of Paul's recommendation rested on his ability to persuade the church that Euodia and Syntyche shared in whatever legitimation he himself had. This point will be considered in greater detail in the next chapter, which examines the way nuptial imagery disrupts gender-based roles in Philippians 1 and 3. For now it is sufficient to take note of the athletic term in 4:3 (συνήθλησαν), since it, like nuptial imagery, addresses the qualification of women for ministry from a provocative and innovative perspective. The σύν-prefix associates Euodia's and Syntyche's ministry with Paul's own, which had been described in agonistic metaphors throughout the letter, as 3:13-14 vividly reminds the reader. Paul's application of athletic imagery to the two women possibly introduced a jarring note to first-century readers. It must be kept in mind that with very few exceptions ancient Greek athletics was a masculine social system. Although there is indeed evidence for women's participation in athletics, it seems to be limited to separate events and running races of virgins; married women were not allowed even to watch events at Olympia.[81] Thus, thinking of Euodia and Syntyche as leaders is like imagining females showing up at the stadium and digging in at the starting line with the men. Yet it is precisely in the athletic prowess (in Philippians a metaphor of longing for communion) they share with Paul that Eudodia and Syntyche excel.

Backing up a few verses to 3:17-18 from the recommendation in 4:2-3, we note that Paul, through the same rhetorical strategy of positive and negative example he had employed in earlier portions of the letter, prepared his readers to help Euodia and Syntyche in spite of the violation of gender-based roles such support would entail. In 3:17, Paul reports that he has seen and approved the way that unnamed leaders, presumably Euodia and Syntyche, conduct themselves, and he exhorts the community to imitate his care in the selection of leaders. Next, he prepares readers to think as favorably of Euodia and Syntyche as they do of him, since he is himself the τύπος of these leaders, who, if I am correct in my interpretation of these verses, make their textual appearance in 4:2-3.

These verses also contain a negative example, as Paul continues his strategy of drawing contrasting portraits. Euodia and Syntyche are in the mold of Paul as he has described himself in 3:2-14, but they are not like the rivals, those of whom he often spoke and over whom he now weeps.[82] Most of all, they are not like "the enemies of the cross of Christ." This last invective, accompanied by the four additional terms of abuse in 3:19 that pick up where Paul left off in 3:2, requires a brief comment, since it has not occurred to interpreters of the letter to connect the rivals' enmity with their envy. Yet this is an easy connection to make, since envy and enmity were interrelated in the ancient imagination.[83] Envy is the "universal enemy."[84] Envy was thought to be the cause of enmity.[85] To be an enemy of Christ's cross is to oppose his longing for communion and to begrudge the benefits that come to the church in anticipation of the future κοινωνία with Christ.

So far, then, I have argued that Phil 3:17-18 reiterates a contrast between two groups of leaders. The envious group is first mentioned in 1:15-18, reappears in 1:28-30; 2:1-4; and 2:14-15, and makes a penultimate entrance in 3:2 with a final showing in 3:18-19, in which "enemies of the cross of Christ" (3:18) is the weightiest of the invectives directed at the rivals throughout the letter. It remains now to show how Paul's other bad-mouthing of his opponents in 3:2 and 3:18-19 pertains to his original assessment that they are motivated by envy (1:15).

First to be considered is the canine allusion in 3:2: "Beware the dogs." This warning seems to come out of the blue, and its abrupt appearance has led many scholars to conclude that Philippians is a compilation of letter fragments. In their view, what we experience as a rough transition between 3:1 and 3:2 is actually the ragged seam of two originally separate letters inelegantly sown together by a later editor.[86] When viewed from the literary history of *phthonos*, however, Paul's warning does indeed cohere with the rest of letter. The long-standing connection in ancient literature between dogs and envy indicates that Paul returns in 3:2 to the strategy of contrasting one group of workers with another.[87] Isocrates constructed opponents in just this way, that is, by showing that envy had turned his rivals into beasts:

> Some men . . . have been so brutalized by envy (ὑπὸ τοῦ φθόνου) and want and are so hostile that they wage war, not on depravity, but on prosperity; they hate not only the best men but the noblest pursuits; and, in addition to their other faults, they take sides with wrong-doers and are in sympathy with them, while they destroy, whenever they have the power, those whom they have cause to envy (φθονήσωσιν).[88]

So what precisely is doglike about envy? First, envious people bite their victims through slander and blame. Although the association of dogs with verbal abuse is Homeric, it was Pindar who made a special point of linking blame with envy.[89] Second, like dogs, who first fawn and then suddenly bite their victims, the envious attack others under the pretense of friendship. When Gregory of Nyssa thought of false friends, he thought of dogs:

> Let no one suppose that of all the evils which are brought about by hatred I reckon anger to be the most serious. In my opinion the condition of envy and hypocrisy is far more serious than the one mentioned, insofar as the hidden evil is more to be feared than the obvious one. We are more cautious about those dogs whose fury is not signaled by a warning bark or a direct assault, but which in a gentle and quiet posture watch for our incautious and unthinking moment. It is the same with the condition of envy and hypocrisy, when on the inside people have hatred like a fire smouldering secretly in the depth of their heart, while their outward appearance is disguised by hypocrisy as friendship.[90]

Finally, the envious eat their victims just as dogs scavenge for food.[91] Like dogs, who mutilate corpses and devour flesh, so the envious eat the famous and fortunate by speaking ill of them. This quite possibly is how the puzzling warning "beware the mutilation (βλέπετε τὴν κατατομήν)" in 3:2 ought to be understood. The opponents, according to Paul, threaten to consume the church with their verbal expressions of envy.[92]

Finally, in 3:19 Paul refers to four internal consequences of envy; these are not unlike envy's twisting of the body he had mentioned in 2:15 (σκολιᾶς καὶ διαστραμμένης).[93] The first allusion to *phthonos* in 3:19 is "whose end is destruction (τὸ τέλος ἀπώλεια)." This phrase plays on the double meaning of τέλος, which might either refer to an intended outcome (the destruction of the one envied) or to an unintended effect (the destruction of the one who envies). Ancient authors never tired of pointing out that envy's desire to destroy the friend, relative, fellow citizen, or coworker always backfired in self-destruction. Menander writes,

> Young man, methinks it has not dawned upon your mind
> That everything is wasted by its native ill,
> That all that brings defilement cometh from within.
> For instance, if you'll notice, rust in iron tools;
> In over-cloak the moths; the wormwood in the wood;
> And then, again, there's envy (φθόνος), worst of evils all,
> The impious propensity of evil souls,
> Which hath consumed, consumes, and shall ever consume.[94]

The motif of selfishness proceeding from envy in Phil 2:4 and 21 returns in a phrase that alludes to the doglike behavior (that is, shamelessness) of the opponents: ὧν ὁ θεὸς ἡ κοιλία.[95] Shamelessness again comes to the fore in ἡ δόξα ἐν αἰσχύνῃ αὐτῶν.[96] And finally, the accusation that the envious themselves have accomplished nothing in their lives and fail to appreciate the excellence in beauty, virtue, wealth, etc. of their victims is expressed in οἱ τὰ ἐπίγεια φρονοῦντες.[97]

CONCLUSION

This chapter has begun to explore the political implications of Paul's erotic transformation of the lordship of Christ. The longing of Jesus for communion is the model of leadership embraced by Paul, and his co-workers Timothy, Epaphroditus, Euodia, and Syntyche. All five embody the politically significant narrative in the Christ Hymn of lordly power defining itself as desire for communion with an absent beloved. In order to underscore longing as a value for leaders, Paul invents a set of rivals in missionary practice whose chief characteristic is envy. Appearing throughout the letter, their resentment, insincere speech, antagonism, fault-finding, biting speech, and enmity stand in stark contrast to Paul's apostolic sweetness and to the yearning for communion in those individuals whom Paul recommends to the church.

Only half of the politics of longing has been addressed, however. What remains is to examine the impact longing had on the problem of legitimation. Paul and his co-workers, it has been suggested in this chapter, did not possess sufficient social status to claim that they were valid leaders. Paul was a prisoner; Timothy was young; Epaphroditus was a homesick slave; and Euodia and Syntyche were women. And yet each could look forward to transformation of their bodies and communion with the Lord, whose status they could claim as their own. Our political interest in Philippians now shifts from *longing* for communion to longing for *communion*.

Notes

1. Phil 3:2.

2. See James A. Smith, *Marks of an Apostle: Deconstruction, Philippians, and Problematizing Pauline Theology,* Semeia 53 (Atlanta: Society of Biblical Literature, 2005), 59–62.

3. My translation.

4. Aside from a few Cynic texts (Heraclitus, *[Ep.]* 5.2 and Diogenes, *[Ep.]* 1.1) and Clement of Alexandria (*Strom.* 4.21.130.5), this term refers to interaction between persons in decision-making contexts rather than an individual's conformity to ethical norms; for example, see Xenophon, *Hell.* 2.4.22, 43. See further Nicole Loraux, "Reflections of the Greek City on Unity and Division," in *City States in Classical Antiquity and Medieval Italy,* ed. Anthony Molho, Kurt Raaflaub, and Julia Emlen (Ann Arbor: University of Michigan Press, 1991), 35. For later developments, see Erich S. Gruen, "The Polis in the Hellenistic World," *Nomodeiktes: Greek Studies in Honor of Martin Ostwald,* ed. Ralph M. Rosen and Joseph Farrell (Ann Arbor University of Michigan Press, 1993), 339–54.

5. Wayne A. Meeks draws attention to the boldness of early Christians naming themselves ἐκκλησία; see his *The First Urban Christians: The Social World of the Apostle Paul* (New Haven: Yale University Press, 1983), 108. For the political dimension of ecclesiology in the early church, see Barbara Ellen Bowe, *A Church in Crisis: Ecclesiology and Paraenesis in Clement of Rome,* HDR 23 (Minneapolis: Fortress Press, 1988), 86–87. By the fourth century B.C.E. this term was contrasted with ὁ ἰδιώτης, a citizen present at the assembly who participated by voting only and not by speaking or by other forms of influence; see Josiah Ober, *Mass and Elite in Democratic Athens: Rhetoric, Ideology, and the Power of the People* (Princeton: Princeton University Press, 1989), 106–9; M. Hansen, "The Political Powers of the People's Court in Fourth-Century Athens," in *The Greek City: From Homer to Alexander,* ed. Oswyn Murray and Simon Price (Oxford: Clarendon, 1990), 231. For the Roman period, see Polybius 23.12.9; Plutarch, *Comp. Dem. Cic.* 3.1; *An seni* 796C–F.

6. Dio Chrysostom, *2 Tars.* 32–33; *SVF* 3.172.18–19; 3.173.19–22; 3.174.26–29; Philo, *Somn.* 1.221–25; Diogenes Laertius, *Vitae philosophorum* 2.89; 6.11, 29; 9.3; 10.10, 119; Epictetus, *Diatr.* 1.23.1–6; Plutarch, *[Lib. ed.]* 12F; *Adv. Col.* 1125C; Marcus Aurelius, Τὰ εἰς ἑαυτόν 4.24.1; Seneca, *On Tranq.* 13.1; *Ira* 3.6.3. Retirement from political engagement had a complex intellectual and social history; see L. B. Connor, *The Quiet Athenian* (Oxford: Clarendon, 1986), 175–98. The debate whether to participate or not appears as a rhetorical exercise at Theon, *Progymnasmata* 123–25.

7. Inscriptions show that the *manner* of political engagement was the critical issue. See David Whitehead, "Samian Autonomy," in Rosen and Farrell, *Nomodeiktes,* 321–29. See also Plato, *Gorg.* 500C; Dio Chrysostom, *Grat.* 44.11; Clement of Alexandria, *Paed.* 3.11.81.2; *Strom.* 4.4.15.4–6. A comparable expression occurs in *1 Clem.* 3.4: πολιτεύεσθαι κατὰ τὸ καθῆκον τῷ Χριστῷ. Yet there is an important difference. Paul uses a narrative term, the gospel of Christ, to designate the

character of the action he exhorts the community to adopt, whereas *1 Clement* employs a moral category drawn from Stoic philosophy.

8. The assumption here is that εὐαγγέλιον in the Pauline epistles sometimes pertains to a series of connected events through which Jesus' identity or character is made known and available for imitation; see Rom 1:1; 1 Cor 9:3; 15:1; 2 Cor 11:4. Philippians 2:6-11 also falls within this definition.

9. The introductory exhortation in 2:5, "have this mind (φρονεῖτε) in you which is yours in Christ Jesus," might have reminded the ancient reader of the chief political virtue φρόνησις. See Aristotle, *Eth. nic.* 6.5.1–6.11.7.

10. See Dale B. Martin, *Slavery as Salvation: The Metaphor of Slavery in Pauline Christianity* (New Haven: Yale University Press, 1990), 86–116.

11. See chapter 1, pp. 11–12.

12. Karl Barth, *Epistle to the Philippians: 40th Anniversary Edition*, trans. James W. Leitch (Louisville: Westminster John Knox, 2002), 113.

13. The translator's comment (Barth, *Philippians*, 113 n. 51) on "barrier" is illuminating: "*Grenzpfahl*, lit. boundary post: the cross is here likened to a post or pole that stands, like a 'halt sign' at the frontier, to mark the limit of human endeavor."

14. See Patricia Bulman, *Phthonos in Pindar*, University of California Publications, Classical Studies 35 (Berkeley: University of California Press, 1992), 10–14. Cf. Basil of Ancyra, *De virginitate* 48 (*PG* 30:764.50–765.7).

15. Chrysippus, *Fragmenta moralia* 104.9–10; Andronicus Rhodius, *De passionibus* 2.1.6–7.

16. Gregory of Nyssa, *De vita Mosis* 2.257: ἡ ἐκούσιος τηκεδών; Stobaeus, *Flor.* 3.38.50. Cf. Ovid, *Metam.* 2.768–815.

17. Gregory Nazianzus, *Carmina moralia* (*PG* 37:582.6).

18. Gregory of Nyssa, *Orationes viii de beatitudinibus* 7.4 (*PG* 44:1288.25–32). Translation is from *Gregory of Nyssa: Homilies on the Beatitudes*, trans. Hubertus R. Drobner and Alberto Viciano, Supplements to Vigiliae Christianae 52; Leiden: Brill, 2000), 81.

19. See Katherine M. D. Dunbabin and M. W. Dickie, "Invida Rumpantur Pectora: The Iconography of *Phthonos /Invidia* in Graeco-Roman Art," *JAC* 26 (1983): 7–8, 19–27; *Seeing the Face, Seeing the Soul: Polemon's Physiognomy from Classical Antiquity to Medieval Islam*, ed. Simon Swain (Oxford: Oxford University Press, 2000), 361–65, 577. See also Adamantius, *Physiognomica* 1.12, 21. Another result of bodily wasting, concave mouths, indicated envy along with malice, intemperance and lust; see Swain, 589.

20. My approach to Paul's nonchalance in Phil 1:18 is different from the one taken by Smith (*Marks of an Apostle,* 120). I would, however, echo his criticisms of the usual explanations of this verse: Paul's broad-mindedness, generosity, and so forth. An attempt similar to my own to read Philippians through the envy motif in an agonistic setting is offered by Christfried Böttrich, "Verkündigung aus 'Neid und Rivalität'? Beobachtungen zu Phil, 1, 12-18," *ZNW* 95 (2004): 84–101. Also emphasizing envy in the Greek culture of competition is Vasiliki Limberis, "The Eyes Infected by Evil: Basil of Caesarea's Homily, On Envy," *HTR* 84 (1991): 163–84. For envy and competition in Roman society, see Michelle Zerba, "Love, Envy, and Pantomimic Morality in Cicero's *De Oratore*," *CP* 97 (2002): 299–301. Ancient writers were of course aware of the competitive cultural context of envy: Isocrates, *Antid.* 302; Lucian, *Cal.* 10, 28.

21. Bulman, Phthonos in Pindar, 4–5; Glenn Most, "Epinician Envies," in Envy, Spite, and Jealousy: The Rivalrous Emotions in Ancient Greece, ed. David Konstan and Keith Rutter, Edinburgh Leventis Studies 2 (Edinburgh: Edinburgh University Press, 2003), 133. In the fourth century, Himerius (Declamationes et orations 69) still complained of envy's attack on polished public speech.

22. Demosthenes, *Epp.* 2.4; 3.28.

23. *Steinepigramme* 19/3/3; 20/5/6; 22/1/2.

24. Pp. 94-98.

25. Envy was a prominent theological explanation for disappointment and the experience of loss. See Aristotle, *Metaph.* 1.2.13; Plutarch, *[Cons. Apoll.]*105B: "For we know that in cases of great prosperity fortune is wont to be jealous." In erotic contexts, personified Envy was blamed for interrupted relationships: Chariton, *Chaer.* 1.1.16; 1.2.1; Heliodorus, *Aeth.* 2.1.3; Lucian, *[Asin.]* 19; Nonnus, *Dion.* 47.331; Nicetas Eugenianus, *De Drosillae et Chariclis amoribus* 1.52–53, 306; 4.252. In early Christianity, Envy entered the garden to corrupt Adam and Eve and their descendants: Theophilus, *Autol.* 2.29; Epiphanius, *Panarion* 3.416.1; Antiochus Monachus, *Pandecta scripturae sacrae* 55. This Christian move was anticipated in Greek literature by Zeus's resentment of humankind (Aristophanes, *Plut.* 87). Cf. Aeschylus, *Pers.* 362, 362; Lucian, *Nav.* 26; *Ver. hist.* 1.12; *[Am.]* 46.

26. See chapter 4, p. 95.

27. Aeschylus, *Frg.* 305; Phocylides, *[Sententiae]* 70; Favorinus, *Frg.* 111; Basil, *Homilia de invidia* (PG 31.379.54–380.21).

28. For other instances of labor in Philippians, see 1:6, 22; 2:12-13, 25, 30; 3:2; 4:3.

29. *Testament of Gad* 4:5-7; Ephraem Syrus, *Sermo de virtutibus et vitiis* 18.4–6; 19.9. The astral imagery of Phil 2:15 (ἐν οἷς φαίνεσθε ὡς φωστῆρες ἐν κόσμῳ) risked an envious response in the social world that Paul constructs. For the death gods' envy of any sort of human progress, see chapter 4, pp. 96–97.

30. Hesiod, *Op.* 24–25; Aristotle, *Rhet.* 2.10.5–11; Dio Chrysostom, *Invid.* 2–6; Lucian, *Cal.* 2; Philostratus, *Vit. soph.* 490–91; Plutarch, *Amic. multi.* 96B. See Bulman, *Phthonos in Pindar*, 16, 82 n. 7; Suzanne Saïd, "Envy and Emulation in Isocrates," in Konstan and Rutter, *Envy, Spite, and Jealousy*, 218. See further Isocrates, *Demon.* 26; *Antid.* 4, 259; *Phil.* 11; Lucian, *[Asin.]* 11; *Philops.* 35; *Merc. cond.* 11, 39; *Somn.* 4, 7; *Abdic.* 32; Cf. Callimachus, *Hymn. Apoll.* 105–13; *Aet.* 1.17; Hippocrates, *[Ep.]* 17.292–93.

31. Aristotle, *Rhet.* 2.9.3–5.

32. Hippocrates, *Praec.* 8.

33. Plutarch, *Inim. util.* 86C. See Demosthenes, *Lept.* 139–40; Isocrates, *Ad Nic.* 46; *Nic.* 18. See also Nick Fisher, "'Let Envy Be Absent': Envy, Liturgies and Reciprocity in Athens," in Konstan and Rutter, *Envy, Spite, and Jealousy*, 181–215.

34. Aristotle, *Pol.* 5.3.7. Polybius (7.8.4–5) writes of Hiero, king of Syracuse, whose way of ruling preserved him from "that envy which is wont to wait on superiority."

35. Lucian, *Cal.* 12.

36. See Isocrates, *Panath.* 15–19.

37. Gregory of Nazianzus, *Carmina moralia* (PG 37.910.8): Χάρις φθονεῖσθαι, τὸ φθονεῖν δ' αἶσχος μέγα. Cf. Plutarch, *Inv. od.* 537.

38. Isocrates was master of this technique; see Philostratus, *Vit. soph.* 505. See also Saïd, "Envy and Emulation," 217.

39. Aristotle, *Rhet.* 1.5.17.

40. Pindar, *Partheneia* 1.8–9. Cf. Demosthenes, *Cor.* 315; Lysias, *Oration* 24.1–3; Plutarch, *Inv. od.* 537E-F; Dio Chrysotom, *Pol.* 1–2; *Invid.* 15–26.

41. See Bulman, *Phthonos in Pindar*, 53–63; Gregory Nagy, *The Best of the Achaeans: Concepts of the Hero in Archaic Greek Poetry*, rev. ed. (Baltimore: Johns Hopkins University Press, 1999), 60–61, 73, 130–31, 218–23, 273, 309–16; Saïd, "Envy and Emulation," 231–32. See also Phocylides, *[Sentences]* 70.

42. Lucian, *Symp.* 19; *Cal.* 10; Gregory of Nazianzus, *Oration* 43.20.1. Ephraem Syrus, *Sermo de virtutibus et vitiis.* 19.4.

43. See Phil 1:9 for a similar association of perception and love.

44. *Griechische Vers-Inschriften* 1:113, 132, 133, 134, 170, 208, 257, 299, 727, 1059. Additionally, an entire section of Peek's collection (1:320–449) is organized under this term.

45. Bulman, *Phthonos in Pindar,* 45–49, 57. Andrew Miller, "*Phthonos* and *Parphasis*: The Argument of *Nemean* 8.19-34," *GRBS* 23 (1982): 116–20; Zerba, "Love, Envy," 301–5. See also Democritus, *Frg.* 302.44–45.

46. See Most, "Epinician Envies," 137. See also Bacchylides, *Epinicia* 5.187–90; Basil, *Homilia de invidia* (PG 31:385.20–26).

47. Aeschylus, *Pers.* 955–66, 1067; *Suppl.* 876, 885; *Eum.* 841, 874; *Prom.* 84; Sophocles, *Frg.* 210.30.

48. Cf. Gregory of Nyssa, *De vita Mosis* 2.258.

49. Plutarch, *Inv. od.* 538C. Basil (*Homilia de invidia* [PG 31:40–43]) made a similar observation: the envious person "awaits only one alleviation of his distress—that, perchance, he may see one of the persons whom he envies fall into misfortune. This is the goal of his hatred—to behold the victim of his envy pass from happiness to misery, that he who is admired and emulated might become an object of pity." Translation is from *Saint Basil: Ascetical Works*, trans. M. Monica Wagner, FC 9 (New York: Fathers of the Church, 1950), 464.

50. See 1 Cor 1:28; 6:4; Rom 14:3; Luke 18:9; 23:11. Suda, *Lexicon* E 1814: ἐξουθενῶ σε: ἀντ' οὐδενός σε λογίζομαι.

51. See n. 10.

52. Philippians 2:26 is the only instance in the New Testament of the coordinated use of ἐπειδή and διότι, but see Philo, *Abr.* 145; *Mos.* 2.100, 104; Plutarch, *Prim. frig.* 952C.

53. See pp. 23–25, 45–52, and 59–63.

54. For association of the term with homesickness, see Plutarch, *Exil.* 601C; *Scholia et glossae in Nicandri theriaca* 427D; Cyrillus Scythopolitanus, *Vita Joannis Hesychastae* 217.1–4; Photius, *Lexicon* A 334; *Greek Anthology* 12.226.

55. Zonaras, *[Lexicon]* A 43.11-14.

56. Plato, *Phaedr.* 251D; Heliodorus, *Aeth.* 3.11.1; 7.4.2.

57. Plutarch, *Tu. san.* 129C.

58. Origen, *Fr. Ps.* 118.28.17–18; Hesychius, *Lexicon* A 1090, 3320; Lexica Segueriana, *Glossae rhetoricae* A 208.21; Suda, *Lexicon* A 459; Zonaras, *[Lexicon]* A 45.18, 49.4-7; Galen, *In Hippocratis librum primum epidemiarum commentarii iii* 17a.178–79.

59. Philo, *Praem.* 151; Hesychius, *Lexicon* A 2393, Λ 1358; Photius, *Lexicon* A 1054; Eustathius, *Commentarii ad Homeri Iliadem* 4.859.20–21; *Commentarii ad Homeri Odysseam* 2.182.42–45.

60. Cf. Xenophon, *Ephesiaca* 5.1.6.

61. See Tragica Adespota, *Frg.* 167.1: τῶν εὐτυχούντων ἀνταγωνιστὴς φθόνος; *Sententiae Pythagoreorum* 156.1–2: Ὁ φθόνος ὥσπερ φαῦλος δημαγωγός, ταῖς καλαῖς ἀντιπολιτεύεται πράξεσιν; Ephraem Syrus, *Sermo de virtutibus et vitiis* 19: "For the one having envy and zeal is ἀντικείμενος to all." See also Basil, *Homilia de invidia* (PG 31:372.28). For the death divinity Envy as an antagonist (ἀντίπαλος), see chapter 4, n.75.

62. This is preferable to the NRSV's decision to ignore the passive voice of ἐχαρίσθη in order to translate ὑπὲρ Χριστοῦ as "privilege" and thus to avoid altogether the phrase τὸ ὑπὲρ Χριστοῦ: "For he has graciously granted you the privilege of not only believing in Christ, but of suffering for him as well." My translation assumes, not unreasonably, that the verb left out in τὸ ὑπὲρ Χριστου is εἶναι.

63. See chapter 2, n. 8.

64. For the political side of σωτηρία, see Arthur Darby Nock, "Soter and Euergetes," in *The Joy of Study: Papers on New Testament and Related Subjects to Honor Frederick Clifton Grant,* ed. Sherman E. Johnson (New York: Macmillan, 1951), 127–48.

65. *Greek Anthology* 10.51; Andocides, *De reditu suo* 6.7–8.

66. See Pindar, *Nem.* 4.39–41: "another, with envious glance, broodeth in darkness over some fruitless purpose (γνώμαν κενεάν) that falleth to the ground." See Bulman, *Phthonos in Pindar,* 24–25. See also Plutarch, *Inim. util.* 91E-F.

67. Plutarch, *Rect. rat. aud.* 39D–F; cf. Plutarch, *Tu. san.* 135E.

68. Bulman, *Phthonos in Pindar*, 6–11, 24–27. See Isocrates, *De pace* 93, on which see Saïd, "Envy and Emulation," 231–32. See also Isocrates, *Phil.* 73. See also Margaret Graver, "Dog-Helen and Homeric Insult," *Classical Antiquity* 14 (1995): 51.

69. Bulman, *Phthonos in Pindar*, 23; Isocrates, *Antid.* 62; *Hel. enc.* 30; Demosthenes, *Cor.* 315.

70. Pindar, *Ol.* 6.73–76: "The cavil (μῶμος) of others that are envious hangeth over all, whoever reach the goal as victors in the race." See Bulman, *Phthonos in Pindar*, 21–23; cf. Bacchylides, *Epinicia* 13.162–65. See also Nagy, *Best of the Achaeans*, 222–26, 250.

71. Bulman, *Phthonos in Pindar*, 6–7, 23; Dunbabin and Dickie, "*Invida Rumpantur Pectora*," 17–27; Limberis, "Eyes Infected by Evil," 171.

72. Bulman, *Phthonos in Pindar*, 27–28, 31. See also Fisher, "'Let Envy Be Absent,'" 181–215. Envy is self-tormenting and crooked (σκόλιος); see Nonnus, *Dion.* 8.34–108.

73. *The Leiden Polemon* B16. See Swain, *Seeing the Face*, 407. Cf. Adamantius, *Physiognomica* B16 (Swain, 523): "The man who has a hunched back and shoulders bent in towards his chest is malicious and spiteful (κακοήθης ἐστὶ καὶ βάσκανος); *Physiognomica* B25 (Swain, 529): "If the nose is very crooked (σκολιαῖς), the thoughts are generally crooked (σκολιά) too." Anonymous Latinus, *Book of Physiognomy* 62 (Swain, 597): "But those whose upper back is curved and turns the shoulders into the chest are malicious and envious, and the more so if the whole body is similarly curved in and turned in."

74. Lucian, *Cal.* 5.

75. Dio Chrysostom, *Invid.* 33. Cf. Plotinus, *Enn.* 1.5.26–30: "Suppose, then, an ugly soul, dissolute and unjust, full of all lusts, and all disturbance, sunk in fears by its cowardice and jealousies by its pettiness (ἐν φθόνοις διὰ μικροπρέπειαν), thinking mean and mortal thoughts, as far as it thinks at all (πάντα φρονοῦσα ἃ δὴ καὶ φρονεῖ θνητὰ καὶ ταπεινά), altogether distorted (σκολιὰ πανταχοῦ), loving impure pleasures, living a life which consists of bodily sensations and finding delight in its ugliness."

76. See, for example, Nils A. Dahl, "Euodia and Syntyche and Paul's Letter to the Philippians," in *The Social World of the First Christians: Essays in Honor of Wayne A. Meeks*, ed. L. Michael White and O. Larry Yarbrough (Minneapolis: Fortress Press, 1995), 3–15. For a refreshing approach that breaks away from gender stereotypes, see Mary Rose D'Angelo, "Women Partners in the New Testament," *JFSR* 6 (1990): 65–86.

77. *The Epistles of Paul the Apostle to the Galatians, Ephesians, Philippians and Colossians*, trans. T. H. L. Parker (Edinburgh: Oliver & Boyd, 1965), 285.

78. See Abraham J. Malherbe, "Exhortation in First Thessalonians," *NovT* 25 (1983): 238–56.

79. For letters of recommendation, see Stanley K. Stowers, *Letter Writing in Greco-Roman Antiquity*, LEC 5 (Philadelphia: Westminster, 1986), 153–65.

80. Cf. 2 Cor 6:14.

81. See Pausanius, *Descr.* 5.16.2–4; 6. 20.9.

82. See p. 112 above on Phil 1:17. For weeping as imprecation, see *Greek Anthology* 7.727. For κλαίω and the impact of ritual crying on the composition of sepulchral epigrams, see *Griechische Vers-Inschriften* 1:429, 646, 660, 715, 718, 729, 819, 861, 924, 957, 977, 1015, 1161, 1188, 1195, 1240, 1357, 1472, 1472, 1874, 1981.

83. See, for example, Philostratus, *Ep.* 43.

84. Demosthenes, *1 Aristog.* 80; Basil, *Homilia de invidia* (PG 31:376.5–9).

85. Bulman, *Phthonos in Pindar*, 25. See also Dio Chrysostom, *Rhod.* 31.96–99; cf. *Conc. Apam.* 40.20–24.

86. See Helmut Koester, "The Purpose of the Polemic of a Pauline Fragment (Philippians iii)," *NTS* 8 (1962): 317–32.

87. A possible reason for naming opponents "workers" was offered above (p. 110). For the good/bad polarity associated with those who envy and those who do not, see Bulman, *Phthonos in Pindar*, 22.

88. Isocrates, *Antid.* 142.

89. For Homer, see Deborah Steiner, "Slander's Bite: *Nemean* 7.102–5 and the Language of Invective," *JHS* 121 (2001): 156–57. For Pindar, see *Nem.* 8.21–22: "Tales are a dainty morsel to the envious, and envy fasteneth on the noble and striveth not with the mean." See also Bulman, *Phthonos in Pindar*, 44–45. In a late source (Manuel Philes, *Carmina* 29.17) that is dependent on Basil's *Homilia de invidia* envy *is* a dog. It is not inappropriate to entertain the possibility that Paul's warning about dogs had to do in some way with Cynic philosophers, since he had contrasted his ministry with that of harsh Cynics in 1 Thessalonians; see Abraham J. Malherbe, "Gentle as a Nurse': The Cynic Background to I Thessalonians ii," *NovT* 12 (1970): 203–17. The name "dog" for this group of philosophers was a much-discussed topic in antiquity; see Heinz Schulz-Falkenthal, "Kyniker—Zur inhaltlichen Deutung des Names," *WZ* 26.2 (1977): 41–49. The epithet was applied, nevertheless, more extensively than to "the envious" alone or to Cynic philosophers, although the one thing both groups had in common—biting speech—was, in addition to shamelessness, the point of the trope. For an exhaustive survey, see Saara Lilja, *Dogs in Ancient Greek Poetry*, Commentationes Humanarum Litteratum 56 (Helsinki: Societas Scientarum Fennica, 1976).

90. Gregory of Nyssa, *Orationes viii de beatitudinibus* 7.4 (PG 44.1285.56–1288.11). Drobner and Viviano, *Gregory of Nyssa: Homilies on the Beatitudes*, 80–81. Cf. Dio Chrysostom, *Invid.* 29–32.

91. Graver, "Dog-Helen and Homeric Insult," 51, 58. See also Bacchylides 3.68.

92. Cf. Gal 5:15-26, and especially δάκνετε καὶ κατεσθίετε in 5:15 in light of φθόνοι in 5:21 and φθονοῦντες in 5:26. For envious persons behaving like dogs (barking, biting, mutilating), see Nagy, *Best of the Achaeans*, 222–31, 312–13; Graver, "Dog-Helen and Homeric Insult," 41–61; Bulman, *Phthonos in Pindar*, 12–13, 44–45, 54–56. See also Pindar, *Pyth.* 2.54; Dio Chrysostom, *Invid.* 29–45; Gregory of Nyssa, *De vita Mosis* 2.258.

93. See p. 117 above.

94. Menander, *Frg.* 540; cf. *Frg.* 634: "The envious man (ὁ φθονερός) is his own enemy; he is forever grappling with vexation self-imposed." See Isocrates, *Antid.* 13; *Evag.* 6; *T. Sim.* 4:7-9; Agathon, *Frg.* 23: "the one who envies those having good things is destroyed." Cf. *Greek Anthology* 10.111: "Envy slays itself by its own arrows." See also Bulman, *Phthonos in Pindar*, 18, 39.

95. See Nagy, *Best of the Achaeans*, 229–31, 260–61; Graver, "Dog-Helen and Homeric Insult,"47.

96. Demosthenes, *Lept.* 139–42; Philostratus, *Vit. soph.* 490–91.

97. Isocrates, *Evag.* 6; Philostratus, *Vit. soph.* 514–15; Plotinus, *Enn.* 1.5.26–30.

6

The Politics of a Manbride

> *But we could also speak of any faithful soul, one to whom, all the same, "to live is Christ," and who has won the kiss and the embrace of the spouse . . . she incessantly yearns for him with the fire of a most genuine love. She has thus gained for herself both the privilege and the name "bride."*[1]

EPITHALAMIUM

If ever there was an occasion for envy to take root, it was the Greek wedding.[2] After removal of the bride's veil but before the couple entered the bedroom, an orator stood up and uttered profuse, envy provoking praise.[3] Both of the young persons were magnified.[4] The groom was extolled for his impressive physical stature, as in these roof-raising lines of Sappho: "On high the roof—Hymenaeus!—raise up, you carpenters—Hymenaeus! The bridegroom is coming, the equal of Ares, much larger than a large man."[5] The bride was praised for her preeminence in beauty:

> O what a maiden in the halls
> Of Aristaenetus
> Her gentle nurture had, our queen
> Cleanthis glorious!
> Superior to other maids
> As many as there be,
> Than Aphrodite prettier
> And Helen eke is she.[6]

The bride, and occasionally the groom too, shone like stars.[7] And it was not only the couple who were praised but also their parents and the institution of marriage itself. This speech was called the *epithalamium*, a reworking of the Greek bridal song (ὁ ἐπιθαλάμιος ὕμνος) sung at the door of (ἐπί) the marriage chamber (θάλαμος). Now, Paul's letter to the Philippians is not an *epithalamium*, but the saturation of its verses with nuptial imagery justifies our reading of it as if were, as if Paul and Christ would soon be wed. That is why, as Paul insinuates throughout the epistle, the rivals envy him so.

The beauty and bliss of the couple risked provoking the envy of those gathered for the celebration.[8] This chapter advances the idea that Paul turns this danger into a framing device for his letter to the Philippians. By casting his relationship to Christ and, by implication, the bonds with Christ also of his co-workers in the language of an anticipated marital union, Paul lays out a new rationale for the legitimation of leaders quite at odds with the dominant, ancient paradigm that held up masculinity and high social status as key requirements. What is legitimating about this longed-for relation to Christ? Difficult as it is to imagine in view of the asymmetry of power within marriage in Aristotle's *Politics*, for example, and in ensuing treatises on household management, marriage in the *epithalamium* and related genres was celebrated as a kind of sharing (κοινωνία), or as a relationship of equality (ἰσότης).[9] Like friends, bride and groom have all things in common, and that feature of marriage too garnered much praise in wedding speeches.[10] Paul turns this feature of the Greek wedding to politics. In Philippians, a longed-for κοινωνία with Christ authorizes Paul's own ministry and undergirds his recommendation of Euodia and Syntyche, whose legitimation for leadership roles rested on their future sharing with Christ as a bride shares all things with the groom.

The *epithalamium* emphasized that this κοινωνία between bride and groom is one of the two moments of perfection in the course of a person's life.[11] If Greek weddings are held in mind, then, it appears that the perfection Paul speaks of in 3:12 (τετελείωμαι) is less a matter of self-discipline as it has usually been conceived and more a vision of human fulfillment in the intimacy of reciprocal desire and communion. This impression will be strengthened in the course of this chapter as other nuptial imagery in the letter is identified. Most interpreters, however, think that in Phil 3:7-14 Paul reports his moral progress, humbly admitting in 3:12 that he has not yet arrived at perfection. Yet, when the nuptial connotation of τετελείωμαι is recognized, Paul's life appears in a transitional state as if he were a bride awaiting perfection in the wedding ceremony. This image of Paul as a male bride disrupts gender-based social roles and opens a space for Eudodia and Syntyche to participate fully in the leadership of the church.

But the wedding in the ancient world marked only one of two great transitions in human life. The other, of course, was death, and much will be made in this chapter of the *conflation* in ancient literature and in Philippians of weddings and funerals. Paul's wedding day, it will be suggested below, cannot be disentangled from his demise. Whether through life or through death (Phil 1:20), as he looks forward to the perfection of sharing all things with Christ, Paul's liminality paradoxically secures political legitimation.[12] Like a bride processing from her father's household to the groom's, Paul has died to his old life according to the autobiography in 3:4-14, but he does not yet live in the new. His is the journey of every bride, as John Chrysostom described the young woman's transition: "For there are two companies, one of the virgins, the other of the married; the one are giving her up, the other receiving her."[13]

Yet not only does Paul exist between times; he lives also between classification systems, including the categories of male and female. Paul is a manbride. In Phil 3:12, he both pursues (the usual male role in Greek culture) and is pursued (the female role) by Christ. By portraying himself as the soon-to-be bride of Christ, who has both been captured by Christ and pursues the Lord, Paul underlines the transitional and therefore indefinable character of a life of faith. The liminal state in which he discovers himself dismisses masculinity, an irrelevant mark of identity. Objection to the ministry of Euodia and Syntyche therefore cannot stand.

Nor can Paul's imprisonment be held against him. In his opponents' eyes, Paul's bondage robbed him of free speech, shamed him into silence, and disqualified him as an apostle (Phil 1:12-20).[14] Paul fought back by wrapping himself in the conflation of death and marriage found in ritual mourning practices in Greek antiquity and in literature, especially among the tragedians, and in grave inscriptions.[15] The dream interpreter Artemidorus also knew of the conflation; he succinctly states the mutual implication of death and marriage, both of which he, in agreement with traditional wisdom, views as perfection of life: "To dream that one is dead, that one is carried out for burial, or that one is buried . . . signifies marriage for a bachelor. For both marriage and death are considered τέλη in a man's life, and one is always represented by the other."[16] So while it might appear to some that he is on his way to death, Paul proclaims his status as a bride awaiting her wedding day. And it is precisely in that waiting that Paul's authority resides.

And what exactly does Paul the bride long for? Philippians 1:23 speaks frankly: Paul wishes "to be with Christ." English speakers share this phrase with the ancient Greeks for the intimacy separated lovers longed to enjoy. In Paul's day the phrase suggested romantic attachment, mutual devotion, and the joy of presence, although admittedly it often just meant having sex.[17] Our interest is the former connotation.[18] The word συνεῖναι summed up the happy *telos* of one romantic novel and was a lover's ruined hope at the beginning of another. Theagenes, the male half of the care-worn couple in Heliodorus's *Aethiopica*, articulated what inspired him to carry on even though fate seemed opposed to his happiness and was determined to interrupt the couple's communion: "'To live in union with another (τὸ μὲν συνεῖναι ἡμᾶς ἀλλήλοις), Charikleia, to possess that which we have come to value above all things and for which we have undergone so many travails, such is our prayer, which I pray the gods of Greece may grant.'"[19] In another novel, Xenophon's *An Ephesian Tale*, such a happy union was not to be for Hippothous and Hyperanthes. The former tells the sad story: "And at last we were able to take our opportunity to be alone with each other (γενέσθαι μετ' ἀλλήλων μόνοι); we were both the same age, and no one was suspicious. For a long time we were together (συνῆμεν), passionately in love, until some evil spirit envied us."[20] "To be with" was such a magnificent state of affairs that it provoked first a rival human lover to intervene and in the end envious Death himself too visited this couple and stole the one from the other.[21] In Phil 1:23 Paul's desire (ἐπιθυμία, often translated in other contexts as "lust") is to "dissolve and to be with Christ (σύν Χριστῷ εἶναι)."[22] The eroticism of the hope expressed in Phil 1:23 was not lost on some later Christian writers who thought that the verse spoke of an intimate union Paul would soon enjoy with Christ.[23]

It must be said, however, that most authors in the centuries following Philippians construed Paul's wish for union with Christ in moral terms, as the apostle's growth in virtue.[24] But I believe Paul's reliance on other poetic motifs in Philippians favors an erotic reading of his stated desire rather than a moral one. For example, not only did Paul wish to be with Christ, but he also wanted to dissolve (ἀναλῦσαι). The notion of dissolving had an important amatory history. The same medieval Christian writers whose readings of Paul's *pothos* in Phil 1:8 and Christ's *kenosis* in 2:7 I consulted in earlier chapters were convinced of Paul's erotic desire in 1:23. They knew what the archaic poets knew: Sleep, Death, and Love loosened, unbound, or dissolved limbs.[25] In effect, they regarded Paul's ἀναλῦσαι in light of Sappho's reapplication of the Homeric term "limb-loosening" (λυσιμελής), an adjective originally applied only to Sleep and Death.[26] Modern translations, however, and even the King James Version (often the faithful transmitter of the apostle's emotions), do not tolerate a Paul who melts in longing for Christ; in these translations Paul desires instead to "depart" or to "be gone." The Vulgate, however, translates ἀναλῦσαι with "dissolve" thus preserving Paul's wish that his body be altered, not removed. To dissolve was to melt; it was to die of love.[27] Paul desired to come undone, and like his Lord his politics is inhabited by his longing.

CUTTING MASCULINITY

The last chapter, which treated the role of envy in Paul's construction of his opponents, ignored a view shared by many Pauline scholars that in Phil 3:2 the apostle's warning "watch out for the mutilation (τὴν κατατομήν)" refers to rival missionaries insisting on circumcision. I do not wish to oppose this opinion directly, only to add a level of complexity that puts into question the larger project scholars usually pursue in conjunction with these verses, that is, the historical reconstruction of Paul's opponents. Rather than following the well-worn path that begins with a word that does appear in the text (circumcision) to one that does not (Judaizers), I wish to take stock of the letter's *invention* of rivals and the chief characteristic Paul attributes to them, envy.

Rhetoric, then, and not history is my concern in pointing out that the word order of κατατομή and then περιτομή in 3:3 allows the reader a brief moment to associate "dog" with "evil workers" *before* the text's playfulness with cutting (τομή) takes over and brings circumcision to mind. In other words, just for an instant readers are confronted with the doglike behavior of the rival Christian workers. Since, as we saw in the previous chapter, slander and blame were sometimes likened to the canine mutilation of corpses, there is, therefore, good reason for present-day interpreters to pause before asserting that here in Phil 3:2 Paul is launching an attack on opponents whose identifying mark is their insistence on Jewish law. In other words, not until περιτομή appears do we have any reason to believe that the rivals have an interest in marking the flesh of the males in the Philippian church for a religious purpose. But if κατατομή is still fresh in the memory as the word περιτομή is read, it is difficult to put out of mind the image of wounded manhood that the combination of the two words creates. And that, I suggest, may have been Paul's intent. The trick of reading Phil 3:2-3, then, and 3:4-14 for that matter, is to entertain the possibility that Paul was drawing attention more to masculinity's role in the customary legitimation of leaders than to the topic of religious affiliation.

The significance of Paul's reference to circumcision in 3:2 must be addressed, of course, but in this chapter the usual approach of reading through it to historical events and persons threatening the church and to reconstruct the opponents as so-called Judaizers will be avoided. Similarly, the autobiographical portion of Philippians (3:4-14) will not be treated as if it were a comparison of Christianity and Judaism, to the disadvantage of the latter. Instead, both circumcision and Paul's curriculum vitae will be interpreted as devices for severing the link, so prominent in the ancient world, between masculinity and leadership. Euodia and Syntyche benefit from this cut on masculinity. If, as I suggested in the previous chapter, Phil 4:2-3 is a letter of recommendation in which Paul asks the church to offer Euodia and Syntyche financial support for their ministry, then it makes sense in 3:2-14 for Paul to anticipate a possible objection based on gender. How then, in addition to the disturbing image of a mutilated penis, do these verses disrupt male prerogative? That is the question the remainder of this chapter seeks to answer.

Paul gives a preview in 3:3-4 of his critique of gender-based legitimation. First of all, he redefines circumcision as the community itself rather than a cut of flesh that qualifies one class of persons for leadership. Marks on the flesh and the piece of flesh that receives those signs of belonging and authority recede, and what takes their place in granting legitimacy is the "we." Now add to this that the "we" of "we are the circumcision" almost certainly was composed of males and females, regardless of whether Paul intended to name his entourage only or the church in Philippi, too. The result is the same: both men and women give meaning to circumcision, which has become a metaphor and no longer the actual cut that qualifies men for public leadership.

Philippians 3:4-6 brings this point out more clearly. Here Paul introduces a key term in ancient philosophy's discourse about the legitimation of political leaders: confidence (πεποίθησις). Confidence is the condition of mind that served as the basis of bold speech (παρρησία), without which no one in antiquity could claim to be a leader.[28] In 3:3, he asserts that "we" carry out religious rites (λατρεύοντες), normally a male activity, and that "we" boast in Christ Jesus and are not confident (πεποιθότες) in flesh, leaving it up to the reader, of course, to imagine what particular part of male anatomy (cf. Gal 3:3) he had in mind that no longer has a bearing on leadership. In short, Paul's boasting in Christ Jesus might be seen as a path to leadership in opposition to the biological facts of his male body. Furthermore, the confidence-granting institutions that Paul enumerates in 3:5-6 have their origin in nonmetaphorical circumcision and therefore recede from the public sphere, as Paul imagines it to be, along with the privileges of marked masculinity.

More needs to be said about the way Paul's boasting in Christ Jesus indirectly supports the ministry of Euodia and Syntyche. Paul's confidence for his own ministry comes from his belonging to a social institution quite different from those that in 3:5 he declines to exploit. As we saw in connection with Phil

1:21, Paul's boasting comes from his future marriage to Christ. Erotic poetry and medieval Christian readings of Phil 3:7-14 encourage us to think that these verses portray Paul as a bride as she awaits her wedding—at which point she will have all things in common with her spouse. Her confidence resides therefore in her future. The nuptial imagery in Philippians 3, however, contributes not only to Paul's standing in the church but also supports his recommendation of Eudodia and Syntyche. How so? If Paul becomes a bride, or more precisely, a manbride, the dichotomy of male and female that justified assignment of men to public spaces and women to the domestic sphere can no longer be sustained. In other words, the indeterminacy of Paul's gender in these verses opens a place of ecclesial responsibility for Eudodia and Syntyche. The implication of Paul's self-presentation for the church at Philippi is this: Eudodia and Syntyche ought not to be denied recognition as leaders on the basis of an obsolescent distinction between soon to be transformed human bodies.

Paul's argument is actually stronger than this, however, since there is a confessional tone in Paul's dissolution of the dichotomy of gender. Euodia and Syntyche *must* not be denied public roles simply because they are women. This I take to be the force of Paul's lacing of the account of his own career with references to Christ's lordship. That is, Paul punctuates his story of legitimacy (and by implication Euodia's and Syntyche's confidence for ministry) with language reminiscent of "Jesus Christ is Lord" in Phil 2:11. An echo of this early Christian confession occurs in 3:8 ("Christ Jesus my Lord"), and, apart from a difference in case ending, the last three words of 3:21 reproduce the confession of 2:11 exactly: κύριον Ἰησοῦν Χριστόν. Moreover, if the puzzling στοιχεῖν in 3:16 is translated as "to agree with," it echoes ἐξομολογήσεται of 2:11, and if the anticipation indicated by the term ἐφθάσαμεν in 3:16 alludes to the community's present confession of Jesus, who will be universally recognized as Lord in the future, one more instance of Paul's confessional framing of his autobiography comes into focus. Finally, the exhortation "stand in the Lord" (4:1), which immediately precedes Paul's recommendation of Eudodia and Syntyche, raises the stakes of the community's response: failure to recognize the two women as leaders is a failure to acknowledge Christ's lordship, because this one is a lord who welcomes all into marital intimacy and communion with himself. To reject Euodia and Syntyche is to reject him.

Captured Bride and Animated Wheel

A dramatic scene decorated numerous ancient Greek vases. A young man or a god chases (διώκειν) a female of marriageable age. (In the rare instances when a goddess engages in such pursuit, a young male flees). The reverse side of the vase depicts a wedding scene or, less frequently, the moment of capture itself. For a reason that will become apparent in a moment, it should be noted that the Greek verb for "capture" here is καταλαμβάνειν. Having captured her, the young man holds his future bride's wrist and leads her away to marriage.[29] Ancient poetry also testifies to the popularity of the motif of erotic pursuit. Frequently we read of the lover who chases his fleeing beloved until she is captured.[30] Initially, διώκειν had its place in the discourse of hunting, but later it often occurred in the context of males acquiring a bride. In iconography the virgin is the quarry. She must be tracked down, captured, and domesticated. Poets transferred the hunt to the lover's pursuit of the beloved, female or male.[31] One pursues and the other flees, and that in miniature is the story of Eros.[32]

Such scenes of pursuit, flight, and capture, whether painted on vases or described in literature, suggest that there is far more eroticism in Phil 3:12 than translators of this verse into English have led us to believe. Paul's term διώκειν, which as I just mentioned had a long and illustrious career in love poetry, in modern translations no longer connotes hunting and the acquisition of a bride and has instead become "press on" (NIV and NRSV).[33] Once scrubbed clean of erotic allusion, the verse was easily turned to ascetical striving aimed at union with (that is, the appropriation of) divine nature.[34]

In other words, without the vantage point that erōs provides, pursuit of Christ and union with him signify renunciation of sin and growth in virtue.

This non-erotic approach goes further awry by intellectualizing the moment of capture, a signal of nuptial intent famously represented in iconography by the groom's hand placed on the bride's wrist: the word καταλαμβάνειν is mistakenly taken to mean "to comprehend."[35] Yet, if the scene Paul describes in 3:12 were pictured on a vase and our perceptions were informed by reading ancient poetry, then we would think of the apostle striding forward like a suitor and Christ fleeing like a distraught young woman. And when we turn the vase around, another scene appears as the hunter becomes the hunted and Paul has been captured by Christ. Christ's hand rests on Paul's wrist and they turn to walk away together. Not wed yet, but they are about to be, both pursuing and both captured. Manbrides both.

Though by no means numerous, some Christian interpreters noticed and welcomed such an erotic interpretation of Phil 3:12. Symeon the New Theologian, for example, forestalls a moral meaning of Paul's pursuit by regarding Christ as "the end of the law" (Rom 10:4). From this perspective, what matters most in Paul's words is not an individual's moral perfection (how can one ever know that this goal has been reached?). What matters is to capture

Christ and to be captured by Christ as Paul himself had been. Symeon addresses Christ:

> He who does not love you as he ought and is not, as he must be, the object of your love, may well run, yet not attain the prize (κατέλαβε), and whoever runs is doubtful until he has completed the race. But he who has laid hold on you or on whom you have laid hold (ὁ δὲ καταλαβών σε ἢ καταληφθεὶς ὑπὸ σοῦ) is certain [of victory], since you are the end of the Law. It is you who surround me and inflame me, you who by the labor of my heart enkindle me with boundless desire (πόθον ἄπειρον) for God and for my brethren and fathers.[36]

Symeon's hot pursuit of Christ spills over into his relations with others. His longing for God and his brothers is infinite.[37] John of Ford interpreted the verse both as Paul's progress toward moral perfection and as erotic pursuit.[38] From the perspective of the latter, Paul pursues Christ in order to lay hold of a *person* and not moral virtue: "O Light most desirable, running so joyfully to meet all who long (*desiderantibus*) for you! You present yourself so sweetly, and above all that those who desire (*desiderantium*) you could hope for, you grant the complete, overflowing enjoyment of yourself." He goes on:

> And yet, by those who enjoy you, you are desired with desire that is always new, and every minute renewed, and they press eagerly forward (*seseque urgentibus desideriis desideraris*). You are sought and you are encircled, and it is as though only for the first time, or better, not even yet, they have fully seized upon you (*apprehenderint*). Who can wonder at it? Since your throat is "most sweet", its indescribable sweetness has devoured them, but at the same time, you are "wholly desirable", and they enjoy you blissfully. They desire (*desiderant*), then, to enjoy unceasingly, so that, as it were in the one kiss of peace, they may experience simultaneously the bliss of desire and the desire of bliss (*felicitas desiderii et desiderium felicitatis*).[39]

As did Symeon before him, John wove Phil 3:12 into a reflection on infinite longing for communion.

Finally, Gilbert of Hoyland's rumination on Song of Songs 3:1 ("In my little bed by night, I sought him whom my soul loves") is very instructive with regard to the themes of pursuit and capture but requires some patient exegesis to arrive at Gilbert's point: "This verse seems most characteristic of cloistered brethren," he observes.[40] The coziness of the bed suggests to Gilbert every monk's spiritual quest for tranquility, and the bed's nocturnal use when nighttime has removed the sleeper from the admiring gaze of others points to humility. Although a fine exposition of the text, Gilbert was not satisfied with his first round of interpretation, since for him there is more to the spiritual life than tranquility and humility. Gilbert makes the case for restlessness, too, and a longing for union with Christ:

> Is this [tranquility and humility] enough? Enough perhaps for a laborer but not for a lover. Sweet indeed is sleep to the laborer. But a lover's fretfulness does not allow him sleep; it dispels drowsiness and brings on wakefulness. Love is made more restless by rest itself. . . . Then its sweet fire grows more vigorous and its devouring flame emerging from its hiding place ranges more freely through the relaxed spirit, penetrating more deeply and consuming more hungrily. Welcoming its chance, love cannot but practice its craft. Love always either enjoys the Beloved when present or yearns for him when absent.[41]

What Gilbert proposes, then, is a spirituality that moves away from regarding God as the omnipotent fulfiller of human needs and instead seeks God as an absent beloved:

> "In the day of my distress", says the psalm, "I sought God with outstretched hands". Far different is the motive for quest which the bride now proposes. Distress does not drive her but affection draws her. The sage in the psalm seeks the Lord to counter his distress; the bride seeks her Beloved for the encounter and delight of love. Yes, both the little bed of repose and the hiding-place of night refer to this, that she may constantly recall her Beloved, calmly savor his wisdom and taste his sweetness. Therefore much more compelling is the motive for search in one enamored than in one in need, though one can rightly claim that with a kind of holy greed love is always in need.[42]

But how might he put this spirituality based on longing further into language?

That question drove Gilbert to employ diction of the ancient poetic tradition and to quote Paul's letter to the Philippians. To get at this spiritual restlessness, Gilbert, on the one hand, selected the image of the wheel, quite famous in antiquity for signifying the torture of unfilled desire and longing for the beloved.[43] On the other hand, for Gilbert the course of Paul,'s life in Phil 3:12-13 embodied longing spirituality:

> Ever on fire for deeper mysteries and disregarding its present possessions, love tumbles forward head over heels to what lies ahead and like a living hoop, light-heartedly, bounds upward with all of its might to the heights, scarcely touching the earth. Even in Paul, love does not consider that it has reached the goal; pressing onward to what lies ahead Paul follows like an animated wheel where the spirit of burning desire sweeps him forward.[44]

I do not know whether Gilbert read Plautus.[45] Yet his manipulation of erotic clichés suggests that he was familiar with *some* ancient writer of amatory lines, possibly Ovid. Or he may just have stumbled upon the widely disseminated legend of Ixion, whose punishment for lusting after Zeus's wife, Hera, was to be affixed to a wheel spinning forever through the sky, a punishment which mirrored the head over heels posture of anyone unlucky enough to fall in love. In any case, here in Plautus's *Cistellaria* is the humorous version of Gilbert's and Paul's very serious spirituality of longing. It is Alcesimarchus, having been separated from his girlfriend by his father, who speaks:

> I believe it was Love who first devised torture among us men. I draw this inference from home, from my own experience—no need to look outside: I outdo and surpass everyone in mental agony. I'm being thrown around, tossed around, pierced, turned on the wheel of love (*amoris rota*); poor me, I'm being destroyed, driven, driven apart, dragged apart, torn apart: so clouded is my mind. Where I am, there I'm not, where I'm not, there my heart is; all my moods are like this.[46]

The complaint continues for a dozen or so more lines. If Gilbert had read Plautus, he would have recognized in this passage something very similar to his own application of the wheel motif to the apostle Paul, also an unfortunate lover, who suffers a much-delayed union with his beloved, Christ. Rolling along after Jesus, Paul is a model of the spirituality of longing.

In the End, *Koinōnia*

I argued in the previous chapter that Paul, quite provocatively by first-century standards, recommended Euodia and Syntyche to the church at Philippi (4:2-3) for leadership roles. The fact that they were women spoke against Paul's desire that the community recognize them as leaders and support them financially. Recall that Paul does three things in Phil 3:2-14 to counter such an objection. First, he puts forward his own life as a model (τύπος) by which the community might recognize leaders. Second, he connects his career to that of Euodia and Syntyche by means of athletic metaphors (3:13-14 and συνήθλησαν in 4:3). Third, he promotes Euodia and Syntyche by an indirect reference ("the ones walking") in 3:17 and by the order of composition itself; that is, 4:2-3 follows almost immediately upon 3:17. I additionally have suggested that Paul's confession of Jesus as Lord works its way through Paul's autobiography in 3:4-14 implying that the community's failure to support Euodia and Syntyche is a denial of Jesus' sovereignty. We are now in a position to see that Paul used nuptial imagery in 3:7-14 to delegitimize masculine hegemony and relocate confidence (πεποίθησις) for ministry away from the possession of a male body to the sharing of Jesus' body. Presenting himself as a manbride of Christ, Paul both fractures the masculine structure of political legitimation and lifts up κοινωνία as the basis and goal of leaders in the church.

Paul places his critique of masculine power and his restructuring of political authority appropriately under the rubric of justice (δικαιοσύνη). An important term in ancient political theory, it might seem that justice has little to do with nuptial imagery, the leading literary feature of this section of Philippians. This would indeed be the case if Paul were only speaking of justice that is in law (3:6) and that pertained to him alone (ἐμὴν δικαιοσύνην, 3:9), but he introduces a different kind of justice, one he associates with faith (τὴν διὰ πίστεως Χριστοῦ . . . ἐπὶ τῇ πίστει). When defined as "faithfulness," Paul's (and Christ's) πίστις goes to the heart of ancient erotic discourse and nuptial imagery.[47] Faithfulness is the question left hanging till the end, for example, in Chariton's novel *Chaereas and Callirhoe,* which narrates the testing of the lovers' loyalty to one another: "Callirhoe proved invincible; she stayed true to Chaereas alone (ἔμενε Χαιρέᾳ μόνῳ πιστή)."[48] Whether Chaereas would remain equally faithful—that question compels the reader to turn the pages.[49]

Justice based on πίστις, we learn from the erotic tradition, is thus a matter of mutual desire, reciprocity, equality, and sharing. Erotic justice is the κοινωνία of lovers or friends; it is the communion that Paul and the community enjoy in 1:7, an ambiguous verse that nevertheless in its double meaning makes this very point about justice as communion. The translation could be "I have you in my heart" just as accurately as "you have me in your heart." Equal ecstasy and the mutual dwelling in the other's heart is the reason Paul gives for his judgment that his thinking about the church is just (δίκαιος). Just such an understanding of justice as communion is found in ancient erotic poetry, novels, and wedding speeches, where loving and being loved in return define justice.[50] Conversely, injustice is unrequited love.[51]

In addition to erotic justice, other instances of nuptial imagery in 3:4-14 point to communion with Christ.[52] In Phil 3:8, Paul writes of his relationship to Christ as if its end were a sharing in Christ and all that is Christ's, in other words, as if marriage were at stake: "I regard everything as loss (ζημίαν) because of the surpassing value of knowing Christ Jesus my Lord. For his sake I have suffered the loss (ἐζημιώθην) of all things, and I regard them as rubbish, in order that I may gain Christ (ἵνα Χριστὸν κερδήσω)." In the middle of the eighteenth century Johann Jakob Wettstein called attention to the remarkable similarity of this verse to a passage from Heliodorus's romance *Aethiopica* in which Theagenes, a young man whose sole purpose in life is to wed Chariklea, makes this heartfelt plea for assistance and summarizes the novel's convoluted plot. "'Save us, Kalasiris,' he said. 'We come to you in supplication, strangers in a foreign land, with no home to go to, who have lost (ἀλλοτριωθέντας) everything in order to win one another (κερδήσωσι).'"[53] The loss (ζημία) that Paul mentions in reference to his past life fits within the nuptial framework, since the term designates the break the young bride must make between her childhood and her relations with parents in order to enter a new life in her husband.[54] Another wedding motif pertaining to this transition of the bride follows in 3:9: "that I might be found in him (εὑρεθῶ ἐν αὐτῷ)." In this passage Paul imagines the relocation of his body to another sphere, Christ. By the first century, the notion of the bride leaving her father's household and dwelling in her husband was not unusual. Greek tragedies provide evidence for the notion that the bride is found in the groom.[55] Before the bride might be given away by her father, however, she must be won by her suitor. In ancient literature, athletic imagery mixed with nuptial narrative to produce the motif of the bride at the finish line.[56]

Ovid imagined, for example, that Paris addressed Helen in this way: "Ah, might the gods make you the prize in a mighty contest, and let the victor have you for his couch!—as Hippomenes bore off, the prize of his running, Schoeneus's daughter, as Hippodamia came to Phrygian embrace, as fierce Hercules broke the horns of the Achelous while aspiring to thy embraces, Deianira. My daring would have boldly made its way in the face of conditions such as these, and you would know well how to be the object of my toils."[57]

The bride was herself the prize (βραβεῖον). She was the goal (σκοπός) obtained through the groom's pursuit (δίωξις), a labor and a straining after victory for which he had received a call or summons (κλῆσις).[58] Similarity of athletic contest (ἀγών) and erotic intention had an application broader than marriage, however, as this passage from Plutarch's *Amatorius* suggests, but the longing (πόθος) for union remains the same, as Eros motivates all contestants in love to achieve their end (τέλος):

> Love, on the other hand, has a function as holy as any you could mention, nor is there any contest or competition (ἀγῶνα) more fitting for a god to preside over and umpire (βραβεύειν) than the pursuit (δίωξιν) and tendance by lovers of handsome young men. Here there is no ignoble compulsion; instead persuasion and favour, prompting truly "A labour sweet, a toil that is no toil," leads the way to virtuous friendship. Not "without a god" does such friendship attain its proper goal (τέλος), nor is the guide to it, to whose dominion it belongs, any other god than Eros, companion of the Muses, the Graces and Aphrodite.[59]

Philippians 3:13 reinforces the nuptial imagery of 3:12 (pursuit, capture, and perfection), and 3:14 completes the union of nuptial and athletic imagery with its mention of the key terms σκοπός, βραβεῖον, διώκω, and κλῆσις. For Paul, Christ is the prize, the much-longed-for bride waiting at the end of the lover's struggle.[60]

WISHING FOR THE IMPOSSIBLE

We conclude our study of the legitimation of Paul's ministry and that of Euodia and Syntyche with an apostolic fantasy in Phil 3:10-11 and 20-21: bodily metamorphosis for the sake of κοινωνία with the beloved. Metamorphosis was a very popular theme in ancient literature.[61] Like Paul, ancient writers fantasized about impossible alterations to their bodies so that the sharing of another's body might take place.[62] Growing wings was a common fantasy in this regard, as Ovid illustrates: "now would I pray for wings to ply—thine, Perseus, or thine, Daedalus—that the yielding air might give way before my rapid flight and I might on a sudden behold the sweet soil of my native land, the faces in my lonely home, my loyal friends, and—foremost of all— the dear features of my wife."[63] If the many lovesick wishes for communion could be gathered into one, it might have sounded like this: Oh, that I were a ring, the wind, a pink rose, Sleep, a dolphin, thrush or blackbird—anything to touch my beloved.[64] Or, as Chloe pined for her Daphnis: "I wish I were his pipes, so he could breathe into me."[65]

It will be recalled that the common problem of Paul and his co-workers, particularly in the case of Euodia and Syntyche, viewed from the prevailing cultural perspective, was the condition of their bodies. In Paul's case, his bound body deprived him of free speech and disqualified him for ministry. For Euodia and Syntyche, their female bodies consigned them to private, domestic roles and precluded their participation in public affairs. To counter the elite, male-oriented objection to their bodies, Paul used the motif of the lover wishing for bodily transformation so that separation from the beloved might be overcome and communion fully enjoyed. In 3:10, Paul writes of a "communion of sufferings (κοινωνίαν τῶν παθημάτων)."[66] This phrase is reminiscent of Paul's sharing in the innards (σπλάγχνα) of Christ in 1:8, and it will be recalled that the latter verse suggested the identity of Christ's and Paul's emotions in a physical way.[67] Physical transformation is reiterated in 3:10, when Paul writes of his being shaped together with Christ's death (συμμορφιζόμενος τῷ θανάτῳ αὐτοῦ) reminding the reader of Christ's crucial shape change into the form of a slave (μορφὴν δούλου λαβών, 2:7). Finally, Paul's wish (εἴ πως) for sharing in Christ's resurrection in 3:11 anticipates the community's eager expectation (ἀπεκδεχόμεθα) in 3:20-21 for the savior's transformation (μετασχηματίσει) of bodies into the same shape (σύμμορφον) as his own glorious body. Paul, his colleagues, and the entire church, though now in transition, will soon possess all the rights and privileges of the Lord's body in their enjoyment of κοινωνία with him.[68] For this reason, to disregard Euodia and Syntyche is to deny the Lord's transforming power.

Notes

1. John of Ford, *Sermon* 77.6. *Sermons on the Final Verses of the Song of Songs, V,* trans. Wendy Mary Beckett, Cistercian Fathers Series 45 (Kalamazoo: Cistercian Publications, 1983), 191. See also *Sermon* 72.7. Theophylact's paraphrase (*In epistolam ad Philippenses* 1.21 [*PG* 124:1153]) recognized the verse's eroticism: "That is, I live a new life, and Christ is all things to me, even breath, life, and light." For "he/she is all things to me" as an erotic motif, see David E. Fredrickson, "God, Christ, and All Things in 1 Corinthians 15:28," *WW* 18 (1998): 254-63.

2. See Dioscorus, *Frg.* 23.21: "Away with you, O Grudging Spirit, from this wedding kindly regarded by God."

3. See Rebecca H. Hague, "Ancient Greek Weddings: The Tradition of Praise," *Journal of Folklore Research* 20 (1983): 131-43. For the "extensive lauding of the couple" among modern Greeks, see J. C. B. Petropoulos, *Eroticism in Ancient and Medieval Greek Poetry* (London: Duckworth, 2003), 12.

4. See Menander Rhetor, Περὶ ἐπιδεικτικῶν 399.21; 403.26–32; 406.11; 410.12–13. See also Dionysius of Halicarnassus, [Rhet.] 4.2. For the praiseworthiness of physical stature in males, see Aristotle, Rhet. 1.5.4. Might Paul's intent to magnify (μεγαλύνω) Christ be understood against this background?

5. Sappho, Frg. 111. Cf. Catullus, 61.16–20, 184–93; Claudian, Epithalamium 270–71; Joannes of Gaza, Anacreontea 3; Choricius, Opera 5.1.1; Dioscorus, Frg. 21.18–25. See also Petropoulos, Eroticism, 31–32, 105–6.

6. Lucian, Symp. 41. For the nuptial motif of the bride surpassing all rivals, see Sappho, Frg. 113; Alcman, Frg. 1.40–49; Theocritus, Id. 18.32–37; Catullus 61.82–86; Statius, Silvae 1.2.83–90, 107–20; See also Petropoulos, Eroticism, 89, 105. The phrase τὸ ὑπερέχον τῆς γνώσεως Χριστοῦ Ἰησοῦ in Phil 3:8 might be understood as a nuptial reference; possibly Phil 2:3 as well.

7. See Sappho, Frg. 96.6–9. See further Petropoulos, Eroticism, 89–90, 109. It is tempting to see an allusion to this motif in Phil 2:15.

8. See Aristophanes, Av. 1720–30; Euripides, Hel. 1433–35; Dioscorus, Frg. 21, 23. See also Petropoulos, Eroticism, 109.

9. For pervasive inequality in philosophic understandings of marriage, see David L. Balch, Let Wives Be Submissive: The Domestic Code in 1 Peter, SBLMS 26 (Chico, Calif.: Scholars Press, 1981), 23–80. For equality and unity in nonphilosophic contexts, see Aristophanes, Av. 1731–41; Theocritus, Id. 18.51–52. See also Petropoulos, Eroticism, 103–9.

10. See Menander Rhetor, Περὶ ἐπιδεικτικῶν 401.29–402.20; 404.23; Greek Anthology 12.103; Catullus, 61.31–35; Choricius, Opera 6.1.40; Theocritus, Id. 18.51–52: ἴσον ἔρασθαι ἀλλάλων. See also Petropoulos, Eroticism, 44.

11. For this reason, the marriage ceremony was itself known as a τελετή. For the τελ- root in wedding terminology, see Menander Rhetor, Περὶ ἐπιδεικτικῶν 405.19; 406.4; 407.1; 408.16; 409.9; 410.7–8, 15, 24; Dionysius of Halicarnassus, [Rhet.] 4.1. Earlier usage is consonant; see Sappho, Frg. 128; Sophocles, Ant. 1240–41: τὰ νυμφικὰ τέλη. Julius Pollux's list (Onomasticon 3.38.5) of terms pertaining to weddings is instructive: "marriage was called a telos and those who got married were called teleioi (τέλος ὁ γάμος ἐκαλεῖτο, καὶ τέλειοι οἱ γεγαμηκότες)." The power of the wedding to perfect the couple is shown in Himerius, Declamationes et orations 9.48: ὁ γὰρ τῷ ἐν γάμῳ τελούμενος; cf. Declamationes et orations 9.54: ὑπ' Ἀφροδίτῃ τελούμενον.

12. For the concept of liminality, see Arnold van Gennep, The Rites of Passage, trans. Monika B. Vizedom and Gabrielle L. Caffee (Chicago: University of Chicago Press, 1960); and Victor Turner, The Ritual Process: Structure and Anti-Structure, Symbol, Myth, and Ritual (Ithaca, N.Y.: Cornell University Press, 1977), 94–130.

13. John Chrysostom, Hom. Col. 12 (PG 62:386.58–62). Translation is from NPNF 13:318.

14. See chapter 5, pp. 105, 112.

15. See Rush Rehm, Marriage to Death: The Conflation of Wedding and Funeral Rituals in Greek Tragedy (Princeton: Princeton University Press, 1994). For death as marriage to Hades in funerary epigrams, see chapter 4, p. 97.

16. Artemidorus, Onir. 2.49. Translation is from The Interpretation of Dreams: Oneirocritica by Artemidorus, trans. Robert J. White (Park Ridge, N.J.: Noyes, 1975), 126. See also Richard Seaford, "The Tragic Wedding," JHS 107 (1987): 106–30.

17. For the latter meaning, see K. J. Dover, "Classical Greek Attitudes to Sexual Behavior," in Women in the Ancient World: The Arethusa Papers, ed. John Peradotto and John Patrick Sullivan, SUNY Series in Classical Studies (Albany: State University of New York Press, 1984), 266; J. N. Adams, The Latin Sexual Vocabulary (Baltimore: Johns Hopkins University Press, 1990), 177.

18. See Euripides, Alc. 473–75. See further Rehm, Marriage to Death, 54.

19. Heliodorus, Aeth. 5.4.6. Translation is from Collected Ancient Greek Novels, ed. B. P. Reardon (Berkeley: University of California Press, 1989), 449.

20. Xenophon of Ephesus, *Ephesiaca* 3.2.4. Translation is from Reardon, *Collected Ancient Greek Novels*, 147. Cf. *Ephesiaca* 5.1.5.

21. Death did not always have the last word, however. For being together *post mortem*, see *Griechische Vers-Inschriften* 1:881, 1111; Heliodorus, *Aeth.* 2.4.2–3.

22. We will not treat here the dilemma (Phil 1:24-25) that Paul's desire creates for him: whether to go and be with Christ or stay and be with the community. For the language of desperation that Paul employs ("to die is gain"), see R. L. Fowler, "The Rhetoric of Desperation," *HSCP* 91 (1987): 5–38. For desperate circumstances of an erotic kind, see Heliodorus, *Aeth.* 6.9.3; see also Anne Burnett, "Desire and Memory (Sappho Frag. 94)," *CP* 74 (1979): 16–27. For the theme of the lover's plight of being caught between two loves yet promising to remain (μένω), see Bion, *Epitaph. Adon.* 42; *Greek Anthology* 5.75; 247; 12.104, 126.

23. See Aelred of Rievaulx, *The Mirror of Charity* 2.6.12. Beatrice experienced Paul's emotions as she suffered the classic symptoms of lovesickness; see *Life of Beatrice of Nazareth: 1200–1268*, trans. Roger de Ganck, Cistercian Fathers Series (Kalamazoo: Cistercian Publications, 1991), 156–57, 185–86.

24. See Clement of Alexandria, *Strom.* 3.9.65.1–3.9.66.1; Origen, *Mart.* 47; Gregory of Nyssa, *De iis qui baptismum differunt* 46.429.1-7.

25. Patricia Rosenmeyer (*The Poetics of Imitation: Anacreon and the Anacreontic Tradition* [Cambridge: Cambridge University Press, 1992], 158) describes the ancient effect of Eros that these later Christian interpreters saw in this verse: "Erotic tension or disillusionment seems to attract images of disaggregation, as each segment of the body and its senses comes into contact with the disturbing power of Eros."

26. See *Od.* 20.57; 23.343; *Scholia in Odysseam* 23.343.1; 4.794.1; Theognis, *Eleg.* 1.838, 1010; 2.1385; Sappho, *Frg.* 130; Archilochus, *Frg.* 196; Alcman, *Frg.* 3.64-68; Euripides, *Heracl.* 602; *Hec.* 438; Moschus, *Europa* 4; *Anacreontea* 13.17, 19.6; Plutarch, *Amat.* 761B; Chariton, *Chaer.* 1.1.14; Julius Pollux, *Onomasticon* 2.62–64. See also Monica Silveira Cyrino, *In Pandora's Jar: Lovesickness in Early Greek Poetry* (Lanham, MD: University Press of America, 1995), 47, 74–76, 83, 136; Froma I. Zeitlin, *Playing the Other: Gender and Society in Classical Greek Literature*, Women in Culture and Society (Chicago: University of Chicago Press, 1995), 58–64.

27. The term ἀναλύω suggests death through liquefaction of the body. See Julius Pollux, *Onomasticon* 6.114; *Steinepigramme* 4/12/4. See further Apollonius of Rhodes, *Argon.* 3.808; Plutarch, *Frg.* 177; Heliodorus, *Aeth* 8.11.4. For λύω as an allusion to death in grave inscriptions, see *Griechische Vers-Inschriften* 1:460, 718, 873, 884, 1979, 1940, 1942, 1979.

28. See David E. Fredrickson, "Παρρησία in the Pauline Epistles," in *Friendship, Flattery, and Frankness of Speech: Studies on Friendship in the New Testament World*, ed. John T. Fitzgerald, NovTSup 82 (Leiden: Brill, 1996), 163–83. For πεποίθησις in particular, see Philodemus, *Lib.* 45; Josephus, *A.J.* 19.317–18.

29. See Seaford, "Tragic Wedding," 107; Christiane Sourvinou-Inwood, "The Young Abductor of the Locrian Pinakes," *Bulletin of the Institute of Classical Studies* 20 (1973): 12–21; *"Reading" Greek Culture: Texts and Images, Rituals and Myths* (New York: Oxford University Press, 1991), 65–70; John H. Oakley and Rebecca H. Sinos, *The Wedding in Ancient Athens*, Wisconsin Studies in Classics (Madison: University of Wisconsin Press, 1993), 32–33, 45; John H. Oakley, "Nuptial Nuances: Wedding Images in Non-Wedding Scenes of Myth," in *Pandora: Women in Classical Greece*, ed. Ellen D. Reeder and Sally C. Humphreys (Baltimore: Walters Art Gallery, 1995), 63–73. See also Julius Pollux, *Onomasticon* 3.69–70; Plutarch, *Amic. mult.* 93D: "in our longing for the person we pursue (ἔρωτι τοῦ διωκομένου), we pass over the one already within our grasp (τὸν καταλαμβανόμενον)." Achilles Tatius, *Leuc. Clit.* 1.5.5. Although the pursuit motif was sometimes found in stories of abduction, weddings themselves were conceptualized as substitutions for rape; see Petropoulos, *Eroticism*, 12–13. The Greeks believed that marriage was

the chief mark of civilization, "the victory of culture over nature" according to Seaford, "Tragic Wedding," 106.

30. For example, Achilles Tatius, *Leuc. Clit.* 8.6.7; 8.13.3; *Greek Anthology* 5.59, 247. See also John D. Marry, "Sappho and the Heroic Ideal," *Arethusa* 12 (1979): 72–73; Eva Stehle, *Performance and Gender in Ancient Greece: Nondramatic Poetry in Its Setting* (Princeton: Princeton University Press, 1997), 296–98.

31. See Anne Carson, *Eros the Bittersweet: An Essay* (Princeton: Princeton University Press, 1986), 19–20; Claude Calame, *The Poetics of Eros in Ancient* Greece, trans. Janet Lloyd (Princeton: Princeton University Press, 1999), 23–24: "This mismatch between the desire of one afflicted by love and the elusiveness of the one who provokes that erotic passion is a feature that pervades all archaic poetry."

32. See Theocritus, *Id.* 11.75; Plutarch, *Frg.* 136; Bion, *Epitaph. Adon.* 52–53; *Greek Anthology* 12.102.

33. The KJV came closer to the ancient sense with "follow after."

34. Although erotic pursuit shows up even in the ascetic interpretation; see, for example, Clement of Alexandria, *Paed.* 1.6.52.2–3; Theodoretus, *Interpretatio in xiv epistulas sancti Pauli PG* 82:581; and Symeon the New Theologian, *Hymni* 29.55–56 (*Hymns of Divine Love: By St. Symeon the New Theologian*, trans. George A. Maloney [Denville, N.J.: Dimension Books, 1970], 154):

> I meant He called me rather to repentance
> and I at once followed the Master
> When He ran, I also ran after Him
> When He fled, I likewise pursued (ἐδίωκεν) Him
> as a hound chasing a rabbit.

35. See Macarius, *[Homiliae spirituals]* 50.26.17: "But the Lord neither has an end nor is he totally comprehended. And Christians do not dare to say, 'We have comprehended', but they are humble night and day in their search. In the changeable world, there is no end to education and no one understands this better than a person who has begun to learn" (*The Fifty Spiritual Homilies; and, The Great Letter: Pseudo-Macarius*, trans. George A. Maloney, CWS (New York: Paulist, 1992), 170. The chief objection to this noetic interpretation of καταλαμβάνειν is that it fails to explain the passive voice in 3:12: "I was κατελήμφθην by Christ." What would be the point of Paul's saying that he had been comprehended by Christ in an intellectual way? Other writers acknowledge the mutual capturing that goes on between Paul and Christ in more erotic and less cognitive terms; see William of St. Thierry, *On Contemplating God* 7 (*On Contemplating God: Prayer, Meditations, I*, trans. Sister Penelope, Cistercian Fathers Series 3 (Spencer, Mass.: Cistercian Publications, 1971), 44: "So I desire to love you, and I love to desire you; and in this way I press forward, hoping to make him my own who has made me his own. That is to say, I hope one day to love you perfectly, you who first loved us, you the love-worthy, you the lovable." Cf. Jacopone da Todi, *Lauds* 91.

36. Symeon the New Theologian, *Catacheses* 1.123–30. Translation is from *Symeon the New Theologian: The Discourses*, trans. C. J. de Catanzaro, CWS (New York: Paulist, 1980), 44. See also Nicetas Paphlago, *Oratio* 16 (*PG* 105:332–33).

37. Jacopone da Todi echoes these themes of heat and infinite love while alluding to Phil 3:12. See *Lauds* 90 (*Jacopone da Todi: The Lauds*, trans. Serge and Elizabeth Hughes, CWS [New York: Paulist, 1982], 261): Outside, I am within; I pursue and am pursued / Love without limits, why do You drive me mad / And destroy me in this blazing furnace?

38. For an example of ascetic reading, see John of Ford, *Sermon* 94.5: "And so the bride, in the same Spirit as Paul, is moved to anxiety about the perfection of her justice or charity, and she too 'presses on', if in any way she may grasp it" (*Sermons on the Final Verses of the Song of Songs, VI*,

trans. Wendy Mary Beckett, Cistercian Fathers Series 46 [Kalamazoo: Cistercian Publications, 1984], 140).

39. John of Ford, *Sermon* 38.5. Translation is from *Sermons on the Final Verses of the Song of Songs, III*, trans. Wendy Mary Beckett, Cistercian Fathers Series 43 (Kalamazoo: Cistercian Publications, 1982), 109. See further John of Ford, *Sermon* 3.4; 26.5.

40. Gilbert of Hoyland, *Sermon* 2.5. Translation is from *Sermons on the Song of* Songs, *I*, trans. Lawrence C. Braceland, Cistercian Fathers Series 14 (Kalamazoo: Cistercian Publications, 1978), 60.

41. Gilbert of Hoyland, *Sermon* 2.5 (Braceland, *Sermons I, 60–61*).

42. Gilbert of Hoyland, *Sermon* 2.5 (Braceland, *Sermons I, 61*).

43. See Aristophanes, *Lys.* 845–46: "Oh, oh, evil fate! I've got terrible spasms and cramps. It's like I'm being broken on the rack (ἐπὶ τροχοῦ στρεβλούμενον)." Cf. *Anacreontea* 30.1–10: "In a dream I seemed to be running (τροχάζειν), with wings on my shoulders, and Love, with shoes of lead on his pretty feet, was pursuing (ἐδίωκε) me and catching me up. What is the meaning of this dream? I think it means that though I have been entangled in many loves and have wriggled free from all the others, I am caught fast in this one." See also *Anacreontea* 31.1–8: "Love, beating me cruelly with a rod tied round with hyacinths, ordered me to run by his side (συντροχάζειν); and as I ran through fierce torrents and thickets and gullies the sweat distressed me, my heart climbed to my nose and I might have perished."

44. Gilbert of Hoyland, *Sermon* 2.6 (Braceland, *Sermons I, 61*). Cf. *Sermon* 14.2.

45. Bits of Plautus, as did other fragments of ancient dramatists, detached themselves from plays and floated freely as proverbs. See, for instance, Gilbert of Hoyland, *Sermon* 16.7. In any case, he might have found the motif of the wheel also in Propertius 3.5.42; Tibullus 1.3.73–74; or in Ovid's tour of Hades in *Metam.* 4.461: "There whirls Ixion on his wheel, both following himself and fleeing, all in one."

46. Plautus, *Cist.* 203–12. Cf. Plutarch, *Amat.* 766A–B; Philostratus, *Vit. Apoll.* 6.40.21–27; Propertius 1.9.20. For more examples, see Netta Zagagi, *Tradition and Originality in Plautus: Studies in the Amatory Motif in Plautine Comedy,* Hypomnemata 62 (Göttingen: Vandenhoeck & Ruprecht, 1980), 68–89.

47. See Calame, *Poetics of Eros,* 103; John Barsby, "Love in Terence," in *Amor Roma: Essays Presented to E. J. Kenney on his Seventy-Fifth Birthday,* ed. S. M. Braund and R. Mayer (Cambridge: Cambridge University Press, 1999), 5–29; Daniel H. Garrison, *Sexual Culture in Ancient Greece,* Oklahoma Series in Classical Culture 24 (Norman: University of Oklahoma Press, 2000), 244–45. See further *Greek Anthology* 5.52; Horace, *Carm.* 2.12.16; Catullus 30.11–12; 87.3–4.

48. Chariton, *Chaer.* 2.8.2. Translation is from Reardon, *Collected Ancient Greek Novels,* 46. Cf. *Chaer.* 6.6.5.

49. See Ryan K. Balot, "Foucault, Chariton, and the Masculine Self," *Helios* 25 (1998): 157. See also Achilles Tatius, *Leuc. Clit.* 2.19.1: "I waited a few days and then said to Leukippe: 'How long will we stop at mere kisses, dearest? The overture is delightful, but now let us add erotic grace notes. We can exchange promises to be faithful to each other (φέρε ἀνάγκην ἀλλήλοις ἐπιθῶμεν πίστεως). Once Aphrodite has initiated us into her mysteries, no other power can contravene her will."

50. See Calame, *Poetics of Eros,* 24–29, 61, 102; Joan B. Burton, *Theocritus's Urban Mimes: Mobility, Gender, and Patronage,* Hellenistic Culture and Society 19; Berkeley: University of California Press, 1995), 83–92; Richard Hunter, *Theocritus and the Archaeology of Greek Poetry* (Cambridge: Cambridge University Press, 2006), 170–71.

51. As in Gal 4:12. Cf. Sappho, *Frg.* 1, on which see Ellen Greene, "Subjects, Objects, and Erotic Symmetry in Sappho's Fragments," in *Among Women: From the Homosocial to the Homoerotic in the Ancient World,* ed. Nancy Sorkin Rabinowitz and Lisa Auanger (Austin: University of Texas Press, 2002), 82–105. See further Theognis, *Eleg.* 2.1283; Euripides, *Med.* 16–28, 265–66, 314–15; Theocritus, *Id.* 11.67; *Greek Anthology* 5.23; 12.103. See also Keith Preston, *Studies in the Diction of*

the *Sermo Amatorius in Roman Comedy* (Menasha, WI: George Banta, 1916), 58–60; Richard Hunter, *Theocritus* (Cambridge: Cambridge University Press, 1999), 240; James H. Schwartz, "Engraved Gems in the Collection of the American Numismatic Society II: Intaglios with Eros," *American Journal of Numismatics* 11 (1999): 19.

52. For the antitype of the reading I am proposing, see Karl Barth, *The Epistle to the Philippians: 40th Anniversary Edition*, trans. James W. Leitch (Louisville: Westminster John Knox, 2002), 99: "Here the meaning of the fact that Jesus Christ is *my Lord* becomes clear and full-toned—also in contradistinction to the use mysticism makes of the same possessive pronoun. Paul, as the sequel shows, would claim the *right* of Christ as *his* right. That, intrinsically, is the aim of the *kērdesō kai heurethō* (in order to gain Christ and be found in him). The right of *Christ*, however, puts Paul in the *wrong*. In order to *gain* Christ and *be found* in him, he must look on *his* right as dung, as *skybala*, that is, *not* look on it any longer." It is Barth who interjects the language of "rights" (inconceivable between lovers!) and accordingly misconstrues mysticism as claiming to have rights over Jesus.

53. Heliodorus, *Aeth.* 4.18.2; cf. *Aeth.* 6.9.3. See Johann Jakob Wettstein, *Novum Testamentum Graecum* (1751–52; repr., 2 vols.; Graz: Akademische Druck- u. Verlagsanstalt, 1962), 2:276.

54. See John H. Oakley and Rebecca H. Sinos, *The Wedding in Ancient Athens,* Wisconsin Studies in Classics (Madison: University of Wisconsin Press, 1993), 12: "The word 'penalty' (zemia) makes it clear that the bride must make an offering to this goddess as compensation for the coming marriage union. Artemis is the virgin goddess who protects young and animals and children, but she is equally capable of using her power to kill them. The bride must win Artemis' acquiescence in order to depart safely from her sphere to the sphere of sexuality belonging to Aphrodite."

55. See Richard Seaford, "The Tragic Wedding," *JHS* 107 (1987): 106–30. See *Greek Anthology* 7.492. For an example of later, erotic interpretation of what it means to enter Jesus, see Jacopone da Todi, *Laud* 90 (Hughes and Hughes, *Lauds,* 264):

> "Love, Love," the world cries out,
> "Love, Love," shouts all creation.
> Love, Love, so inexhaustible are You
> That he who clasps You close desires You all the more!
> Love, Love, perfect circle, he who enters into You
> With his whole heart loves you forever. For You are warp and woof
> Of the robe of him who loves You, filling him with such delight
> That he calls out again and again, "Love!"

56. See Thomas F. Scanlon, *Eros and Greek Athletics* (Oxford: Oxford University Press, 2002), 219–26.

57. Ovid, *Her.* 16.263–70. See also Statius, *Silvae* 1.2.38–45, 85–86; Musaeus, *Hero et Leander* 197. See Leah Rissman, *Love as War: Homeric Allusion in the Poetry of Sappho,* Beiträge zur klassischen Philologie 157 (Königstein/Ts.: Hain, 1983), 101–3.

58. Three texts vividly illustrate the same overlap of nuptial and athletic imagery that is found in Phil 3:14-15: Heliodorus, *Aeth.* 4.1.1–4.4.4; Menander Rhetor, Περὶ ἐπιδεικτικῶν, 406.13–24; and Chariton, *Chaer.* 1.2.1–2 (on which see Balot, "Foucault, Chariton," 144–54). See further Petropoulos, *Eroticism,* 95, 102.

59. Plutarch, *Amat.* 758 B–C.

60. For this identification, see Gregory of Nyssa, *Orationes viii de beatitudinibus* 8.6 (*PG* 44:1301.1–26).

61. Extensively treated in Petropoulos, *Eroticism,* 74–85.

62. See Rosenmeyer, *Poetics of Imitation,* 160–66; Sarah Mace, "Utopian and Erotic Fusion in a New Elegy by Simonides," in *The New Simonides: Contexts of Praise and Desire,* ed. Deborah Boedeker and David Sider (New York: Oxford University Press, 2001), 185–207. Synesius (*Ep.* 152) traced the notion back to Plato. See also Theocritus, *Id.* 11.54–55; Bion, *Epitaph. Adon.* 64–66.

63. Ovid, *Tristia* 3.8.5–10. See also *P. Giess.* 17 (*Select Papyri, I,* trans. A. S. Hunt and C. C. Edgar, LCL [Cambridge, MA: Harvard University Press, 1932], 309–11): "I beg you, my lord, if it please you, to send for me; else I die because I do not behold you daily. Would that I were able to fly and come to you and make obeisance to you; for it distresses me not to behold you."

64. See Ovid, *Am.* 2.15; *Greek Anthology* 5.83, 84; 12.52, 142.

65. Longus, *Daphn,* 1.14.3. Translation is from Reardon, *Collected Ancient Greek Novels,* 294.

66. I call attention to the possibility that the sufferings referred to by παθήματα in 3:10 are emotions associated with longing desire, as, for example, in the Greek title of Parthenius's *Narrationes amatoriae*: Περὶ ἐρωτικῶν παθημάτων. Cf. *Narrationes amatoriae* 13.1; Euripides, *Hipp.* 570. If this is the case, then the emotions Paul seeks to share with Christ are those narrated in Phil 2:6-8, for which see chapter 3.

67. See chapter 2, pp. 35–36.

68. See Paulinus of Nola, *Epp.* 11.2; 45.5.

Conclusion

I end this book wishing to express gratitude to two groups of writers whose deaths long ago preserve them from the embarrassment, consternation, or perplexity that my thankfulness might otherwise occasion. One group illustrates for me the sufficiency of an intermittent courage of conviction: a few fourth-century Christians and a few more middle- and late-Byzantine authors and Latin writers of the Middle Ages *sometimes* allowed themselves to hear echoes of ancient amatory poetry in the language of Paul's letter to the Philippians. They confirmed a figure I had glimpsed in the letter—an erotic Paul—but was hesitant to speak about until others within the Christian tradition first took the risk. They paved the way for construing the apostle's emotion as the *erōs* of secular literature, even though they knew such readings were unsuitable and offensive to theologians of sovereignty, before whose critical gaze these pages now, apprehensively, give themselves to viewing.

To the other group, to Sappho and her many admirers/imitators who shared with her, and with Homer's Penelope, a strangely mixed *erōs*, a desire for communion combined with the dangerous experience of heating, melting, and finally emptying of one's body—to these writers I owe an even greater debt. The poetry I have appealed to throughout this book, culminating in the amazing epigram on infinite longing by Paulus Silentiarius, confirms that my Christian co-conspirators, John of Ford, Gilbert of Hoyland, Baldwin of Ford, and the rest, were on the right track when they read Paul in light of longing desire. And thanks are due to these love poets for a reason beyond the writing of their poetry, and this is perhaps the most important reason for my gratitude: their troubling of the too-tidy commonplace, which admittedly they often also promoted, that *erōs* is love when the beloved is present and *pothos* is love when the beloved is absent. They teach us that there is no escape from the vulnerability to loss and to grief written inside of love. That is to say, there is no dichotomy that can insulate love from longing. For coming to know that awe-filling truth I am grateful. To project it into God is why I wrote this book.

Such a projection of longing desire into God has been made difficult, however, by the many interpreters of Paul's letters who protect divine equilibrium by encircling God with three rings of defense. The outer ring is the illusion of epistolary presence. Then comes Paul's authoritative apostleship. Finally, scholars have erected a version of Paul's Christology, whether intentionally or not I cannot say, the effect of which has been to ward off self-consuming desire from ever infecting the Godhead. God appears to be unassailable. Yet, in the first four chapters, I tried to show how these three lines of defense rebel against the prophylactic use to which scholars and theologians have attempted to put them and, in spite of themselves, actually welcome longing and seek to pass it on from one ring to the next and finally to the center, to God, who then of course becomes decentered as anyone one who has lost a love would be. In the last two chapters, in a very preliminary way I attempted to describe what difference a god in mourning might make for the politics of the Philippian community.

The outer ring: epistolary presence. There is a view widely held today that Paul's letters were instruments of apostolic control—itself a faint copy of divine sovereignty. Even though recent emphasis on Philippians as a letter of friendship lends warmth to Paul the teacher, theologian, and moral director and softens the portrait of a domineering Paul and, by implication, the impressions we have of Christ and of God, the underlying structure of the letter as a platform for authority remains in contemporary criticism. In conformity to ancient epistolary theory, Philippians is taken to be a substitute for Paul's presence and voice through which he effects change in readers. Although I affirm the insight that Philippians is a friendly letter, I nevertheless want to challenge the idea that this letter, or any letter for that matter and least of all a letter full of expressions of longing, delivers the presence of the author and nothing more needs to be said about its emotional effects on readers. Many letter writers in the first thousand years of the common era were, in fact, as ambivalent about letters as I am. While joyous letter recipients touted the miraculous appearance of the absent writer, their jubilation often turned to grief as they realized, as they themselves often said, that the fictive presence they held in their hands actually turned them more deeply to the absence of their loved one. As a result of this epistolary duplicity, longing desire breached the first line of defense laid down by Paul's interpreters to protect divine sovereignty. In other words, the Paul that Philippians makes present is a Paul who is not there.

This incursion merits closer inspection. In one sense, the letter to the Philippians, as an instance of writing, suffered and still suffers the fault that Plato ascribed to all writing at the end of the *Phaedrus*: it outlives the author, and because of its longevity it is freed from the stabilizing force of the author's intentions, which in this instance were buried with Paul—assuming that he had clarity about them when he was alive. For this reason, ancient epistolary theory was naïve, or perhaps very cunning, to claim that letters delivered presence and voice without countervailing effects, and modern Pauline interpreters are equally naïve, or again maybe very shrewd, when they claim to have discovered Paul's intentions in a letter and then use the letter to prove their claim. They read his writing as the expression of his ideas or the contents of his commands, and thus the letter itself necessarily shapes an authoritative Paul, benevolent or otherwise, whose expertise concerning his own mind cannot be surpassed. But Philippians (whether Paul did this intentionally or unintentionally, I do not know) makes epistolary theory's claim about his presence and modern scholars' view of the letter as an instrument of control quite problematic, especially so by the eroticization of friendship motifs. That is, the letter not only points to Paul's absence in a commonsense way (why would he write if he were not gone?) but all the more so when it, in the company of numerous other letters in the first thousand years of the common era, declared the writer's longing; called upon a divine witness to attest to grief over separation; characterized the recipients as longed-for ones; and acknowledged the heart as host, visitant, scripted surface, and space for carrying about the absent beloved. Longing has broken through the ring of epistolary presence and, feeling its growing power, heads off for the corruption of apostleship.

The middle ring: apostleship. If it is the case that Paul heightened the *philia* of the epistle by the grief that lurks inside of *erōs*, *pothos* in other words, then it is necessary to rethink the phrase "apostolic authority," which is often associated with Paul's reputation in contemporary scholarship, whether he is despised for patriarchy or admired for the mission-oriented control of congregations. Philippians 1:8 ("We long for all of you in the innards of Christ") suggests that in Paul's case "authority" may not be the correct word to pair with "apostolic." His declaration of longing for the Philippians puts Paul's apostleship in a new light, especially if we understand it against the background of longing in the poetic tradition beginning with Homer and Sappho and ending, for the purposes of this study, with Paulus Silentiarius. By his application of the Sapphic motif "sweet-bitter love" to Paul's declaration of longing in Phil 1:8, John of Ford lends credence to my hunch that poetry's exploration of the emotion growing out of grief over a separated beloved is a possible background for interpreting Paul's relationship with the Philippian community.

The picture of Paul as mourning lover contrasts sharply with the one drawn by many of today's interpreters, who regard him either as a dogmatist, a rhetor, a disciplinarian, or perhaps a combination of all three. The Paul of Phil 1:8, as I suggested in light of the prominence of *pothos* in poetry from the eighth century B.C.E. to the sixth century C.E., experienced the wounding, piercing, heating, and melting of his body. From the poetic perspective, the physicality of Paul's self-portrait emerges forcefully, and because Paul's longing for the Philippians occurs "in the innards of Christ," what we discover by way of a doctrine of Paul—that he cannot be known apart from his longing for the Philippians—pertains directly to his doctrine of Christ. In other words, Christology and Paulology are twin disciplines of Pauline theology, although it is not possible to say which of the two was born first.

THE INNER RING: CHRISTOLOGY

With a letter so full of longing and an apostle yearning for communion, Christ is God's last line of defense against an emotion that, if it should ever cross over into Godhead, would ruin God's sovereign freedom from need and freedom to dispose of creation according to the divine will. For this reason, a large number of Christian interpreters tell the story of Christ Jesus in Phil 2:6-11 as if it were an object lesson about human obedience to God. This form of Christology may well have begun with Clement of Alexandria, whose comments on the Christ Hymn turned Christ's longing for humans into a divine intention to save humans. The Christian tradition developed Clement's idea supplanting *erōs* with philanthropy. Christ, the New Adam, restores humanity to its place under God's throne by illustrating humble submission to the will of the Father. He empties himself of divine substance, all the privileges and powers of God, in order to play the human role with conviction. Unaided by his divine nature, which had temporarily been put aside or, perhaps, merely masked, for our sake Christ became a slave to God and obedient even to the point of death. For his exemplary behavior, Christ was rewarded by the Father with resurrection from the dead, and he ascended to the position he held before the object lesson began—only now he is tolerant of human shortcomings since he remembers just how difficult life can be and how inscrutable the movements of the sovereign God often are.

But such a reading of the Christ Hymn is by no means as self-evident as many interpreters assume. I could discover no evidence from ancient literature to support the notion that "he emptied himself" refers to humility. Moreover, it may very well be the case on grammatical grounds that "he took the form of a slave" preceded "he emptied himself," thus distancing *kenōsis* from incarnation and attaching it instead to Christ's body. And since there is no stated referent for either Jesus' slavery or for his obedience, there is no overriding reason to think of the Christ Hymn as an illustration of humble submission to God as master. Yet there is support (spotty but not to be ignored) both from the history of interpretation and from the popular poetic motif *servitium amoris* that Christ's taking on the "form of a slave" worked hand in glove with the longing-oriented interpretation of *kenōsis* I have made. In addition to these exegetical objections to the prevailing interpretation, there is a moral one: the notion of self-limitation is itself very problematic, since it presumes a self to limit. The set of christological ideas known as kenotic theory, with its focus on the *voluntary* act of divine self-limitation, sets a moral standard of humility before the poor and marginalized, which they are, structurally, never able to live up to but to which they perpetually are held accountable by those who have power and privilege and who have comforted their own consciences by telling tales of sacrifice in imitation of the obedient Son of God.

All that changes when Christ's *kenōsis* is interpreted as a physical event, the result of melting and the final outcome of longing desire. Ancient physicians posited that the warming and subsequent liquefaction of the body and its draining away were the origin of pain. Similarly, poets recognized that the absence of the beloved melted the innards, the seat of the emotions, and liquefied the grieving lover. Philological evidence points in the same direction: Christ's so-called self-empting was not a voluntary act of humility but a wasting away in longing for communion. Later writers such as Bernard of Clairvaux, Hadewijch of Antwerp, Gilbert of Hoyland, Isaac of Stella, Nicholas Cabasilas, and Jacopone da Todi came very close to the erotic interpretation of the Christ Hymn that I have offered in these pages. Poetry, medicine, philology, and the works of a handful of interpreters from the Middle Ages therefore give us reason to think that if in Philippians the purpose of Christology, the inner ring around God, was to preserve divine sovereignty, then it has failed.

Yet if it is Christology's purpose, as I believe it is in Paul's letter to the Philippians, to project longing into God, then it has taken full advantage of its proximity to theology, and we might now, on the basis of Paul's words, think of God and think of longing for communion at the same time. Longing and divinity, not sovereignty and divinity, are, in the wake of Philippians, the new dogmatic coupling. In fact, that is the way Christ Jesus himself thought about theological matters, since we read that "he did not regard erotic abduction to be equal to a god." What *is* equal to a god, however, is the taking of a slave's form in the unreasoning and undignified loss of control love brings to the lover, in other words the unintended but fully willed subjection of the lover to the frailty of the beloved's flesh. To borrow (but also to bend to the point of breaking) the Christian church's language invented centuries after the composition of the Pauline epistles, we might say that the second person of the Trinity pioneered a new (but not new with respect to the Hebrew Bible) way of being ὁ θεός. It is not without *theo*logical significance, then, that the subject of the verbs in Phil 2:6-8 is not God but Christ Jesus. God, it seems, awaited Christ's erotic innovation in what it means to be divine.

No rings left: God. Recall that I joined with other scholars in rejecting the translation of μορφὴ τοῦ θεοῦ in Phil 2:6 as "essence" or "nature of God." Yet in an unusual move I also argued that it is possible to retain the *visual* aspect of μορφή and still make sense of the text. I went on to document that, when Greek authors mentioned divine form, it was usually to praise someone's beauty, which for the Greeks meant youth, and youth in turn signified ageless and undying life. When Paul begins to tell the story of Christ Jesus by saying that he existed in divine form, ancient readers might well have thought that he meant freedom from death or from any other sort of limitation. And they might have been correct. In fact, Paul might have counted on them to read into "the form of God" this common construal of divinity, as unfettered power, in order to set up Christ's momentous rejection of it.

And reject it Christ did. Paul got the attention of his readers by narrating Christ's disregard of a very characteristic feature of divine freedom in the ancient world: the abduction of humans. In order to make this claim about Phil 2:6, that Christ rejected being θεός in the way of sexual violence, I had to do three things: first, to insist on the meaning of ἁρπαγμός as erotic abduction and not "thing to be grasped" or "thing grasped after"; second, to translate 2:6 as "he did not regard erotic abduction to be equal to a god"; and, third, to document just how deeply the motif of sexual violence permeated the foundational cultural and religious myths and the social practices (specifically, marrying and burying) of the ancient Greeks. There is not much more I can say about the first two points; if either is faulty, then of course the third, the one I find most interesting from a theological perspective, is not worth considering. But I think a good case has been made, and if the third point about the general perception of the gods as abductors holds, then it may be said that Christian theology, to the extent that it desires to be Pauline, ought to have this mind in it, which was also in Christ Jesus, who refused to be God by being sovereign in the sense of dominating the world and treating it as an object for his control, but having lost control, having fallen in love with mortal and sinful flesh he longed for communion even to the point of death. The longing one is the one God calls lord. In that confession of Jesus' lordship, the sovereignty of God begins to come to an end.

And in this beginning of sovereignty's demise, politics of a Pauline sort has its chance. That is, in Philippians the doctrine of the church, and particularly the problem of defining the quality and the legitimacy of its leaders, hinges on Christ's disregard for snatching, his vulnerability to longing desire, and God's reputation as Father depending on the world's joining with God to give the name of Lord to the slave of love. What does this opening for politics look like in the letter to the Philippians? If the longing Christ is Lord, then Paul would have committed a colossal performative contradiction had he passed over Euodia and Syntyche, Timothy and Epaphroditus, and indeed even himself in chains, and had instead recommended for leadership roles others who possessed higher social status and the power that accompanies it. Yet the silenced (and therefore useless) apostle and his lowly, young, homesick, and, in the case of two of them, female colleagues had this going for them: all five repeat the political drama of the Christ Hymn and embody the power—if that is what it can still be called—of desire for an absent beloved. In order to overcome the natural objection to his recommendation (really, what community would want its leaders heartsick and pining away for the other?), Paul invents a rival set of leaders whose chief characteristic is envy, an emotion that mimicked the effects of *pothos* on the body but also closed off any affection for the other. Traces of their resentment—for this is what ancient envy was—can be found throughout the letter, culminating in Paul's reference to the "enemies of the cross of Christ" (3:18).

"Here's your choice in leaders," Paul might have said less poetically than he did say, "choose those who begrudge you or choose those whose love for you is so tender that your very presence puts them in mind of your absence." Yet, was there more to Paul's politics than imitation of Christ's longing? Yes, something of immediate, practical consequence. Paul's desire for communion with Christ opened a social space in which slaves, women, those imprisoned and deprived of voice could recognize themselves and be recognized as fully legitimate leaders. Paul's desire turned him into a manbride, an impossible being that dissolved the dichotomy of male and female and ruined the path to leadership built on that distinction. His deployment of nuptial imagery exploited the liminality of the bride with unmistakable parallels to the liminality of the corpse. He canceled the confidence-granting power of high status and masculinity and replaced them both with two things that are, in fact, little more than sweet nothings: a wish for a transformed body and a desire to dissolve and be with Christ.

Bibliography

Adams, J. N. *The Latin Sexual Vocabulary*. Baltimore: Johns Hopkins University Press, 1990.

Albis, Robert V. *Poet and Audience in the Argonautica of Apollonius*. Greek Studies: Interdisciplinary Approaches. Lanham, MD: Rowman & Littlefield, 1996.

Alexander, Loveday. "Hellenistic Letter-Forms and the Structure of Philippians." *JSNT* 37 (1989): 87–101.

Auanger, Lisa. "Glimpses through a Window: An Approach to Roman Female Homoeroticism through Art Historical and Literary Evidence." In *Among Women: From the Homosocial to the Homoerotic in the Ancient World*, edited by Nancy Sorkin Rabinowitz and Lisa Auanger, 211–55. Austin: University of Texas Press, 2002.

Avagianou, Aphrodite. *Sacred Marriage in the Rituals of Greek Religion*. European University Studies: Series XV, Classics 54. Bern: Peter Lang, 1991.

Bagnall, Roger S., and Raffaella Cribiore. *Women's Letters from Ancient Egypt: 300 BC–AD 800*. Ann Arbor: University of Michigan Press, 2006.

Balch, David L. *Let Wives Be Submissive: The Domestic Code in 1 Peter*. SBLMS 26. Chico, CA: Scholars, 1981.

Balot, Ryan K. "Foucault, Chariton, and the Masculine Self." *Helios* 25 (1998): 139–62.

Barringer, Judith M. *Divine Escorts: Nereids in Archaic and Classical Greek Art*. Ann Arbor: University of Michigan Press, 1995.

Barsby, John. "Love in Terence." In *Amor, Roma: Love & Latin Literature*, edited by Susanna Morton Braund and Roland Mayer, 5–29. Cambridge: Cambridge Philosophical Society, 1999.

Barth, Karl. *The Epistle to the Philippians: 40th Anniversary Edition*. Translated by James W. Leitch. Louisville: Westminster John Knox, 2002.

Beckett, Wendy Mary. *Sermons on the Final Verses of the Song of Songs, II*. Cistercian Fathers Series 39. Kalamazoo: Cistercian, 1982.

———. *Sermons on the Final Verses of the Song of Songs, III*. Cistercian Fathers Series 43. Kalamazoo: Cistercian, 1982.

———. *Sermons on the Final Verses of the Song of Songs, V*. Cistercian Fathers Series 45. Kalamazoo: Cistercian, 1983.

———. *Sermons on the Final Verses of the Song of Songs, VI.* Cistercian Fathers Series 46. Kalamazoo: Cistercian, 1984.

Beecher, Donald A., and Massimo Ciavolella. *A Treatise on Lovesickness: Jacques Ferrand.* Syracuse: Syracuse University Press, 1990.

Bell, David N. *Baldwin of Ford: Spiritual Tractates, II.* Cistercian Fathers Series 41. Kalamazoo: Cistercian, 1986.

Bergren, Ann L. T. "The Homeric Hymn to Aphrodite: Tradition and Rhetoric, Praise and Blame." *Classical Antiquity* 8 (1989): 1–41.

Berry, Ken. "The Function of Friendship Language in Philippians 4:10-20." In *Friendship, Flattery, and Frankness of Speech: Studies on Friendship in the New Testament World*, edited by John T. Fitzgerald, 107–24. NovTSup 82. Leiden: Brill, 1996.

Bettini, Maurizio. *The Portrait of the Lover.* Translated by Laura Gibbs. Berkeley: University of California Press, 1999.

Beye, Charles Rowan. "Jason as Love-hero in Apollonios' *Argonautika.*" *GRBS* 10 (1969): 31–55.

Bickerman, E. J. "Love Story in the Homeric Hymn to Aphrodite." *Athenaeum* 54 (1976): 229-54.

Biesterfeldt, Hans H., and Dimitri Gutas. "The Malady of Love." *JAOS* 104 (1984): 21–55.

Blass, F., and A. Debrunner. *A Greek Grammar of the New Testament and Other Early Christian Literature.* Translated by Robert W. Funk. Chicago: University of Chicago Press, 1961.

Blum, Owen J. *The Letters of Peter Damian: Letters 61–90.* FC: Medieval Continuation 3. Washington, DC: Catholic University of America Press, 1989.

Borthwick, E. K. ΦΥΛΛΑΣΩ or ΛΑΦΥΣΣΩ? A Note on Two Emendations." *Eranos* 77 (1979): 79–83.

Børtnes, Jostein. "Eros Transformed: Same-Sex Love and Divine Desire." In *Greek Biography and Panegyric in Late Antiquity*, edited by Tomas Hägg and Philip Rousseau, 180–93. Transformation of the Classical Heritage 31. Berkeley: University of California Press, 2000.

Böttrich, Christfried. "Verkündigung aus 'Neid und Rivalität'? Beobachtungen zu Phil, 1, 12-18." *ZNW* 95 (2004): 84–101.

Bowe, Barbara Ellen. *A Church in Crisis: Ecclesiology and Paraenesis in Clement of Rome.* HDR 23. Minneapolis: Fortress Press, 1988.

Bowman, Alan K. *Life and Letters on the Roman Frontier: Vindolanda and Its People.* London: British Museum, 1994.

Braceland, Lawrence C. *The Works of Gilbert of Hoyland: Sermons on the Song of Songs, I.* Cistercian Fathers Series 14. Kalamazoo: Cistercian, 1978.

Bruss, Jon Steffen. *Hidden Presences: Monuments, Gravesites, and Corpses in Greek Funerary Epigram.* Hellenistica Groningana 10. Dudley, MA: Peeters, 2005.

Bulloch, A. W. *Callimachus: The Fifth Hymn.* Cambridge Classical Texts and Commentaries 26. Cambridge: Cambridge University Press, 1985.

Bulman, Patricia. *Phthonos in Pindar.* University of California Publications. Classical Studies 35. Berkeley: University of California Press, 1992.

Burnett, Anne. "Desire and Memory (Sappho Frag. 94)." *CP* 74 (1979): 16–27.

Burton, Joan B. *Theocritus's Urban Mimes: Mobility, Gender, and Patronage.* Hellenistic Culture and Society 19. Berkeley: University of California Press, 1995.

Calame, Claude. *The Poetics of Eros in Ancient Greece.* Translated by Janet Lloyd. Princeton: Princeton University Press, 1999.

Campbell, Malcolm. *A Commentary on Apollonius Rhodius Argonautica III 1–471.* Mnemosyne 141. Leiden: Brill, 1994.

Carr, David M. *The Erotic Word: Sexuality, Spirituality, and the Bible.* Oxford: Oxford University Press, 2003.

Carson, Anne. *Eros the Bittersweet: An Essay.* Princeton: Princeton University Press, 1986.

———. *If Not, Winter: Fragments of Sappho.* New York: Alfred A. Knopf, 2002.

Clarke, G. W. *The Letters of St. Cyprian of Carthage.* ACW 43 (New York: Newman, 1984.

Coakley, Sarah. "Kenosis: Theological Meanings and Gender Connotations." In *The Work of Love: Creation as Kenosis,* edited by John Polkinghorne, 192–210. Grand Rapids: Eerdmans, 2001.

———. *Powers and Submissions: Spirituality, Philosophy and Gender.* Challenges in Contemporary Theology. Oxford: Blackwell, 2002.

Connor, L. B. *The Quiet Athenian.* Oxford: Clarendon, 1986.

Conte, Gian Biagio. *Genres and Readers: Lucretius, Love Elegy, Pliny's Encyclopeadia.* Translated by Glenn W. Most. Baltimore: Johns Hopkins University Press, 1994.

Corso, Antonio. "Love as Suffering: The Eros of Thespiae of Praxiteles." *Bulletin of the Institute of Classical Studies* 42 (1997–98): 63–91.

Countryman, William L. *Love, Human and Divine: Reflections on Love, Sexuality, and Friendship.* Harrisburg, PA: Morehouse, 2005.

Culler, Jonathan D. *On Deconstruction: Theory and Criticism after Structuralism.* Ithaca, NY: Cornell University Press, 1982.

Curkpatrick, Stephen. "Apostrophic Desire and Parousia in the Apostle Paul's Epistles: A Derridean Proposal for Textual Interpretation." *BibInt* 10 (2002): 175–93.

Cyrino, Monica Silveira. *In Pandora's Jar: Lovesickness in Early Greek Poetry.* Lanham, MD: University Press of America, 1995.

Dahl, Nils A. "Euodia and Syntyche and Paul's Letter to the Philippians." In *The Social World of the First Christians: Essays in Honor of Wayne A. Meeks,* edited by L. Michael White and O. Larry Yarbrough, 3–15. Minneapolis: Fortress Press, 1995.

D'Angelo, Mary Rose. "Women Partners in the New Testament." *JFSR* 6 (1990): 65–86.

Darrouzès, Jean. *Épistoliers Byzantins du Xe Siècle.* Archives de l'orient chrétien 6. Paris: Institut français d'études byzantines, 1960.

deCatanzaro, Carmino J. *The Life in Christ.* Crestwood, NY: St. Vladimir's Seminary Press, 1974.

de Ganck, Roger. *Life of Beatrice of Nazareth:1200–1268.* Cistercian Fathers Series 50. Kalamazoo: Cistercian, 1991.

De Pretis, Anna. "'Insincerity,' 'Facts,' and 'Epistolarity': Approaches to Pliny's *Epistles* to Calpurnia." *Arethusa* 36 (2003): 127–46.

de Verger, Antonio Ramírez. "Erotic Language in Pliny, *Ep.* VII 5." *Glotta* 74 (1999): 114–16.

Dover, K. J. "Classical Greek Attitudes to Sexual Behavior." In *Women in the Ancient World: The Arethusa Papers,* edited by John Peradotto and John Patrick Sullivan, 143–57. SUNY Series in Classical Studies. Albany: State University of New York Press, 1984.

Drobner, Hubertus R. and Alberto Viciano. *Gregory of Nyssa: Homilies on the Beatitudes.* Supplements to Vigiliae Christianae 52. Leiden: Brill, 2000.

Dunbabin, Katherine M. D. and M. W. Dickie. "*Invida Rumpantur Pectora*: The Iconography of *Phthonos/Invidia* in Graeco-Roman Art." *JAC* 26 (1983): 7–37.

Elsner, Jaś, ed. *The Verbal and the Visual: Cultures of Ekphrasis in Antiquity.* Ramus 31. Bendingo North, Victoria: Aureal, 2002.

Evans, Gillian R. *Alan of Lille: The Art of Preaching.* Cistercian Fathers Series 23. Kalamazoo: Cistercian, 1981.

Evans-Grubbs, Judith. "Abduction Marriage in Antiquity: A Law of Constantine (*CTh* ix.24.1) and Its Social Context." *JRS* 79 (1989): 59–83.

Fisher, Nick. "'Let Envy Be Absent': Envy, Liturgies and Reciprocity in Athens." In *Envy, Spite, and Jealousy: The Rivalrous Emotions in Ancient*

Greece, edited by David Konstan and Keith Rutter, 181–215. Edinburgh Leventis Studies 2. Edinburgh: Edinburgh University Press, 2003.

FitzGerald, Augustine. *The Letters of Synesius of Cyrene*. London: Oxford University Press, 1926.

Fitzgerald, John T. "Philippians in the Light of Some Ancient Discussions of Friendship." In *Friendship, Flattery, and Frankness of Speech: Studies on Friendship in the New Testament World*, edited by John T. Fitzgerald, 141–60. NovTSup 82. Leiden: Brill, 1996.

Ford, Gordon B., Jr. *The Letters of St. Isidore of Seville*. 2nd ed. Amsterdam: Adolf M. Hakkert, 1970.

Fowl, Stephen E. *Philippians*. Two Horizons New Testament Commentary. Grand Rapids: Eerdmans, 2005.

Fowler, R. L. "The Rhetoric of Desperation." *HSCP* 91 (1987): 5–38.

Fredrickson, David E. "Παρρησία in the Pauline Epistles." In *Friendship, Flattery, and Frankness of Speech: Studies on Friendship in the New Testament World*, edited by John T. Fitzgerald, 163–83. NovTSup 82. Leiden: Brill, 1996.

———. "God, Christ, and All Things in 1 Corinthians 15:28." *WW* 18 (1998): 254–63.

———. "Natural and Unnatural Use in Romans 1:24-27: Paul and the Philosophic Critique of Eros." In *Homosexuality, Science, and the "Plain Sense" of Scripture*, edited by David L. Balch, 197–222. Grand Rapids: Eerdmans, 2000.

———. "Passionless Sex in 1 Thessalonians 4:4-5," *WW* 23 (2003): 23–30.

Furley, David J., and J. S. Wilkie. *Galen on Respiration and the Arteries*. Princeton: Princeton University Press, 1984.

Garrison, Daniel H. *Mild Frenzy: A Reading of the Hellenistic Love Epigram*. Hermes Einzelschriften 41. Wiesbaden: Steiner, 1978.

———. *Sexual Culture in Ancient Greece*. Oklahoma Series in Classical Culture 24. Norman: University of Oklahoma Press, 2000.

Goitein, S. D. *Letters of Medieval Jewish Traders*. Princeton: Princeton University Press, 1973.

Goldhill, Simon. "The Erotic Experience of Looking." In *The Sleep of Reason: Erotic Experience and Sexual Ethics in Ancient Greece and Rome*, edited by Martha C. Nussbaum and Juha Sihvola, 374–99. Chicago: University of Chicago Press, 2002.

Graver, Margaret. "Dog-Helen and Homeric Insult." *Classical Antiquity* 14 (1995): 41–61.

Grebe, Sabine. "Marriage and Exile: Cicero's Letters to Terentia." *Helios* 30 (2003): 127–46.

Green, Peter. *The Argonautika.* Hellenistic Culture and Society 25. Berkeley: University of California Press, 1997.

Green, Robert Montraville. *A Translation of Galen's Hygiene (De sanitate tuenda).* Springfield, IL: Thomas, 1951.

Greene, Ellen. "Subjects, Objects, and Erotic Symmetry in Sappho's Fragments." In *Among Women: From the Homosocial to the Homoerotic in the Ancient World,* edited by Nancy Sorkin Rabinowitz and Lisa Auanger, 82–105. Austin: University of Texas Press, 2002.

Grenfell, Bernard P. and Arthur S. Hunt, eds. *The Oxyrhynchus Papyri: Part 14.* London: London Exploration Society, 1920.

Grmek, Mirko. *Diseases in the Ancient Greek World.* Baltimore: Johns Hopkins University Press, 1989.

Gruen, Erich S. "The Polis in the Hellenistic World." In *Nomodeiktes: Greek Studies in Honor of Martin Ostwald,* edited by Ralph M. Rosen and Joseph Farrell, 339–54. Ann Arbor: University of Michigan Press, 1993.

Gutzwiller, Kathryn J. *Poetic Garlands: Hellenistic Epigrams in Context.* Hellenistic Culture and Society 28. Berkeley: University of California Press, 1998.

Hague, Rebecca H. "Ancient Greek Weddings: The Tradition of Praise." *Journal of Folklore Research* 20 (1983): 131–43.

Hallett, Judith P. "The Vindolanda Letters from Claudia Severa." In *Women Writing Latin: From Roman Antiquity to Early Modern Europe,* edited by Laurie J. Churchill, Phyllis R. Brown, and Jane E. Jeffrey, 1:93–99. Women Writers of the World. New York: Routledge, 2002.

Hamilton, Edith, and Huntington Cairns, eds. *The Collected Dialogues of Plato, Including the Letters.* Bollingen Series 71. Princeton: Princeton University Press, 1961.

Hansen, M. "The Political Powers of the People's Court in Fourth-Century Athens." In *The Greek City: From Homer to Alexander,* edited by Oswyn Murray and Simon Price, 215–43. Oxford: Clarendon, 1990.

Hardie, Philip. "Another Look at Virgil's Ganymede." In *Classics in Progress: Essays on Ancient Greece and Rome,* edited by T. P. Wiseman, 333–61. British Academy Centenary Monographs. Oxford: Oxford University Press, 2002.

Hart, Columba. *Hadewijch: The Complete Works.* CWS. New York: Paulist, 1980.

Hawthorne, Gerald. "In the Form of God and Equal with God." In *Where Christology Began: Essays on Philippians 2,* edited by Ralph P. Martin and Brian J. Dodd, 96–110. Louisville: Westminster John Knox, 1998.

Hoover, Roy. "The Harpagmos Enigma: A Philological Solution." *HTR* 64 (1971): 95–119.

Hughes, Serge, and Elizabeth Hughes, *Jacopone da Todi: The Lauds.* CWS. New York: Paulist, 1982.

Hunter, Richard. *Theocritus and the Archaeology of Greek Poetry.* Cambridge: Cambridge University, 1996.

———. *Theocritus.* Cambridge: Cambridge University Press, 1999.

Hutchinson, G. O. *Cicero's Correspondence: A Literary Study.* Oxford: Clarendon, 1998.

Jouanna, Jacques. *Hippocrates.* Translated by M. B. DeBevoise. Medicine & Culture. Baltimore: Johns Hopkins University Press, 1999.

Kambylis, Athanasios. *Symeon Neos Theologos: Hymnen.* Supplementa Byzantina 3. Berlin: Walter de Gruyter, 1976.

Karlsson, Gustav. *Idéologie et cérémonial dans l'épistolographie byzantine: Textes du Xe siècle analysés et commentés,* Acta Universitatis Upsaliensis, Studia Graeca Upsaliensia 3. Uppsala: Almqvist & Wiksell, 1959.

Koester, Helmut. "The Purpose of the Polemic of a Pauline Fragment (Philippians iii)." *NTS* 8 (1962): 317–32.

Kortus, Michael. *Briefe des Apollonius-Archives aus der Sammlung Papyri Gissenses: Edition, Übersetzung und Kommentar.* Berichte und Arbeiten aus der Universitätsbibliothek und dem Universitätsarchiv Giessen 49. Giessen: Universitätsbibliothek, 1999.

Koskenniemi, Heikki. *Studien zur Idee und Phraseologie des griechischen Briefes bis 400 n. Chr.* Suomalaisen Tiedeakatemian toimituksia B, 102.2. Helsinki: n.p., 1956.

Kost, Karlheinz. *Musaios, Hero und Leander: Einleitung, Text, Übersetzung, und Kommentar.* Bonn: Bouvier, 1971.

Kramer, Bärbel, John C. Shelton, and Gerald M. Browne. *Das Archiv des Nepheros und verwandte Texte.* 2 vols. in 1. Aegyptiaca Treverensia 4. Mainz am Rhein: P. von Zabern, 1987.

Lattimore, Richmond. *Themes in Greek and Latin Epitaphs.* Urbana: University of Illinois Press, 1962.

Lefkowitz, Mary R. "Seduction and Rape in Greek Myth." In *Consent and Coercion to Sex and Marriage in Ancient and Medieval Societies,* edited by

Angeliki E. Laiou, 17–37. Washington, DC: Dumbarton Oaks Research Library and Collection, 1993.

———. "'Predatory' Goddesses." *Hesperia* 71 (2002): 325–44.

Lidov, Joel B. "The Second Stanza of Sappho 31: Another Look." *AJP* 114 (1993): 503–35.

Lilja, Saara. *Dogs in Ancient Greek Poetry.* Commentationes Humanarum Litteratum 56. Helsinki: Societas Scientarum Fennica, 1976.

Limberis, Vasiliki. "The Eyes Infected by Evil: Basil of Caesarea's Homily, On Envy." *HTR* 84 (1991): 163–84.

Loraux, Nicole. "Reflections of the Greek City on Unity and Division." In *City States in Classical Antiquity and Medieval Italy*, edited by Anthony Molho, Kurt Raaflaub, and Julia Emlen, 33–51. Ann Arbor: University of Michigan Press, 1991.

Luck, G. "Panaetius and Menander." *AJP* 96 (1975): 256–68.

Ludwig, Walther. "Platons Kuss und seine Folgen." *Illinois Classical Studies* 14 (1989): 435–47.

Luibheid, Colm. *Pseudo-Dionysius: The Complete Works.* CWS. Mahwah, NJ: Paulist, 1987.

MacCoull, Leslie S. B. *Dioscorus of Aphrodito: His Work and World.* Transformation of the Classical Heritage 16 (Berkeley: University of California Press, 1988.

Mace, Sarah. "Utopian and Erotic Fusion in a New Elegy by Simonides." In *The New Simonides: Contexts of Praise and Desire*, edited by Deborah Boedeker and David Sider, 185–207. New York: Oxford University Press, 2001.

Malherbe, Abraham J. "'Gentle as a Nurse': The Cynic Background to I Thessalonians ii." *NovT* 12 (1970): 203–17.

———, ed. *The Cynic Epistles.* SBLSBS 12. Atlanta: Scholars, 1977.

———. "Exhortation in First Thessalonians." *NovT* 25 (1983): 238–56.

———. "Paul's Self-Sufficiency (Philippians 4:11)." In *Friendship, Flattery, and Frankness of Speech: Studies on Friendship in the New Testament World*, edited by John T. Fitzgerald, 125–39. NovTSup 82. Leiden: Brill, 1996.

———. *The Letters to the Thessalonians: A New Translation with Introduction and Commentary.* AB 32B. New York: Doubleday, 2000.

Maloney, George A. *Hymns of Divine Love by St. Symeon the New Theologian.* Denville, NJ: Dimension, 1975.

———. *The Fifty Spiritual Homilies; and, The Great Letter: Pseudo Macarius.* CWS. New York: Paulist, 1992.

Marry, John D. "Sappho and the Heroic Ideal." *Arethusa* 12 (1979): 71–92.

Martin, Dale B. *Slavery as Salvation: The Metaphor of Slavery in Pauline Christianity.* New Haven: Yale University Press, 1990.

Martin, Dale B. *Sex and the Single Savior: Gender and Sexuality in Biblical Interpretation.* Louisville: Westminster John Knox, 2006.

McCaffry, Hugh. *Isaac of Stella: Sermons on the Christian Year.* Cistercian Fathers Series 11. Kalamazoo: Cistercian, 1979.

McGinn, Bernard. *The Growth of Mysticism: Gregory the Great through the Twelfth Century.* Vol. 2 of *The Presence of God: A History of Western Christian Mysticism.* New York: Crossroad, 1994.

———. "God as Eros: Metaphysical Foundations of Christian Mysticism." In *New Perspectives on Historical Theology: Essays in Memory of John Meyendorff,* edited by Bradley Nassif, 189–209. Grand Rapids: Eerdmans, 1996.

———. *The Flowering of Mysticism: Men and Women in the New Mysticism, 1200–1350.* Vol. 3 of *The Presence of God: A History of Western Christian Mysticism.* New York: Crossroad, 1998.

———. *Symeon – The New Theologian: The Practical and Theological Chapters and The Three Theological Discourses.* Cistercian Studies Series 41. Kalamazoo: Cistercian, 1982.

McGuire, Brian Patrick. *Friendship and Community: The Monastic Experience, 350–1250.* Cistercian Studies Series 95. Kalamazoo: Cistercian, 1988.

Meeks, Wayne A. *The First Urban Christians: The Social World of the Apostle Paul.* New Haven: Yale University Press, 1983.

Miller, Andrew. "*Phthonos* and *Parphasis*: The Argument of *Nemean* 8.19-34." *GRBS* 23 (1982): 111–20.

Miller, John F. "Reading Cupid's Triumph." *Classical Journal* 90 (1995): 287–94.

Moltmann, Jürgen. "Perichoresis: An Old Magic Word for a New Trinitarian Theology." In *Trinity, Community, and Power: Mapping Trajectories in Wesleyan Theology,* edited by M. Douglas Meeks, 111–25. Nashville: Kingswood, 1990.

Monks of Mount Saint Bernard Abbey. *Guerric of Igny: Liturgical Sermons.* 2 vols. Cistercian Father Series 8, 32. Spencer, MA: Cistercian, 1970, 1971.

Most, Glenn. "Epinician Envies." In *Envy, Spite, and Jealousy: The Rivalrous Emotions in Ancient Greece,* edited by David Konstan and Keith Rutter, 123–42. Edinburgh Leventis Studies 2. Edinburgh: Edinburgh University Press, 2003.

Murgatroyd, Paul. "*Servitium Amoris* and the Roman Elegists." *Latomus* 40 (1980): 589–606.

————. "Amatory Hunting, Fishing and Fowling." *Latomus* 43 (1984): 362–68.

Nagy, Gregory. *The Best of the Achaeans: Concepts of the Hero in Archaic Greek Poetry.* Rev. ed. Baltimore: Johns Hopkins University Press, 1999.

Nock, Arthur Darby. "Soter and Euergetes." In *The Joy of Study: Papers on New Testament and Related Subjects to Honor Frederick Clifton Grant,* edited by Sherman E. Johnson, 127–48. New York: Macmillan, 1951.

Oakley, John H. "Nuptial Nuances: Wedding Images in Non-Wedding Scenes of Myth." In *Pandora: Women in Classical Greece,* edited by Ellen D. Reeder and Sally C. Humphreys, 63–73. Baltimore: Walters Art Gallery, 1995.

Oakley, John H., and Rebecca H. Sinos. *The Wedding in Ancient Athens.* Wisconsin Studies in Classics. Madison: University of Wisconsin Press, 1993.

Ober, Josiah. *Mass and Elite in Democratic Athens: Rhetoric, Ideology, and the Power of the People.* Princeton: Princeton University Press, 1989.

O'Brien, Peter T. *The Epistle to the Philippians.* NIGTC. Grand Rapids: Eerdmans, 1991.

Olsson, Bror. *Papyrusbriefe aus der frühesten Römerzeit.* Uppsala: Almqvist & Wiksell, 1925.

Onians, Richard Broxton. *The Origins of European Thought about the Body, the Mind, the Soul, the World, Time, and Fate: New Interpretations of Greek, Roman, and Kindred Evidence, Also of Some Basic Jewish and Christian Beliefs.* 2nd ed. Cambridge: Cambridge University Press, 1954.

Padel, Ruth. *In and Out of the Mind: Greek Images of the Tragic Self.* Princeton: Princeton University Press, 1992.

Parássoglou, George M. "Four Papyri from the Yale Collection." *AJP* 92 [1971]: 652–66.

————. "Five Private Letters from Roman Egypt." *Hellenica* 26 (1973): 271–81.

Parker, T. H. L. *The Epistles of Paul the Apostle to the Galatians, Ephesians, Philippians and Colossians.* Edinburgh: Oliver & Boyd, 1965.

Parsons, P. J., ed. *The Oxyrhynchus Papyri: Volume 42.* Oxford: Oxford University Press, 1974.

Parsons, Sister Wilfrid. *Saint Augustine: Letters.* FC. Washington, DC: Catholic University of America Press, 1951.

Penelope. *On Contemplating God: Prayer, Meditations, I.* Cistercian Fathers Series 3. Spencer, MA: Cistercian, 1971.

Petropoulos, J. C. B. *Eroticism in Ancient and Medieval Greek Poetry.* London: Duckworth, 2003.

Posset, Franz. *Pater Bernhardus: Martin Luther and Bernard of Clairvaux.* Cistercian Studies Series 168. Kalamazoo: Cistercian, 1999.

Preston, Keith. *Studies in the Diction of the Sermo Amatorius in Roman Comedy.* Menasha, WI: George Banta, 1916.

Pringle, John. *Commentaries on the Epistles of Paul the Apostle to the Philippians, Colossians, and Thessalonians.* Grand Rapids: Eerdmans, 1948.

Rabinowitz, Nancy Sorkin. "Excavating Women's Homoeroticism in Ancient Greece: The Evidence from Attic Vase Painting." In *Among Women: From the Homosocial to the Homoerotic in the Ancient World,* edited by Nancy Sorkin Rabinowitz and Lisa Auanger, 106–66. Austin: University of Texas Press, 2002.

Reardon, B. P., ed. *Collected Ancient Greek Novels.* Berkeley: University of California Press, 1989.

Reed, J. D. *Bion of Smyrna, The Fragments and the Adonis.* Cambridge Classical Texts and Commentaries 33. New York: Cambridge University Press, 1997.

Rehm, Rush. *Marriage to Death: The Conflation of Wedding and Funeral Rituals in Greek Tragedy.* Princeton: Princeton University Press, 1994.

Reumann, John. "Philippians, Especially Chapter 4, as a 'Letter of Friendship': Observations on a Checkered History of Scholarship." In *Friendship, Flattery, and Frankness of Speech: Studies on Friendship in the New Testament World,* edited by John T. Fitzgerald, 83–106. NovTSup 82. Leiden: Brill, 1996.

———. *Philippians: A New Translation with Introduction and Commentary.* Anchor Yale Bible 33B. New Haven: Yale University Press, 2008.

Richlin, Amy. "Fronto + Marcus: Love, Friendship, Letters," In *The Boswell Thesis: Essays on Christianity, Social Tolerance, and Homosexuality,* edited by Mathew Kuefler, 111–29. Chicago: University of Chicago, 2006.

Rissman, Leah. *Love as War: Homeric Allusion in the Poetry of Sappho.* Beiträge zur klassischen Philologie 157. Königstein/Ts.: Hain, 1983.

Roberts, C. H., ed. *The Antinoopolis Papyri, Part I.* London: London Exploration Society, 1950.

Roos, A. G., ed. *Papyri groninganae: griechische Papyri der Universitätsbibliothek zu Groningen.* Amsterdam: Noord-Hollandsche Uitgevers-Maatschappij, 1933.

Rosenmeyer, Patricia. *The Poetics of Imitation: Anacreon and the Anacreontic Tradition.* Cambridge: Cambridge University Press, 1992.

———. "Love Letters in Callimachus, Ovid, and Aristaenetus, or, The Sad Fate of a Mailorder Bride." *MD* 36 (1996): 9–31.

———. "Tracing *Medulla* as a *Locus Eroticus,*" *Arethusa* 32 (1999): 19–47.

Ross, David O., Jr. "Nine Epigrams from Pompeii (*CIL* 4.4966–73)." *Yale Classical Studies* 21 (1969): 127–42.

Saïd, Suzanne. "Envy and Emulation in Isocrates." In *Envy, Spite, and Jealousy: The Rivalrous Emotions in Ancient Greece*, edited by David Konstan and Keith Rutter, 217–34. Edinburgh Leventis Studies 2. Edinburgh: Edinburgh University Press, 2003.

Scanlon, Thomas F. *Eros and Greek Athletics*. Oxford: Oxford University Press, 2002.

Schulz-Falkenthal, Heinz. "Kyniker—Zur inhaltlichen Deutung des Names." *WZ* 26.2 (1977): 41–49.

Schwartz, James H. "Engraved Gems in the Collection of the American Numismatic Society II: Intaglios with Eros." *American Journal of Numismatics* 11 (1999): 13–45.

Seaford, Richard. "The Tragic Wedding." *JHS* 107 (1987): 106–30.

Seremetakis, C. Nadia. *The Last Word: Women, Death and Divination in Inner Mani*. Chicago: University of Chicago Press, 1991.

Shapiro, H. A. "Eros in Love: Pederasty and Pornography in Greece." In *Pornography and Representation in Greece and Rome*, edited by Amy Richlin, 53–72. New York: Oxford University Press, 1992.

Sharrock, Alison. *Seduction and Repetition in Ovid's Ars Amatoria II*. New York: Oxford University Press, 1994.

Sherwin-White, A. N. *The Letters of Pliny: A Historical and Social Commentary*. Oxford: Clarendon, 1968.

Sider, David. *The Epigrams of Philodemus: Introduction, Text, and Commentary*. Oxford: Oxford University Press, 1997.

Smith, Christopher. "'Ἐκκλεῖσαι' in Galatians 4:17: The Motif of the Excluded Lover as a Metaphor of Manipulation." *CBQ* 58 (1996): 480–99.

Smith, James A. *Marks of an Apostle: Deconstruction, Philippians, and Problematizing Pauline Theology*. Semeia 53. Atlanta: Society of Biblical Literature, 2005.

Sourvinou-Inwood, Christiane. "The Young Abductor of the Locrian Pinakes." *Bulletin of the Institute of Classical Studies* 20 (1973): 12–21.

———. "Erotic Pursuits: Images and Meanings." *JHS* 107 (1987): 131–53.

———. *"Reading" Greek Culture: Texts and Images, Rituals and Myths*. New York: Oxford University Press, 1991.

Stehle, Eva. *Performance and Gender in Ancient Greece: Nondramatic Poetry in Its Setting*. Princeton: Princeton University Press, 1997.

Steiner, Deborah. "Slander's Bite: *Nemean* 7.102–5 and the Language of Invective." *JHS* 121 (2001): 154–58.

Stewart, Andrew. "Rape?" In *Pandora: Women in Classical Greece*, edited by Ellen D. Reeder, 74–90. Princeton: Trustees of the Walters Art Gallery/Princeton University, 1995.

Stiegman, Emero. *Bernard of Clairvaux: On Loving God.* Cistercian Fathers Series 13B. Kalamazoo: Cistercian, 1973.

Stirewalt, M. Luther, Jr. *Paul the Letter Writer.* Grand Rapids: Eerdmans, 2003.

Stowers, Stanley K. *Letter Writing in Greco-Roman Antiquity.* LEC 5. Philadelphia: Westminster, 1986.

———. "Friends and Enemies in the Politics of Heaven: Reading Theology in Philippians." In *Pauline Theology,* vol. 1: *Thessalonians, Philippians, Galatians, Philemon,* edited by Jouette M. Bassler, 105–21. Minneapolis: Fortress Press, 1991.

Swain, Simon, ed. *Seeing the Face, Seeing the Soul: Polemon's Physiognomy from Classical Antiquity to Medieval Islam.* Oxford: Oxford University Press, 2000.

Swete, H. B. *Theodori Episcopi Mopsuesteni in Epistolas B. Pauli Commentarii.* 2 vols. Cambridge: Cambridge University Press, 1880.

Taylor, A. E. *A Commentary on Plato's Timaeus.* Oxford: Clarendon, 1928.

Thraede, Klaus. *Gründzuge griechisch-römischer Brieftopik.* Zetemata 48. Munich: Beck, 1970.

Tōmadakēs, Nikolaos. ΒΥΖΑΝΤΙΝΗ ΕΠΙΣΤΟΛΟΓΡΑΦΙΑ. Thessaloniki, 1993.

Toohey, Peter. "Dangerous Ways to Fall in Love: Chariton I 1, 5-10 and VI 9, 4." *Maia* 51 (1999): 259–75.

———. *Melancholy, Love, and Time: Boundaries of the Self in Ancient Literature.* Ann Arbor: University of Michigan Press, 2004.

Turner, Victor. *The Ritual Process: Structure and Anti-Structure.* Symbol, Myth, and Ritual. Ithaca, NY: Cornell University Press, 1977.

van Gennep, Arnold. *The Rites of Passage.* Translated by Monika B. Vizedom and Gabrielle L. Caffee. Chicago: University of Chicago Press, 1960.

Vermeule, Emily. *Aspects of Death in Early Greek Art and Poetry.* Sather Classical Lectures 46. Berkeley: University of California Press, 1979.

Wack, Mary Frances. *Lovesickness in the Middle Ages: The Viaticum and Its Commentaries.* Middle Ages Series. Philadelphia: University of Pennsylvania Press, 1990.

Wagner, M. Monica. *Saint Basil: Ascetical Works.* FC 9. New York: Fathers of the Church, 1950.

Walsh, Kilian. *Bernard of Clairvaux: On the Song of Songs II.* Cistercian Fathers Series 7. Kalamazoo: Cistercian, 1976.

Walsh, Kilian, and Irene M. Edmonds. *Bernard of Clairvaux: On the Song of Songs III,* Cistercian Fathers Series 31. Kalamazoo: Cistercian, 1979.

Walsh, P. G. *Pliny the Younger: Complete Letters.* Oxford: Oxford University Press, 2006.

Welch, Claude, ed. *God and Incarnation in Mid-Nineteenth Century German Theology: G. Thomasius, I. A. Dorner, and A. E. Biedermann.* Library of Protestant Theology. New York: Oxford University Press, 1965.

Wettstein, Johann Jakob. *Novum Testamentum Graecum. 1751–52.* Repr., 2 vols. Graz: Akademische Druck- u. Verlagsanstalt, 1962.

White, John Lee. *The Form and Function of the Body of the Greek Letter: A Study of the Letter-Body in the Non-Literary Papyri and in Paul the Apostle.* SBLDS 2. Missoula, MT: Scholars, 1972.

White, L. Michael. "Morality between Two Worlds: A Paradigm of Friendship in Philippians." In *Greeks, Romans, and Christians: Essays in Honor of Abraham J. Malherbe,* edited by David L. Balch, Everett Ferguson, and Wayne A. Meeks, 201–15. Minneapolis: Fortress Press, 1990.

White, Robert J. *The Interpretation of Dreams: Oneirocritica by Artemidorus.* Park Ridge, NJ: Noyes, 1975.

Whitehead, David. "Samian Autonomy." In *Nomodeiktes: Greek Studies in Honor of Martin Ostwald,* edited by Ralph M. Rosen and Joseph Farrell, 321–29. Ann Arbor: University of Michigan Press, 1993.

Worman, Nancy. "The Body as Argument: Helen in Four Greek Texts." *Classical Antiquity* 16 (1997): 151–203.

Worp, K. A., ed. *Greek Papyri from Kellis: I (P. Kell. G.) Nos. 1–90.* Oxford: Oxbow, 1995.

Youtie, Herbert C., and John G. Winter, eds. *Michigan Papyri,* vol. 8: *Papyri and Ostraca from Karanis.* Ann Arbor: University of Michigan Press, 1951.

———. "P. Mich. Inv. 241: ΕΔΟΞΑ ΣΕ ΘΕΩΡΕΙΝ." *ZPE* 22 (1976): 49–52.

Zagagi, Neta. *Tradition and Originality in Plautus: Studies of the Amatory Motifs in Plautine Comedy.* Hypomnemata 62. Göttingen: Vandenhoeck & Ruprecht, 1989.

Zanker, Graham. "The Love Theme in Apollonius Rhodius' Argonautica." *Wiener Studien* 13 (1979): 52–75.

Zeitlin, Froma I. *Playing the Other: Gender and Society in Classical Greek Literature.* Women in Culture and Society. Chicago: University of Chicago Press, 1995.

———. "Living Portraits and Sculpted Bodies in Chariton's Theater of Romance." In *The Ancient Novel and Beyond,* edited by Stelios Panayotakis, Maaike Zimmerman, and Wytse Keulen, 71–83. Mnemosyne 241. Leiden: Brill, 2003.

Zerba, Michelle. "Love, Envy, and Pantomimic Morality in Cicero's *De Oratore.*" *CP* 97 (2002): 299–321.

Zimmerman, Clayton. *The Pastoral Narcissus: A Study of the First Idyll of Theocritus.* Greek Studies. Lanham MD: Rowman & Littlefield, 1994.

Index

Biblical Index